DOWN AND BACK

DOWN AND BACK

ON ALCOHOL, FAMILY, AND A LIFE IN HOCKEY

JUSTIN BOURNE

VIKING

VIKING

an imprint of Penguin Canada,
a division of Penguin Random House Canada Limited

Canada • USA • UK • Ireland • Australia • New Zealand • India • South Africa • China

First published 2023

www.penguinrandomhouse.ca

LIBRARY AND ARCHIVES CANADA CATALOGUING IN PUBLICATION

Title: Down and back : On Alcohol, Family, and a Life in Hockey / Justin Bourne.
Names: Bourne, Justin, author.
Identifiers: Canadiana (print) 20220142181 | Canadiana (ebook) 20220142211 | ISBN
9780735245006 (hardcover) | ISBN 9780735245013 (EPUB)
Subjects: LCSH: Bourne, Justin. | LCSH: Hockey players—United States—Biography. |
LCSH: Sportswriters—United States—Biography. | LCSH: Sportscasters—United
States—Biography. | LCSH: Hockey coaches—United States—Biography. | LCSH:
Recovering alcoholics—United States—Biography. | LCSH: Bourne, Justin—Family. |
LCSH: Fathers and sons—United States. | LCGFT: Autobiographies.
Classification: LCC GV848.5.B68 A3 2022 | DDC 796.962092—dc23

Book design by Talia Abramson
Cover design by Talia Abramson
Cover images: (author) © Brianna and Charlie Bourne; (teammates Mike Bossy #22 and
Bob Bourne #14 celebrate winning Game One of the 1982 Stanley Cup Finals, May 8,
1982) © B Bennett / Contributor / Getty Images Sport Classic

Printed in Canada

10 9 8 7 6 5 4 3 2 1

Penguin
Random House
VIKING CANADA

To my family. In my darkest days you inspired the
mission statement "I will live with the care of those
closest to me in my heart"—I have since, and I will forever.
I love you all. Honest Jell-O.

Feed the good wolf.

CONTENTS

1

THE RETURN
OF THE RING

When the NHL playoffs approach each spring, we go down the list of talented greybeards who've had great careers and pinpoint those we deem most deserving of "getting their ring," and the sport as a whole seems to root for them. We talk vaguely about "being a winner," and we talk about the team pursuit of winning the Cup, but in the context of individual hockey players it's common to refer to their championship pedigree as including— or not including—*rings*.

I grew up with an innate understanding of the magic of the ring. My father, Bob Bourne, earned four of them as an integral part of the New York Islanders' Stanley Cup dynasty in the early 1980s. For as long as I can remember, those rings have been part of our family history.

My perception of the ring has changed over the years. I share the reverence for the ring as some historical tomb that holds the magic of greatness past, a piece of fossilized amber to be handed down through generations, containing something capable of bringing old stories forward to the present moment. They're larger than life (both figuratively *and* literally these days), and almost supernatural, like something action heroes fight over in comic books. Within hockey, they're proof of immortalization.

For me, though, other adjectives exist, too, others that are generally unfamiliar in the daily orbit of a Cup ring. There's disappointment, there's hurt and mistrust, and more specifically, there's the pains of addictions and their consequences. I still revere *rings*, but there's a heaviness beyond their physical weight.

I was young during my dad's heyday—too young to fully appreciate the skills, talent and determination that made him a success. But I was fortunate that we spent enough time together at events and in dressing rooms as I got older to gain an understanding of what made him special to his teams and his teammates. I saw the way a grinning Al Arbour—the long-time coach of the Islanders, and fifth-winningest coach in NHL history— would shout an affectionate "Shithead!" when Dad would pop up years later, moments before they'd share a warm embrace. That particular brand of nickname comes from the special bond you form when you've been to the sport's mountaintop together, having pushed and pulled with another person to get the most out of them, to achieve the type of goal you immortalize with gold.

I saw the numerous friends that would come through to be a part of Dad's charity events years after retirement. I watched old VHS tapes and heard enough stories to appreciate what Life Before Me had been like. It had been successful, and it had been good, mostly.

During his career my dad banked respect away from the rink to go with what he earned on it. The scrapbooks and trophies around our family home in my early years spoke volumes about his character. In one corner, a Bill Masterton Trophy for perseverance and dedication to hockey. In another, a *Sports Illustrated*

Sportsman of the Year award for his work to raise money for children's health care, a pursuit that grew from the needs of my incredible brother, Jeff, who was born with spina bifida. (Jeff's life has been worthy of a non-hockey Bill Masterton, as his endurance through nearly 40 surgeries and navigating life in a chair has truly defined perseverance and dedication.) And we had a closet filled with "Good Guy" awards from the New York media, who annually recognized him for being an athlete who could be counted on for honest, straightforward answers after a win or a loss.

What you wouldn't see in our family home was a complete set of my dad's four Stanley Cup rings, in part because he was generous with his success. He presented his first ring to his father, Victor Bourne. Grandpa Bourne raised his family on a farm near the dozen-person town of Netherhill, Saskatchewan, about two hours west of Saskatoon. The second ring went to his father-in-law, Jim Juba. Grandpa Juba was another solid prairie farm guy with an endearing Ukrainian accent who naturally vibed with my dad. It was a measure of love that my dad shared those rings with two men who had a big influence on his life. (In time, both of those rings would find their way back to him.)

In that same spirit, Dad eventually passed on one his rings to Jeff at his high school graduation, a family treasure meant to last a lifetime.

In the year 2000, it was my turn.

Dad left when I was about eight and Jeff was eleven, and so by high school graduation, my mother, Janice, had spent years with us, grinding over the day-to-day details of life. Mom was lovely, and the picture of patience and commitment through some days that weren't easy. Because of that, I admit to feeling like she got jobbed out of some much-deserved attention the day my ring came. She had put in the work as a single mom for roughly a decade by that point. It was in June and at my high school graduation—an event I see as a triumph over the mundane details of daily life—when a day known for celebrating the rote turned its attention to the rare. It was a substantial piece of gold, with two sizable diamonds (to represent the second Islanders Cup) set in the middle of an Islander-blue stone, and it instantly became the star of the show.

To a 17-year-old kid, it was an incredible gift. You might think the weight of something like that could crush a kid that age, particularly one with some hockey aspirations, but not for a second did I consider it something to live up to. It was so far beyond where I was in the sport that it didn't even feel like it was earned in the same field. I wasn't on track for the draft (I didn't even know when that was); I was off to see if I could crack a Junior A team (I did not, that first summer), with the grand end goal of having some university pay for my education (that I did eventually manage to accomplish).

Maybe it would've been different had I grown up in a house with my dad, or had he coached my hockey teams or something along the way, but the field in which that ring was earned somehow felt entirely separate from whatever it was I was doing. I was beyond proud to have it.

That generosity and connection meant a lot then, but even more later. Life after hockey has not been easy for my dad. A variety of factors affected his life, his demeanour and his personality. Concussions and alcohol are a part of that story—he'd tell you the same—and good luck untangling which to hold accountable for what. It's also well established that children of alcoholics have a much greater likelihood of developing their own issues with alcohol. Let's just say if your father is both an alcoholic and a Stanley Cup winner, your odds of following in his footsteps down one path is far more likely than down the other.

If life ever leads you to the epiphany that it's time to boil a frog, apparently there are some loose guidelines to help you on your way. I'm told that if you boil the water first, then drop the amphibian in, it will jump directly out. The contrast from its previous normal is just too much. But if you put one in a pot on the stove and turn the heat up ever so slowly, a degree at a time, it won't notice the temperature increases, and before you know it, voilà, you've made frog legs.

That seems relevant when discussing my relationship with Dad in the years after he retired. Intermittent incidents became part of the increasing temperature of the water, and I never jumped out, strange as that might have seemed to those on the outside. I probably looked like the frog in the water, continuing to put up with the ever-rising heat, even if just a degree at a time. I assure you, though, that wasn't the case. I never got used to the new temperatures that came with Dad's struggles, period. I just consciously chose to tolerate them, because what was the alternative—not having a relationship? I usually saw the next small heat increase coming, and steeled myself yet again rather than hopping free. I'm not sure that choice, which I made over and again, was ever right or wrong. I still don't know.

Today I make a living analyzing hockey. I imagine the reason I'm at least somewhat useful in that gig is that I've always excelled at reading the play, both on the ice and off. It's what got me as far as I did as a professional player, and what led to me being hired as a video coach in the American Hockey League. Show me how a breakout is unfolding at one end, or a forecheck, and I can make a reasonably accurate guess as to how things will unfold over the next 10 seconds, even if they end up 200 feet away.

With that attribute as a strength, it's possible I knew Dad was going to take the ring even before he did.

His mind hadn't been right for a while, but he was particularly unwell then, and so avoiding disaster on his visit to Toronto from Kelowna in 2013 seemed unlikely even before he'd arrived. We were on high alert. But the odd range of what could go sideways didn't hit me until we were five steps inside my apartment and he asked to try on the Stanley Cup ring he had given me for high school graduation over a decade before.

The ask to try it on was odd phrasing, coming from the person for whom it was sized. And it was an odd interest coming from the man who at some point had three more similar rings in a sparkling quartet.

Since something was off, and it was Dad, I had reason to worry it might be the start of something bad. By then, the trust was gone.

I considered that he might have asked for nostalgia's sake, and fought back the type of doubts that could cloud the opening hour of his week-long visit. I wasn't ready for trouble—particularly where, I hoped, it might never come.

At the time, that 1981 New York Islanders Stanley Cup ring sat in a cloudy Plexiglas display case that was made for an autographed baseball, tucked inside an open ring box atop a flimsy brown IKEA shelf in our bathroom. I had bigger plans for it, someday, but given my financial situation at the time, the presentation had seemed sufficient.

My relationship with Dad had shifted more to the "drinking buddies" side in those days, and so I did what I'd become accustomed to doing: I simply agreed to *whatever* to avoid any type of confrontation, handed over the ring, and encouraged the procession to move down to the Foggy Dew. The Dew, you see, was a fully functioning Irish pub located on the bottom floor of our apartment building, so it was essentially in the basement of our living quarters at the time. A fireman pole from our worn green living room couch would've taken you to a spot directly in front of the leading taps at a V-shaped bar, taps that were generally stocked with Guinness and a decent IPA, two of my favourites at the time.

A basement pub—that should've been fine, right? As the famously naive *Simpsons* quote goes, "Nothing could possibli go wrong."

And so my dad, a large man with a large past, brought the large ring down with him that first day.

Each of his Stanley Cup rings had been sized for a different finger so that he could wear all four at once, and so the second one didn't quite fit his ring finger but rather his middle finger, which might have made for an awkward wear in isolation, but man, did it make for a great recurring joke when inquiring patrons asked to have a look. Gleefully flipping off those asking for a view was particularly hilarious to the types of people who sit along the wood at Irish pubs, so after a couple of beers the ring felt less out of place and more like an old friend: welcome. The laughs came easily.

The conversations it inspired that first day and night—and a few others during his visit—really drove home the point of something I already knew: that ring was a really cool thing to have. Beyond that, though, it was good to have Dad around in general.

He'd spent a lot of my early life on the road, away playing hockey, and then after retirement and the divorce, away coaching hockey around the US in the minors—first in Texas, then Las Vegas, then Utah. By the time he returned home to Kelowna once and for all, I was on the road at the start of my own hockey adventures. In sum, spending a week together wasn't something we'd done much of, well, ever. And of course, drinking was something we both excelled at, much to my lovely wife's chagrin.

Still, I recognized the ring's presence at the bar that first night as at least the tip of an iceberg of concern. I'd never seen him wear a Stanley Cup ring outside of his house before, at least not for a non-hockey-related event, so something just felt off. Combining that with his struggling for money back then and flying cross-country to see my wife and me (not a common occurrence), in short order I had put together a theory for the genesis of his visit.

It's why I hedged with "it's *possible*" that I knew he'd take the ring before he even knew he was going to do it. Because if he didn't show up in town with the intent of taking it, I definitely knew first. The second he slipped it on that first day, he might as well have been Frodo Baggins with it and disappeared. Its fate was sealed. But if reclaiming the ring was the real incentive for the random visit, then yeah, safe to say it wasn't me who knew first.

Like many former Islanders and other NHLers from back in the day, Dad had discovered the potential financial relief the sports memorabilia marketplace offered. Not many players from the 1970s and '80s had been paid the kind of dollars that set them up for life, so it was understandable. Those years beyond hockey cost real money, and it just so happened that a 1981 New York Islanders ring could deliver a quick payday in the ballpark of $15,000.

The ring itself, he could have it. *Of course* he could have it. It was never mine to begin with; he won it, and I would've been grateful for the chance to help him at all, as momentarily sad as moving on from something so meaningful would've been if faced head on. I spent a lot of that week hoping he'd just outright ask to have it back. Hoping that he'd tell me he was struggling, he was in a financial bind, and there were no easy avenues for getting back to comfortable in the foreseeable future. In the fantasies where that conversation sprang up, maybe there would be a plan, a whole, real plan in place that he'd been working on behind the scenes to help him work towards a healthy purpose. Behind every interaction we'd had for the previous 10 or 15 years was just me searching for signs of the start of something good for him. I think he felt that I wanted that for him.

The thing with those fantastical hopes of mine is that they didn't spring to life from the void; they'd been constantly running in my personal background like some imaginary phone app slowly sapping my mental battery. Without knowing exactly which variety was ahead, his slow-motion course of life felt inevitably drawn towards disaster. This ring thing wasn't some crisis in isolation, not at all, but rather the 14-karat straw that broke the camel's back, emotionally speaking.

Having to pretend I didn't see it coming that week, even in the moment of its actual "reclaiming" . . . that ripped one final tear in a relationship I'd been trying to care less about but just couldn't. I had to find a way to not care, because if I was honest about how much I did care, it might devour me from the inside out.

Spoiler alert: I did not find a way to not care.

On the trip's final day, we sat in the Foggy Dew while the clock ticked closer to Dad's departure, a sloppy week behind us, but with disaster by and large avoided.

Maybe he'd leave it, and he'd never even considered taking it, and I should feel terrible for ever having suspected he might.

What's the expression in *Ted Lasso*—"It's the hope that kills you"?

I think part of me wanted him to have it. I must have, or surely I would've spoken up. I just couldn't imagine coming all that way to get it, then running into a scolding roadblock right before the finish line, particularly if he was banking on the money. Particularly when *it was his to begin with*. I feared an end-of-trip blow-up. It's not that he was prone to that sort of thing with me—far from it, in fact—it's just that things were not going great for him back home, and I really didn't want to be the one to make his life harder. I didn't want things between us to be awkward if I had the ring despite him wanting it. And so I let it happen.

Dad had left his bags up in our apartment above the bar to be grabbed before his Uber to the airport arrived. Some 15 minutes after Dad's ride arrived, he retrieved his bags and departed, and my wife and I finished our drinks and went back upstairs to our apartment. He was gone, and yeah, the ring was gone, and my hopes were, too. I sent a barely confrontational text, something to the effect of *If you needed it, you could've just asked, I'd have said yes*. I have a vague recollection of immediately volunteering my blessing to sell the thing before the lies could start—those inevitable lies, first about it being an accident, then later about how it had mysteriously disappeared. I went there right away because I'd played the movie well out in my mind, and had to protect myself from more hope and pain in the future.

That's what alcoholism does to families. It prepares them for lies, and the hurt of being lied to, and makes them distrust even the truth, which becomes unrecognizable even when present. It shatters trust.

I don't remember the exact details but remember that he wrote back right away and acknowledged having the ring. I remember that the conversation died after a few messages, and we never spoke of it again, as if it had never happened. It was just . . . gone, left to become a greater symbol of the things we left unspoken over those years.

We would spend a week at my mom's every summer, we didn't pause our visits with him then or after, and he eventually visited Toronto again (another trip that ended poorly, for different reasons).

I know he went to rehab for alcohol the first time in the winter of 2017, which was two years before he'd go for the second time, which was pretty close to when I'd go to rehab in 2019— for the last time, fingers crossed. That visit of mine was two years before Dad would go for the third time.

Turns out the fighting doesn't always stop when the playing days are over.

The ring was gone, but it was just a thing, just another tangle in an already snarled knot. Hockey, and the universe around it, gave to my family for a long time—money, fame, opportunity— before it started taking away. At first it happened slowly, like gentle erosion. But by this time we were losing great chunks, hulking glaciers finally giving way to warming conditions.

I've never been one to blame hockey for those losses, considering all it's done for my family. I'm grateful for nearly every aspect of the game, every day of my life. But it's wilfully blind to not acknowledge that our chosen industry of hockey has affected us in some ways, and it's worth looking at how this has shaped the way I've come to view a life within the game.

When you're a hockey player, each day offers a clean sheet and a chance to write a new story, if you stay zoomed in to that present moment. Fresh ice always was, and remains, my number one favourite thing about being a player. The first satisfying cuts into unspoiled slate, feeling the cool air on my face, and dumping a bucket of pucks to begin anew was just so pure. Handling that first puck and physically expressing your best-developed talent is therapeutic. Anything can happen, and that freedom feels exhilarating.

But when you zoom out, most lives lived within hockey have a more consistent and contained arc, and that's where my interests lie now. *My* life within hockey may be unique, but overall, the general path for those of us who love this game shows similar themes.

2

A HOCKEY KID IN
HAPPY TIMES

I can't imagine there are many kids age five or under who look around at their own life and reflect, "Well, gosh, this is all rather peculiar relative to societal norms, now, isn't it?" I was no different. Nothing about growing up as the son of an NHLer was weird, because the other kids around me were NHL sons and daughters. We all had tiny jerseys and team-branded mini-sticks and dads who signed autographs, so whatever, right?

In hindsight, though, maybe it actually was kinda cool.

Despite common impressions, I wasn't exactly "raised in NHL dressing rooms." You just have to look at the timeline. I was born in 1982, on 12/12 at 12:12 a.m. (my birth certificate claims it was 12:10, which my dad assures me is incorrect, so I roll with 12:12 . . . I wore number 12 for a reason).

Dad retired from the Los Angeles Kings in April of 1988, meaning I would've been a whopping five and a half years old at the time. That's old enough to have memories from a couple years, but not old enough to really appreciate that Dad had an "actually kinda cool" job.

That understanding first started crystallizing many miles from Long Island and well north of Los Angeles, many years after his playing days. My parents retired to Kelowna, British Columbia, when hockey came to an end. It's wild now to realize that they were just 34—six years younger than I am at the time of this book's publication—and had been left to figure out what to do with the rest of their lives, with a wave of big successes and big cities behind them. I can't shake how daunting that must have felt.

These were once prairie people, plucked from Saskatchewan into a life where hockey gave and gave, and gave to them yet again. They were dropped into New York at the tender age of 20, figured it out, got comfortable with faster-paced lives—and then, after an insane 15 years, had to drop it back into a lower gear after hockey. Where would you begin? Where would *I* have begun? At some point, hockey players become like Brooks from *The Shawshank Redemption*, totally dependent on the lifestyle and schedule restrictions that have shaped their whole lives. When that's gone, *now what?* is a monumental question.

Just how unique the previous years had been manifested itself in the form of autograph seekers, few though they were. Our family's new life started out in the type of house you'd expect a recently retired NHL family to retire to. It was big, the view was beautiful, and it had a pool. It sat on a cliff overlooking Okanagan Lake, fairly near the bridge in what was then known as Westside, now tidied up to "West Kelowna."

They didn't come in droves or with much regularity, but what stood out to me from those days is that any came at all. I remember watching two random strangers walking down the long driveway to our door with hockey cards, asking for Dad, hoping to get his signature. Those few moments were so far removed from the usual context where I'd seen Dad sign autographs before. Despite the absence of jerseys, other players, an actual hockey game or even ice, people still wanted to claim some small part of something big that happened years ago.

Whatever those events were, I thought, they must have been pretty special.

The dog's name was Benson, but not even Lassie could have done a better job of saving the kid with the little quad motorcycle idling atop his chest.

Two brilliant brothers had decided to play tag, with the older boy mounted on that little 50cc quad—a glorified Power Wheels machine, really—and the younger on his own two feet, with the result being entirely predictable were any adults around to catch it before it got there. The older boy "caught" the younger one and mowed him over, and before the wheels could go clean over the younger brother, they were lifted off the ground, and so Benson had to bark a rapid alarm to bring out the nearest adults.

Those "nearest adults" were New York Islander veterans Clark Gillies and Bob Bourne, best friends and next-door neighbours at the time, who had been sitting on one of their adjacent back decks while my brother and I played in the front. Dad heard Benson barking for help and ran out and picked Jeff and the machine up off of me, which in all likelihood was a far more dramatic scene in my own mind.

There were actually five kids between the two dads, with Clark and his wife, Pam, having three daughters of comparable ages, and so you can excuse a couple of parents in the '80s letting their five kids run around the neighbourhood with their friends. It was a safe, great place to roam free. Maybe putting the kid who used a wheelchair on a motorized pursuit device, and then leaving, wasn't the savviest call, but the rest was excusable.

Those were the early days of life growing up in a house beside the Gillieses. The youngest daughter, Brianna, was about my age, which meant we were in kindergarten together, at each other's birthdays, and at the core of both our "first memories on earth," which definitely didn't include playing doctor—nope, definitely not, don't ask.

We also ended up in our fair share of pictures that would only later become wildly interesting, like me throwing my arm around her while we posed for a picture with some guy on our dad's softball team, Tony Danza.

Brianna, Justin, and Tony Danza.

Good times.

It hadn't always seemed like it would be *five* kids playing in the yard. Before the driver of that rogue machine—my brother, Jeff—was born, they didn't have the technology to foresee the medical issues that would be evident upon his delivery. He arrived with spina bifida, scoliosis and hydrocephalus, which meant that at birth most of his back was essentially a hole, and his survival was far from certain. Clark was the first person my dad called, crying so much that he was unintelligible, which left Clark believing my mother had passed away during childbirth.

Days later, with Jeff clinging to survival, Clark again spoke to my parents. The doctors weren't optimistic about what life would look like for Jeff if he survived the days after his birth. My parents were given dark prognostications about Jeff's expected mental and physical capabilities. In a moment of profound importance, Clark simply said, "You have to give him a chance."

They gave him a chance.

I had heard that story before and heard it again in 2019, when Clark recounted it over the microphone at my brother's wedding to his lovely wife, Sarah. By that time, Jeff's life history included 41 surgeries, medals at the BC Games, friends everywhere and a full life my parents couldn't have imagined for him those first few days. I was his best man that day, as he was on my own wedding day. Even though we live provinces apart—and the trivial detail that he tried to murder me with a quad motorcycle—we're still best friends.

Photoshoot the day of Jeff's wedding.

———

It's not like the first puck I shot went in; it probably took a dozen. The problem wasn't so much that Islanders goaltender Kelly Hrudey was trying to stop my shots, or that he was even aware I was taking them from the other end of the ice at all. The issue with my quest to score on him for the express purpose of being able to claim "I scored on Kelly Hrudey" was more that it was after practice, and there was enough snow on the rink that I needed curling sweepers to get the damn thing all the way down the rink. I was only four years old, so my strength would not have been the highlight of my combined performance (nor would it ever be).

It's one of my first real memories, period, and my first hockey memory definitively. Hrudey was staying out after practice, working on positioning, and my brother and I were tossed on the ice at the empty end, something I grew to love over the years. If you talk to a kid who grew up with a dad in the NHL in those years, this experience seems to be one of the shared staples—we were all granted chunks of pre- or post-practice ice on which to futz around.

I cashed in on this more when Dad coached in the minors and I was a little older, and I'll never forget that feeling of getting to skate onto the rink inside a *professional* hockey arena. It's just a little different than skating in like, Lumby, British Columbia, or whatever your local small-town point of reference would be. Being out there before practice and feeling the presence of the rising seats from beyond the boards while waiting for the first of the players to take the ice felt like being a Roman gladiator awaiting the release of the lion. It all felt so *big*, even to older me, and light years different from how the game felt back home in Mount Boucherie Arena in Kelowna.

The first time you skate in pro buildings can be jarring, considering the arenas where most of us grew up playing. You know those proper minor hockey rinks—pucks off the glass echo deep like church bells, the boards have all the give of retaining walls, and they're usually kept at a temperature level somewhere between "Siberian winter" and Kelvin's absolute zero. Most pro buildings are weirdly quiet (particularly for practice, where sounds just disappear into the abyss), the boards feel deader and the temperature is unfamiliar. It doesn't even feel like proper hockey at first; it feels like ball hockey in an open gym.

I'm not sure what the complete list of advantages looks like for being the son or daughter of a pro, but being immediately comfortable in those settings felt like an advantage during my younger playing days. There's some sort of spatial awareness that's just different there, and I usually thrived in bigger buildings. Players who skate in the Winter Classics describe having challenges getting their bearings, given the different views on the periphery. It's like that going from the rinks on which you grow up to the grown-up rinks, too.

It couldn't have been long after the memory of scoring that first goal—I eventually got my satisfaction by plunking one off the post that may or may not have hit the back of the net—when Dad's teammates started getting us involved in their pranks, because hey, you can't get mad at the kids. My lingering recollection of 1980s NHL dressing rooms consists of copious amounts of nakedness, the lingering miasma of spray deodorant, and the full complement of childish pranks.

Nothing humanized the men—men who might have been superheroes on TV to some—quite like seeing them giggle over harassing their own teammates. I'm convinced that knowing just how human the best athletes are helped my eventual climb feel more attainable. I always knew my talented opposition was made up of flawed weirdos, just like my team.

You remember '80s hair, obviously. It was glorious. As I understand it, the style goal was simply to have the most of it, full stop. Ideally you'd have it absolutely everywhere it could possibly be visible—up, out and poofed like a poodle's. The aforementioned Kelly Hrudey had some iconic looks, but he wasn't alone in that. Back then, a young Luc Robitaille was either in the midst of a 45-goal rookie campaign or a 53-goal sophomore year (damned if I remember the year), both feats that paled in comparison to his beautiful coif.

This is from 1991, but it's the best I can do for proof. You're gonna have to believe me when I say it was large and fluffy then, as if an over-conditioned marmot had fallen asleep while climbing his head. At least he kept the bangs short. Wouldn't want it to look untidy.

Luke Robataille's beautiful mane.

There's nothing quite like the anticipation of a whole dressing room waiting for a prank to play out, though at that time I surely had no idea what I'd done. As requested by a teammate of Dad's while waiting for him after practice, I had dumped a hearty pile of baby powder into the waiting hair dryer by the sink. After some help cleaning up the presentation, it was left where it usually was, while young Luc finished showering up. It's rare that pranks go unidentified right up until they're unveiled and go exactly to plan, but I can still see the cloud of talcum powder enveloping the future Hall of Famer.

Poof.

The house came roaring down behind him. Robitaille headed back to the showers to start over. As you would expect, he was more than a good sport, and went on to treat my brother and me as well as anyone Dad played with. Years after Dad retired, we went to a Kings game in Vancouver, and we went down to the dressing room before the game. Robitaille let me tape one of his sticks, and while I'm *sure* he didn't use it, he claimed he did, and he put up two goals and an assist that night, which I take to mean my online hockey profile should include two NHL assists.

After the game, Wayne Gretzky autographed his game-used silver aluminum Easton, making it out to my brother and me, and home we went.

So, yes, there were some perks to being the son of an NHLer.

When you're five, all the risk of pushing around an eight-year-old in a wheelchair belongs to everyone else. My brother, Jeff, couldn't really feel his legs (he describes it as "patchy"), and I was too young to be held liable anyway, so that all combined for a big green light. It was entirely on everyone else to get the hell out of the way of the human plow I would race around.

That licence to maim was made worse by the fact that at that age, I couldn't actually see over Jeff's big head, so I had to lean around him like Ace Ventura with the broken windshield, meaning some 50 per cent of my field of vision was compromised, had I even had the desire to drive well. But I was too little to be yelled at for what, on its face, would've appeared to be an act of altruism gone reckless. I mean, I was just a tiny widdle boy pushing around his big brother in a wheelchair—would *you* have lectured me? (Oh, how my brother and I wielded that appearance for gain over the years.)

With an invitation and this unmitigated freedom, I began piloting my brother towards the Calgary Flames dressing room at the Los Angeles Forum in 1988. You may remember the Flames of those years: they were what analysts in those days called "very good." Here are their top 15 scorers from that year. This group doesn't include goalie Mike Vernon, who wasn't far from making the list with seven assists that year.

RK	PLAYER	AGE	POS	GP	G	A	PTS
1	Håkan Loob	27	RW	80	50	56	106
2	Mike Bullard	26	C	79	48	55	103
3	Joe Nieuwendyk	21	C	75	51	41	92
4	Gary Suter	23	D	75	21	70	91
5	Joe Mullen	30	RW	80	40	44	84
6	Al MacInnis	24	D	80	25	58	83
7	John Tonelli	30	LW	74	17	41	58
8	Joel Otto	26	C	62	13	39	52
9	Jim Peplinski	27	LW	75	20	31	51
10	Brett Hull	23	RW	52	26	24	50

RK	PLAYER	AGE	POS	GP	G	A	PTS
11	Brad McCrimmon	28	D	80	7	35	42
12	Carey Wilson	25	C	34	9	21	30
13	Gary Roberts	21	LW	74	13	15	28
14	Lanny McDonald	34	RW	60	10	13	23
15	Perry Berezan	23	C	29	7	12	19

A quick Google search shows that they played the Kings in LA four times that year, scoring a total of 24 goals in those games. So, no wonder they were so friendly when we arrived.

My brother and I had been invited into the room before the game (imagine such a thing today?) so we could go around collecting autographs from the biggest stars. I remember meeting Mike Vernon and Lanny McDonald, though I draw a blank on the rest of the sea of faces.

As I pushed Jeff around the locker room, banking him off random sticks and shins like a shot from the point through a screen, someone on the Flames wanted to autograph my brother's Kings jersey, and that autograph took a curiously long time. The inscription was longer than just a signature, too, and they sent us back into the Kings room with an express purpose. This was not standard "Can you please sign my program" behaviour from the team in red.

My dad greeted us then, and that longer autograph got some attention from his teammates and apparently inspired another autograph from a Kings player—also on Jeff's Kings jersey—along with instructions to go back into the Flames dressing room and seek that same player out.

It seems my brother had become a rolling message board.

By now, people were making room the width of a Zamboni as my brother and I Ping-Ponged through the halls, HOV lane–style, back to the Flames room without any idea of what to expect when we got there. But that doubt was immediately erased—they were expecting us, and they were eager to see what else had been written on the jersey.

And so it went.

From one dressing room to the other, right up until game time, my brother became a human chat room, delivering messages that I'm certain rivalled the kind of Mark Twain–like wit we see in digital ones today. I say that cynically, but we can't really be sure it wasn't genius-level stuff, because that jersey was removed from my brother and presumably thrown into an incinerator before we could get in the elevator to go and watch the actual hockey game.

That jersey remains the single NHL item I would wish to have if you gave me the chance to get one back . . . save for maybe an item mentioned in the first chapter.

I've never forgotten the laughter among what were supposed to be grown-ass men each time we'd show up in their respective dressing rooms with a new message. Looking around at those guys then, how could you not feel the love the game of hockey offered? That vibe nestled within me then, and deeply. *Team* seemed to mean so much to them then, and that sentiment seemed to extend beyond the room to the families, from what I could tell.

Imagine being a highly paid professional with big expectations on you, but being patient enough to let your teammate bring his kids onto the ice while you worked on your game after practice? Or letting random kids in on the jokes played on teammates before the games? And lordy, allowing the opposition's kids into the dressing room, and ending up even demonstrating a shared bond with the opposition? It all became such a big part of what made up hockey to me at the time. It was all something aspirational and positive. Everyone was in on the same jokes, it seemed. It's where my hockey roots were fertilized, nurtured and set. I don't know if it had to be hockey specifically that I grew to be a part of, but I knew I wanted to be a part of *that*, to find that bond with the people I worked with towards some common goal.

Age and experience eventually revealed that the game wasn't welcoming for everyone then, and the sorting of who got to be a part of those things could be abjectly cruel. But to a kid, what I saw of hockey and the life it presented, full of laughs and friendship . . . I wanted to be a part of *that*.

The Bob Bourne Charity Classic of the early '90s was an alcohol tournament that served some golf, and it brought celebrities big and small to Kelowna to raise money for the family charity. Like most of these events, while the charity was the beneficiary, most of the people were just there for the party. I remember meeting Canadian music star Tom Cochrane there—for some reason he stands out—but more than anything, it was a glut of former NHLers who came to participate.

There were bottles just everywhere, and near constant laughter. God, it looked fun. I remember being coached to sit off some distance and ignore the F-bombs, but refusing to actually go inside while the entertainment was clearly on the outside.

I had lived next door to Clark Gillies for years in New York as a kid, but one of my first memories of him was in our Kelowna backyard, standing where the property gave way to the cliff above Okanagan Lake at dusk, smashing golf balls like Bryson DeChambeau, deep into what I can only assume was Ogopogo's lair at its immeasurable bottom. Because my dad was a lefty,

Clark had flipped his driver upside down to swing it righty, mashing the first one, then turned himself around and actually hit the ball lefty, launching it from the other side of the ball what looked like a kilometre. The man was an athlete, and the crew around him was in awe at the free entertainment.

Dad and Clark's relationship had its roots in baseball—not hockey or golf. They had both been drafted by the Houston Astros when they were just 16 and had played rookie-league ball together in Covington, Virginia, and so my dad had seen this whole show of athleticism before. Clark was nothing if not a showman, and we were watching a show—along with the leftover humans from that day's golf who had spilled back into our backyard, and "spilled" seems like an apt choice of words here.

That moment serves as something of a stepping stone between what are essentially hockey islands in my memory bank. A big piece of "Hockeyland" was the early part of my life when Dad still played, and the next started with my own career, somewhere around my last year of midget hockey. These "island" moments are reference points in what seemed like an ocean of time where hockey wasn't an everyday priority in my life. Having NHLers around at that point seemed unusual and cool because I was older, but also because I'd been removed from the everyday-ness of it for a while.

I consider the golf tournament a reference point because it was one of the first times I'd seen the "hockey lifestyle" play out away from the rink, and what I saw looked an awful lot like days I would eventually grow up to have . . . in both good ways and bad.

If this is the first memory I have of alcohol in my life, I guess it's fitting that it starts with a backyard gathering of hockey teammates. But it may come as a surprise to know that alcohol was not at all a part of my life as a child. That's mostly because I was eight at the time of that party, and my parents divorced when I was nine, separating on the very day of the next year's charity tournament, in 1991.

After the divorce, that's not what life looked like for our family. My mom, brother and I had moved to a much smaller house in a different-income neighbourhood by the time I was ten, and that's where I did most of my growing up. That's where my mom dug in and signed up for courses to get a full-time job as a lab technician, drawing blood during the weeks while raising a boy and his disabled brother, driving me all over creation to keep up with my sporting interests.

And so, given that my mom rarely had more than a glass of wine in those days, booze wasn't something that played a role in my day-to-day life at home while I was growing up. As you can likely guess, everything she did became about raising us. (Of course I understand why, but I've always felt a frustration with how I've been presented throughout the years, as the "son of an NHLer," when so much of my journey has been guided by her.)

In those years after the divorce, things changed as you'd expect. My brother and I got older and our lifestyles changed, and life with just Mom became our normal. The life I remember most, what I consider "growing up," was done with her, away from hockey except to play the game for fun during the winter like many Canadian kids

Meanwhile, Dad had his first real bouts of struggling—small things at first, but it started to become clear he needed a new direction.

We had been spending every other weekend at Dad's, but in the summer of 1993, he started down a path that seemed to do him good: he got back into hockey.

At first, he just dipped a toe in. He accepted a job as the assistant coach of the Las Vegas Thunder of the International Hockey League (alongside former teammate Butch Goring), leading to me being the only kid growing up in Kelowna with a poster of an IHL player on their bedroom wall that said something like "RaBonkulous" or "Radekal" or something to that effect (because Radek Bonk ruled, obviously).

The minor-league rosters Dad coached then were filled with the names of coaches you know now: Brad Lauer, Marc Habscheid, Todd Richards and even referee Wes McCauley played for him.

After Vegas, Dad took an offer that would shape the next part of his life, and give me some great memories: coaching in the heart of Texas. Man, oh man, did he love Texas. When we stopped at a roadside display on my first day there and he bought enough cheap fireworks to take down a small island nation, I immediately loved it, too. (My brother loved it less when I lit the fuse on a box of 24 "rockets" and knocked it over as I ran away, and he had to spend the next minute with his head buried in his shirt while they ricocheted off the spokes of his tires. Sorry, man.)

Texas was the first of my hockey islands that came via Dad's coaching pit stops, one that brought pro hockey back into my world in a significant way. If, of course, you can count the Western Professional Hockey League of the mid-'90s as professional. It's in the name, so I'm counting it. It was also the right level of "professional" to see hockey culture at its purest, because nobody was there for the money, and it wasn't so professional that a couple of teenagers couldn't be everywhere at all times, including team meetings.

One of the Central Texas Stampede's biggest rivals was from the hockey hotbed of El Paso, the big, bad Buzzards. Most hockey fans are familiar with the local traditions of throwing things on the ice, yeah? There's the octopuses in Detroit, we've seen the catfish in Nashville, and we've seen plastic rats in Florida. El Paso's fans kept it regional, like Nashville, and threw green chili peppers. It couldn't have been more on the nose for the location and league; plus, I imagine they were easier to smuggle in than catfish.

Fans of NHL teams think they know passion, but leagues like the WPHL breed fans similar to those that root for college sports—since they're often the only show in town, fans will *kill* for their local team. Which led to a 14-year-old me pushing my brother's wheelchair around the main walkway above the lower bowl of the El Paso rink (much more ably now than in the Flames story), dressed in Stampede jerseys, and the two of us getting intermittently dinged about the ears with green peppers. I half-expected Yosemite Sam to shoot at my feet and shout, "Now dance!" at intermission.

At that age, I was in my second year of Bantam B rep hockey. I was not an All-Star. I had actually been cut that year, but got called up around Christmas because some kid moved. (Why I underperformed during tryouts reveals just how non-existent my hockey aspirations were at the time: I showed up in new skates that literally had never been sharpened. My mom and I either assumed they came sharpened, or worse, had never even considered it at all. I could just barely stand on my blades that day, after having played on the B rep team the season before. The metal was straight-up flat on the bottom, with no edges. I kept checking for tape on the bottom, and only realized the problem near the end of the embarrassing practice. While a complete public shaming, it's great context for how much I skated leading up to tryouts and where my hockey life was at.) So to me, WPHL hockey was just about the greatest hockey I'd ever seen (without for a second thinking it was the greatest *actual* hockey I'd ever seen). It was just so fun. It was my local Kelowna Rockets junior team, but on steroids—I don't mean that literally, but I'm not ruling anything out. At one point, the Stampede's Jacques Mailhot got into a fight so intense, the force of a collision blew the Zamboni room doors open. His opponent escaped through those doors, which lead to Mailhot chasing him on the cement like a WWE wrestler.

There was something about Dad coaching hockey in Texas that seemed to bring out something he'd been missing in Kelowna. For one thing, it was a lot of fun—I think for him, too. But also he had a purpose, something he'd been searching for. And with that, too, I wonder if he hadn't recaptured something that he'd gotten used to and then lost—a little bit of fanfare. He had a knowledge of the game better than anyone in the state, and was revered as such.

That's something to consider about athletes who leave the limelight for a quieter life. Most have had people telling them they're wonderful nearly daily for years (fans, coaches encouraging confidence, media recounting their better moments). There has to be some emptiness when that dries up. No particular moment would be worse for not having it, but after a while, you might miss that dopamine boost.

When it came to positive reinforcement, Dad got it aplenty there. Coaches in the United States are held at a different level of reverence than what's offered in Canada (outside of a few legends). When I was in junior hockey, the University of New Hampshire flew me down to see their campus, and one of the features of that trip was breakfast with the coach, the legend Dick Umile. We walked into a diner and you'd have sworn it was small-town Texas and we were in *Friday Night Lights*. He was a local celebrity. It was "Hi, Coach" and "Good morning, Coach" every time he moved—God forbid anybody used his real name.

The southern US in particular elevates coaches, and Dad embraced that. On the second day of our visit to Texas, the Stampede had a pep rally—I mean, straight out of the whole college sports playbook. The fans came and cheered, speeches were given, and my brother and I were floored.

The way home was along a straight road that took you to a stop sign at a T-shaped intersection where you had to merge onto the upper part, and it wasn't easy to get in. At some point Dad got a little aggressive and maybe cut someone off, and that maybe *definitely* pissed someone off.

The truck behind us pulled up fast to our bumper and laid on the horn, and Dad's girlfriend begged him not to flip the driver the bird. "This is Texas, they'll shoot you," she explained, to no avail. After more interplay, Dad had had enough. He was pulling over and getting out and it was about to get real.

At this point, his girlfriend was near tears—"This is *Texas*, and there is a very real chance you are going to get shot." As the doors of the truck opened behind us, Dad had a moment of lucidity and closed his, and we sped off.

They chased.

As we neared home, his girlfriend explained that we absolutely could not go to the house and show whoever it was back there where we lived, so we passed our exit and kept driving with them on our tail. She pulled out her phone and began to call the cops, and as she did, four cop cars sped up on all sides of our vehicle with lights a-blazing.

It turns out that in the vehicle behind us were . . . undercover police officers, and Dad was in trouble.

In theory.

The tone of the police officer's voice changed completely when he realized he was dealing with "Coach," and Dad's status turned out to be our absolute salvation (of a kind that I recognize most people are not so lucky to experience).

We were not only free to go, we were apologized to, and Lord knows how differently that could've gone had Dad not been Dad. Whatever the case may be, we were lucky.

All I know was that in Texas, it seemed like Dad had found a standing he'd been missing; meanwhile, I'd been inspired by life in the minors, which looked like a fun way to live a life, even though light years from the NHL.

We both plowed forward, and with Dad's success in the WPHL—the team went 35–27–0–2 and made the WPHL finals—he now had an ascendent coaching career ahead of him. That season made it seem as though hockey was ready to give to him and our family again, after having done so for so many years before.

Dad's partnership with Butch Goring dated back a few years before Vegas, and his desire to climb up the ranks made his next move a no-brainer. He rejoined Butch's staff, this time in Salt Lake City, Utah, for another crack at the IHL.

Those years of Dad's career would impact me more from a hockey standpoint than the Islanders years, as I was at a perfect age to absorb it all. He was Butch's assistant that year, then took a head coaching job with the Las Vegas Thunder of the same league for a year, then came back to Utah as head coach and GM of the Grizzlies for two more seasons.

My brother and I went down to wherever he was for at least a week each season, usually two, and at that point I was a sponge.

His teams were successful, too (no championships, but they were playoff teams), and I loved seeing how decisions were made. When the games were over and Dad was done for the night, we always thought it was cool that we got to stay up and go into the busy bar with him while he had a beer or two and chatted with some of the Grizzlies' biggest fans.

One thing I took away from that time, and it has never left me, is how remarkably human personnel decisions end up being. This is less commentary on how Dad coached and more on the experience of seeing how all decisions were made at the higher levels. The "remarkably human" thing isn't meant to be synonymous with "compassionate and thoughtful"; I mean "flawed and filtered through our biases," like emotion. Some moves—and I imagine this is more the case in the minors, where salaries are small and less attention is paid—really did get made because "fuck that guy, that's why." Dad always considered all the options and listened to other opinions. I realized that there's rarely some computer program or jury that makes major decisions, so every life-altering decision for the players comes down to the opinion of a person or three. I think that insight has allowed me to knowledgably criticize the choices that hockey teams make today. Things can be rushed, things do get missed.

When dealing with the media, organizations like to frame their decision-making within a *Wizard of Oz*–like grandeur because it insulates them from criticism. And in fairness to the media, they generally buy in because they're operating with less information than the teams have. But more often than not, bad moves get made simply because one of us sentient meat bags has to make the call, and most of us are just out here making our best guesses.

Hockey's hard to break down because the games and their outcomes aren't as clean as in, say, baseball. Sometimes the right decisions ("We should pair these two Ds") elicit the wrong results (two bad bounces cause them to get scored on twice), which sends back the wrong information about the original decision ("That didn't work—we'd better change course"), and your decision-making gets worse despite your having more information to process.

That's why I regularly complain on the radio that hockey is a "dumb game" (it's actually not), and why the nauseating mantra of "process over results" has merit. You first have to assess what a team was *trying* to do before you can decide whether they executed their plan well enough—or even properly judge the plan at all. Becoming an expert in anything takes an ungodly number of hours, and I'm grateful I learned to start looking for "plans" at a young age. The sport doesn't defy analysis, but it sure does its best to obfuscate it.

Beyond the learning, though, those years were just cool because the players on those teams made my brother and me feel like we belonged. We'd roll through the room and grab mittfuls of Dubble Bubble, pound the "juice" (sports drinks) and tell the trainer "great mix today" just like the players would, and we'd loiter around and hear the stories.

That I got to play for that same Utah team in that same dressing room exactly 10 years later would've blown the mind of 15-year-old me. As a young player, I could always score, but I had only recently grown, and as a teenager, hockey still didn't seem like a very viable life path. More than anything, that room made me feel like a hockey spy, soaking in all the little details I could.

That double-agent vibe would never fully go away for me, even as I climbed the ranks (which likely explains how I ended up in media). You'd think I'd be perfectly comfortable in dressing rooms, having spent a life in them, and I am, but more in the sense of how you feel at a friend's house than the way you feel in your own. It always felt like I was just visiting someone else's cool little world—and really, I was at the time, given that I hadn't earned my way there yet—so I wanted to preserve as much as possible in my brain before they kicked me out. Maybe I was meant to do *this*, this media thing, after all.

Dad's coaching days ended, though, and I'll move on from them swiftly and without explanation—a metaphor of sorts, because from my perspective that's the way a lot of things ended for Dad in the mid-'90s: abruptly and without review, never to be visited again. During his last gig, he was a head coach/GM in one of the NHL's feeder leagues at age 45 and with a big-time résumé, and was going head to head with future NHL coaches like Dave Tippett and Randy Carlyle. In his last year, 2000–01, his team had a respectable 38–36–0–8, but when the season was over, that was just . . . it.

To understand how I see hockey's culture and its influences, it's important to understand how my views were shaped, and the path my Dad took after his playing days. When you look back at a few of his years both before and after coaching, he dipped his toe into a lot of pools without ever becoming a full-time swimmer. A nine-to-five job was not something he wanted, and given how his life had gone up until then, I understand why he sought other avenues. He was in a unique situation, given his past, which had seen him earn well from the unconventional and unsustainable path of pro sports. It left him with measures of lingering celebrity that offered more open doors to unique opportunities than for your average middle-aged guy looking for a career change. But long-term plans were something he was neither making nor executing then, which is why I think it's fair to introduce the word *concussions*—plural. My wife works in brain trauma and I've learned the shared challenges of some of her patients, many of whom no longer have the ability to make and execute long-term plans. It could be some of that (he has told me he believes he has chronic traumatic encephalopathy, or CTE), or with Dad, maybe things just didn't work out—that's possible, too. Whatever the causes, it's worth noting how things seemed to come together several times before ending abruptly.

These were tough years to process for a kid who had almost exclusively seen his dad praised. As humans, we're not great at adjusting our opinions after we form first impressions. Multiply that by a great deal when you grow up learning that your dad is a (sporting) hero to many, a guy worthy of the cover of *Sports Illustrated*.

Immediately after his NHL days in 1989, Dad returned to New York while we got set up in Kelowna so that he could finish his certification to become a stockbroker, which he accomplished. He had always been a smart, capable guy, so that shocked nobody. He spent a little time as a broker back in Kelowna, but it involved cold-calling and a more scheduled lifestyle that must've seemed jarring in the immediate wake of the NHL, and it didn't last.

He had studied golf-course management prior to coaching, too, and passed the courses necessary to become certified. He got hired as the general manager of a golf course in Kelowna—Shannon Lake, on the Westside, where I would one day be a junior member—which surely wasn't easy to accomplish. But shortly after that he wasn't the GM there anymore, chalking it up to differences among those in ownership and his not wanting to be a part of their circus.

In the years after coaching, he got his real estate licence and sold houses around Kelowna, and he was into that, but it never quite took, either. He'd keep his licence updated for a good number of years, maybe a decade, but it doesn't feel accurate to say he was a real estate agent over that time. He did it the longest, but I don't know that it was ever a focused career identity.

In the years leading up to his summers running the Hockey Greats Fantasy Camp—a camp where paying participants got to take the ice with former NHL stars—Dad played on Legends of Hockey tours that brought in decent appearance fees but boy, they seemed like some kind of lifestyle. Those guys had a blast touring small-town Canada, but my impression is that each tour was more or less an off-ice party with intermittent stops at arenas to sweat it all out. As nice as it was for the pocketbook, it didn't provide a set schedule or long-term plan to lean on (or a real purpose). Relationships never lasted too long, he started to flip the houses he lived in and move every year or two, and for a while the only permanent thing in his life became impermanence.

As I moved on from high school in 2000 and Dad moved on from coaching, our relationship grew strained. I became more wary of his direction and lifestyle. From experience, I can tell you there's one generalization that would get no pushback from the population at large: alcoholics are not reliable sorts, nor overly honest ones. Years before I developed my own problem, I was on the wrong end of that relationship with exasperating frequency. When someone is struggling with a condition, be it alcoholism or brain trauma or mental health or anything else, how much can you forgive while you're getting hurt?

While I don't exactly know why none of the aforementioned ventures stuck, I don't think it's unfair to wonder if, with Dad, they didn't coincide with the rise of a wave that would eventually crest in a debilitating way. Being more sympathetic to the heavy undertow of alcoholism now, I view some of the developments above differently than I did as teenager.

The timelines and locations of our lives were strangely asynchronous. Dad's last season coaching was in 2001, which brought him back to Kelowna full-time. That year was also my first in junior hockey, which pulled me from Kelowna at the same time.

That was really the beginning of a hockey journey that would take me out of Kelowna for good. I spent one season with my first junior team in Osoyoos, which was 80 minutes away, and the next two in Vernon, which was closer to a 45-minute drive from our front door.

My mom missed maybe three games over those three years; Dad travelled with his Legends tours and made appearances when he could, maybe a handful of times per year when I was in Vernon. He and I fell into a summer routine of beers at the pub and beers on the golf course, and we always enjoyed our time together . . . and our beers. It's not like we didn't bond or that there wasn't a lot of love there—there absolutely was, and still is. But those who've loved—or have been—alcoholics can tell you how priorities get obscured in the tough years.

As hockey drifted from my dad's focus, it became mine, and my reflections on the game and the world around it (including cultural themes like alcohol and concussions) changed dramatically as I earned my way into those same rooms I'd stepped inside many times before, though with much smaller feet.

3

FINDING MYSELF AS A PLAYER AND A VICE SEEKER

The wind hit me like a trainer trying to snap a prone boxer back to their senses, slap after sturdy slap in the face. I was unfazed, though. I was having a moment, the type you mostly have as a teenager, the type that feels profound and meaningful—and maybe it is, but more often it's just some combination of hormones and a decent song. Regardless of which it was, it felt like it mattered then, and sitting alone on the top deck of a chilly ferry from Vancouver across to the Island, I felt like I had made the first decision that mattered in my life. I was heading to my first junior hockey tryout, and whether it went well at this one or not, a few summer "showcase" skates against players with the same aspirations had convinced me I was good enough to play junior *somewhere* (whether in the league above or below the Junior A team I was aiming at, I didn't know), so it was going to be my first real year focusing on hockey.

Sometimes symbolism in your life shows up quietly and with delicate nuance. Other times, you make a bold life decision to focus on hockey and the rink at your first destination greets you with, quite literally, the world's biggest hockey stick.

The world's largest hockey stick, in Cowichan Valley.
© Brendan Kergin

Subtle like a sledgehammer.

In retrospect, though, that decision to dive headlong into hockey *did* matter. Maybe it wasn't just the Jimmy Eat World playing on the ferry after all.

I cannot emphasize enough how much my mom and I were flying blind, heading into that tryout. All we really knew was that the best junior players got college scholarships, and since the NHL didn't seem a realistic option, a scholarship—while still a long shot—seemed like a conceivably attainable goal. I could be the worst player at the camp or the best; it could be very professional or an utter joke. We really had no idea what we were walking into.

In those years, "Mom and I sorting things out" had sort of become the theme. Dad was a willing ear on the phone when we'd chat, but he hadn't been around and didn't have much input to offer. Mom had met someone a handful of years earlier, Glenn Fawdry, who was super supportive and good to me over the years. My brother had my back whatever I chose, and always offered his two cents' worth. But as of 2000–01, when the internet was still mostly useless for finding junior hockey information (not that I considered the internet a useful source for learning then), my life course was being charted by my mom, myself, and whatever word of mouth we could pick up.

Cowichan Valley? Sure, let's do it.

Most elite players are identified early. People prepare them for the landscape that lies ahead from a young age. For me, being good at hockey—even *trying* to be good at hockey—was new, and my knowledge about the ladder I'd have to try to climb felt thin, given that I was 17 years old and had spent a sum total of zero mental energy on it. I was just gonna go play hockey and let the chips fall where they may. Seeing how those chips fell led me to the insight that roster decisions from "tryouts" are rarely meritocratic outcomes born of a clean slate.

This camp was for a Junior A team in the BCHL, and Cowichan Valley was one of dozens of teams that had expressed interest after my minor hockey days. After dealing with the letters and phone calls and invites, I decided I was going to Cowichan's camp strictly because they seemed the most interested. That was at least 99 per cent of what was going on. I was told to "tattoo the team logo on my ass" in the months leading up to the camp, which you can imagine put some weight behind the belief that I could make the team.

I was cut from the team before I could even find a parlour for that ass tattoo, let alone unpack my bags at the hotel.

I'd likely still follow the impulse to go where I seemed most wanted today, despite that outcome. But it was an early lesson about hockey as a career, and how those beyond the most shining prospects have to prove their worth every single day. (And in some cases, you have to learn to see through people who are really good at *pretending* they want you.)

———

Growing up in Kelowna's minor hockey system (more specifically, Westside), I had just played where they put me and enjoyed
it, with absolutely zero thoughts of hockey as a potential "career."
I didn't play at the top levels of pee wee or bantam (I usually
played B rep), and that, combined with being an athletic guy
who was more than familiar with the game, meant I tended to
score a lot. Since I was always playing at a level that matched my
development, I was always among the top few in goals and
points, which contributed to a love for playing. I can't imagine
that struggling to keep up at the highest level you can play without embarrassing yourself is a great time, nor is pining for more
ice time. In my first year of midget hockey, at 15, I got a nice
surprise: enough players had given up on the game—as they do
at that age—that I made the A rep team, though I assure you it
was a numbers thing. I think there was one total cut, two at the
most, that first year.

That was my first crack at integrating with the recognizably
good players at my high school—those guys who wore their
hockey tracksuits to school and for whom *Hockey Player* was
part of their personal identities. You'd think that would've been
me, too, given my upbringing, but if I was at all perceived that
way, I certainly never felt the part. All that blue and orange and
Stanley Cup stuff felt like artifacts of my childhood, not something connected to my own playing.

For someone outside of that group, looking up from the
divisions below, the culture felt intimidating—the constant ball-
busting, the (perceived) unshakable confidence. When hockey
gets accused of not being welcoming, I immediately understand
the vibe as something like what I felt then, even though I'm not
at all someone the game wouldn't welcome with open arms.
I was fortunate enough to know that when I tried to get in, the

initial reaction would be to give me a chance, and I recognize that not everyone gets to start there.

And I learned that, as with exclusive clubs, it's usually fun once you're in, but getting in comes with friction for many.

My first-year midget team was unremarkable, aside from the surprise that I still scored at as good a clip as I had in lower leagues. Something else changed, too. Somewhere within that year, I had one of those growth spurts you hear about a lot from athletes, where I grew like six inches in a year and suddenly my résumé went from "scores a lot" to "scores a lot and is six feet tall at 16 years old"—and apparently scouts liked that combination.

I played well enough and carried myself well enough in that first year of midget to be named captain in year two. (To this day, I'm certain that one of the coaches didn't want to be seen as picking his own very deserving son, so I'll give a shout-out to Brad and Brandon Miller for defaulting to me as the next choice.) And boy, oh boy, did we have a year, from the drop of the puck to the end.

We won and won and won, and before you knew it, little Mount Boucherie Arena was packed with high school kids on game nights. We were a deep-scoring team, including from the back end, and it's there that I laid the foundation of my understanding of the "start-of-season snowball." When a team wins early, players start to believe in one another, and believe in what the coach is saying. It simplifies things when you know you just have to execute the plan, instead of wondering if the plan (or talent) is good enough. Thinking back to how I felt during the high-stakes games at the end of the season, I can't believe my heart rate ever came down. In the end, we won the league championship in front of our raucous school friends and parents.

Our terribly bleached-blond group became the first team from our area to win a provincial championship, and I'm not sure there's a game I played after those tournament games that mattered as much to me on game day as those ones did.

Those championships you win at the minor hockey level are just so different from those at the junior or college or pro level. There's a case to be made that they *mean* more. The players you win with in minor hockey aren't just teammates; in many cases, they're the kids you grew up with. I'll never forget the tears in the eyes of one of my closest friends, Dave Cunning, before the final game, talking about the chance to win something like that together after so many years playing side by side.

The Stanley Cup is the pinnacle of our sport, the greatest accomplishment a hockey player can put on his résumé, and so, in turn, winning it is a wildly emotional experience for players. It's everything in our game, right? But far more people have won championships as kids with profound emotional meaning, given what the title meant to them and their friends around them, in that moment. These people, myself included, feel an attachment to those championships as strongly as if they were Stanley Cups, because they mattered then as if they were. This was my first experience with real hockey success, at least at a meaningful level, that didn't belong to someone else. While it was the end of the season, it was also the start of something.

We make light of people who won't let go of big moments from sporting "glory" days of yore, but they matter so much because you only get a crack or two at each respective level on the way up, and once you age out of the hockey system, it's extremely uncommon to replicate the forging of team bonds with adults the way you do as kids with your teammates. The endorphin rush is no less significant when you win at the lower levels on your way up. It's made more meaningful by the fact that, for kids, bigger trophies are still on the table down the road. Beer-league trophies are a cool win, but the success ends there. As a kid winning a title, you've won all you are eligible to win . . . for now. "There could be better ahead" is the positive backdrop of childhood titles.

I scored our first goal in that provincial final, but we were down 2–1 halfway through the third period when two of our defencemen, Travis Parro and Travis Martell, found the back of the net, and we hung on. I put home an empty-netter to cap it off, and at long last Westside took its first—and still only—province-wide title.

It's funny. I still often cry when I see the Stanley Cup handed out and players achieve their lifelong dreams. I know how meaningful it is, and I've explicitly seen how it can change the lives of those who win it. Part of the reason I get so happy for guys is that I know that to get there, they've had to navigate more than just hockey—there's politics and luck and the whole business of the game. The wins in minor hockey, while not without the occasional bit of politics along the way, mostly have a greater purity.

That championship remains one of my most meaningful hockey accomplishments, so I'll give a shout-out to a great group of guys from what's now West Kelowna.

That season, I scored 53 goals and 118 points in 56 games. I was captain of a championship team. I had grown both mentally and physically, coming to see myself as a *Hockey Player*. For the first time, I felt like there might be more out there for me within the game.

In previous summers, I had mixed in a single week at some sort of hockey camp (namely Dave Roy's Edge of Excellence and the Okanagan Hockey School, my future summer employer), but I dreaded them. No disrespect to those camps, which were well run and informative, but summer as I knew it was not for hockey—not for me, anyway. Prior to hockey *mattering*, under the summer sun I was first and foremost a golfer, having won a couple of junior club championships when I was 16. (Junior memberships were essentially teenage daycare, and they were cheap—my dues were about $200 for a summer, and I averaged well over 18 holes a day.)

In those years, Mom was working full-time, so my friend and I would get dropped off at the course before our moms went to work. We'd stay all day, hitting at the driving range to fill the time after golf, getting picked up on our way home. That was the first portion of every summer day. Then I'd head to the Earls across from the sails in Kelowna to bus tables, and do it all again the next day. That's what my off-seasons had consisted of up until the age of 17. I wasn't a draft pick, or on anyone's radar at all. I wasn't fast-tracked into any training program. Nobody sent me a binder with a workout plan or asked me how my progress was in the gym or told me how to lift to improve. I was the son of a former NHLer, but I was 17 years old the summer I got my first gym membership and started eating a bit more protein and pawing at the weights. The results were far from drastic—I don't know if I could do a chin-up before I was 20—but it turned out the improvement from "almost no training" to "some" mattered a significant amount.

It's not a great sign when you're at a training camp for a junior hockey team—that being Cowichan—and you mention a concurrent opportunity somewhere else and they *encourage* you to go. But that's how it went at that first tryout, ass tattoo and all. In pursuit of that college scholarship, I really wanted to play

Junior A hockey. I figured if I made a team at that age, I'd have a few years to get better and try to make that happen (I had three years of junior eligibility ahead). But surprisingly, one of the few opportunities I had to play major junior in the Western Hockey League came that year, in Kelowna, with the Rockets.

How could a player turn down even a slim chance to play for their hometown team?

When camp in Cowichan started, I let them know about that WHL camp I had been invited to, and they all but sent someone to the hotel to help pack my suitcase. I had initially accepted the Rockets invite with the reasoning that if Cowichan solidly wanted me, I wouldn't be going anywhere. Alas, I don't think I made so much as a single memorable play, I never had any sort of mojo going, and I can't exactly explain what went wrong. Nothing happened, and then it ended. Part of it, I think, is that my strengths have always been most visible in game play, with my brain and hands, and so I wasn't that impressive in drills. That's also just how it goes sometimes in hockey; the puck doesn't bounce your way, and as a winger there's only so much you can do to change your fortunes over a small sample. Whatever the case, after less than a week I was back on the ferry with the wind smacking me in the face, though this time it felt less profound and more like a personal indignity, so I dejectedly went inside and searched for different music.

Having not been good enough at the Junior A camp, I wasn't overly enthusiastic about my WHL chances. In more direct terms, I expected to get smoked in Kelowna.

The Rockets were already a good team. But from whatever confluence of circumstances—that aforementioned luck, being in the flow from a previous camp, whatever—I couldn't *not* score at that camp. Everything I shot went in. It culminated in an intrasquad game in front of a few thousand people at Kelowna's new-ish Prospera Place (which was a pretty big deal for me), where I scored twice in a 3–2 win for my side.

I was in a Rockets jersey, in the big-boy rink in my hometown, hearing my name announced after scoring goals. That didn't hurt the ol' confidence.

They cut the roster down and cut the roster down and cut it down some more, and I remained. One day, I looked around the dressing room before a practice and it felt like we had roughly the number of bodies required to ice a hockey team. We were, in fact, damn near down to roster numbers when they called me in to have a more serious talk about what was going on. I was told the decision was basically down to me and two other players. (I had sussed out that it was probably Randall Gelech and Tyler Mosienko. Rockets fans should be very glad they stuck instead of me, given their being very good players and the whole winning-the-Memorial-Cup thing.) They wanted me to play exhibition games to help them make their final decisions.

Sounds exciting.

Somewhere along the way, it occurred to me I was just 17, and if I made the WHL then, I was suddenly on a path much more in line with the one my dad had followed—with great success. The problem was, if you play exhibition games at the major junior level, you lose NCAA eligibility.

Sounds like a pretty life-defining, less exciting proposition.

The rule at the time was that you would lose a year of eligibility, plus however many games you played in the Canadian Hockey League, even just for exhibition games. I was already old in terms of a college prospect, and knew that no school would like me enough to give me a scholarship if they also had to sit me on the sidelines for a year. The whole reason I was playing junior was to pursue a scholarship, but again, this was the WHL and my hometown, and wasn't I improving fast? And then there's the deal that every year you play major junior, they'll look after a year of education at a Canadian school. That didn't hurt as a selling feature, either, as much as I'd always been set on playing hockey at an NCAA school. My brother and I had gone to countless Rockets games as kids, with the owners (much love to the Hamiltons) inviting my brother to attend the games to keep stats for them. I felt strong ties there.

The decision makers with the Rockets understood my hesitation but encouraged me to dress for exhibition games with a sweetener: they would throw out the game sheet if I played. Nobody would ever be able to track that I'd dressed in a CHL game, I was told (I still don't know how this sort of thing could have been checked up on then, had anybody cared to). I believed it was somewhat commonplace at the time, and that was all I needed. I suited up for the Kelowna Rockets in Kamloops against the Blazers, which I thought was insanely cool because I knew a lot of the names on the opposing team from watching Rockets games.

I still think about a play where I was backchecking as the very last man up the rink, and a turnover saw me get a quick pass in behind the D to go the other way, leaving me with minimal speed but nobody between me and the goalie. Sometimes you make a garbage move and it works; sometimes you make a great move and it doesn't, and this was the latter. I dropped a shoulder and froze the goalie (I was always Team Deke over Team Shoot, because I hadn't yet developed a shot), and went to slide it into the empty net, which would've worked easily at every other level I had played up to that point. The 'tender made a desperation dive back, though, and got his paddle down, swatting it back out like Dikembe Mutumbo. The only thing missing was the finger wag. (The save was ice cold, though; he really should've done the wag.) I swore never again to assume a puck was in, even if I was almost certain the goalie was down and out. Turns out "almost certain" isn't certain enough.

I still wonder what would've happened had I scored there. It's a fun thought exercise. Does the future of any player hang in the balance of a single failed or executed play? (After years around the game, I have concluded yes.) Would mine have? (Years later, I have concluded that scoring probably keeps me with the team a little longer.) And if so, Lord, am I glad that guy made that save. There's no chance I'd have been relevant on that Josh Gorges–captained Rockets team that went on to win the Memorial Cup, I mean zip, zero, zilch, nada. Those guys were *good*. I didn't exactly get cut after that game, but given how well my direct competition played, combined with the hesitance my mom and I felt about playing exhibition games without a solid promise of making the team, my time with the Rockets came to a close. I didn't directly get cut, but they couldn't promise more for me without seeing me in more games, and the risk of damaging my dream of a college scholarship was just too great. Junior camps all over were winding down, and it was time to move on to the next plan.

Maybe you'd expect some sour grapes about how my first run of tryouts had gone, but I don't blame Cowichan or the Rockets for saying certain things so that they could see more of me before deciding I wasn't for them. You can't promise away unearned spots, and I never saw any malice in it. I believe Cowichan did want me there, and that I just disappointed when the time came. (Should they have given me more time to sort it out? That's a debate about the player choices their management made, and not about a broken system.) I don't fault the Rockets for pushing for more viewings of me—my results had been so much better than expectations that seeing whether I could sustain it made sense.

Teams get seen as manipulative and dishonest, and hey, many are. By no means am I claiming it doesn't happen. But they're also trying to build the best teams possible. "Fairness" is nearly impossible in competitive sports, and so eventually the onus has to be on the player to perform.

At that point, I had been with the Rockets for weeks. Junior A rosters were set, and I wasn't really sure what to do, now that I realized I was probably good enough to play at that level but nobody was requesting my services. (I wasn't as *sure* I was good enough to play in the Junior A BCHL as much as I suspected it.) I think because I had chosen Cowichan, the other teams in the league that had been interested had stopped following my progress (I wasn't some prodigy, after all), so I ended up having my pick of Junior B teams, which were still assembling. I figured if I lit it up there someone would find me. We chose the one closest to Kelowna, which ended up working out brilliantly, much like the B rep teams of the past had fit me. Hello, Osoyoos Heat, and a year that was crucial to my development, offering me big minutes and a big role and exactly the type of spot I should've been in if I wanted to get better.

OSOYOOS HEAT, 2000–01

I was somewhat oblivious to junior hockey culture. I had been in plenty of NHL dressing rooms, but they were populated by grown men who'd "made it." Let me tell you, junior hockey 20 or so years ago wasn't tidy.

That year, I wasn't really exposed to much of it off the ice because to say I kept my nose clean at that age would be an all-time understatement. I had enrolled in a college course online, I still didn't drink, period, and I had had a girlfriend for a few years (it would be a long-distance relationship that year, as she went away to school). I mentioned having a year to focus solely on hockey, and when I say "focus on hockey," I mean I focused *solely* on hockey.

I was 17 (turning 18 in December), and the bulk of the players at that level were either 16 or 17 and in high school, or 20 and on some other wavelength—I guess just playing to play (and often working at jobs in town). That meant that during the day, I had time others didn't, and I'd occasionally go down to the rink and just skate by myself while others were in school. Having access to a rink like that feels like something that would never happen today. Some days, it was just . . . mine.

In retrospect, it would've done me a lot of good to, I dunno, lift a single weight that season, but I did not (not a single one, not one time). That will give you context about the level I was at, and the degree of attention we received. But I played a shit-ton of hockey, thought about hockey and watched hockey.

Junior B hockey is wild, because amidst the players who have bright futures (Shea Weber was on the Sicamous team that year), you get a mix of kids who are super talented but have no interest in focusing that ability (booze and drugs started to have a visible effect on some), and some kids who, well, are blessed with neither talent nor a bright hockey future who fill out the bottom rosters. As the guy showing up late from WHL camp (with the omnipresent reality of having an NHLer as a dad), I was judged immediately because people assumed I thought I was too cool to be there. That was actually verbalized by our assistant coach on day one. But I had barely thought about any hockey stuff prior to that summer, and was just flying by the seat of my pants. I had no idea how good the level would be, or if I'd even be good there.

The good news was, in Junior B terms, I was *very* good.

It's possible that I just got off to a rough start in Cowichan a number of weeks earlier, and that I found my stride a couple of weeks too late to have ended up in the right league, but in retrospect, focusing on hockey while being one of the best players in a league was great for my development. I played tons of minutes and in the biggest offensive situations, and scored and scored and scored again. When it was all said and done, I led my conference in scoring, finishing second in the league to Andrew Ebbett, who went on to have a nice little NHL career.

It was nice getting the feel of junior hockey culture—the bullshit, the machismo, the faux-alphaism run amok—on a level I was obviously good enough to play at, because it insulated me from the fear that would've made me hesitant in social situations. Teammates don't take many runs at the team's leading goal scorer.

By mid-season, I had a sense of where I fit into the league. I also had a moment where I might have gotten a little too big for my britches.

In the third period of a game in which I had two goals and four assists, I was looking to add my first career fight to the day's accomplishments. I was finally at a level where you wore a visor instead of a cage, and fighting was not just allowed but encouraged. It was a badge of honour to be a guy who's willing to fight, and frankly, I'd never fought. I mentioned junior hockey culture— well, I really didn't wanna be the guy in the room who was seen as too scared to go at a guy.

I sought out a smaller guy because inexperienced fighters shouldn't pick huge guys for their first opponent, but a word of advice: if you're seeking "small" to fight someone, maybe consider dimensions other than height? The guy I chose would eventually walk onto my college team three years later. His name was Ryan McMullan. He was not tall, no, but he was built like a fire hydrant and had actually thrown a punch before in his life, unlike me. Turns out he was an Alaskan (*red flag, Bourne*). I asked him to fight the only way I knew how, as dictated by my understanding of hockey culture, which was by saying, "Wanna go?" and I swear he hit me square in the nose three times before I ever got my gloves off. My visor was opaque with blood.

Sunglasses have never sat square on my nose ever since. I can't help but think about my poor mother watching Ryan paint the inside of my helmet with the contents of my own sinuses.

I don't know if I thought he and I would take time to legislate the particulars of the engagement before doffing our gloves ("'Kay, no head shots, and the safe word is 'pineapple'"), but if you both ask someone to fight in hockey and lose before you can drop your gloves, maybe you were ill prepared for the battle.

I would never drop my gloves second in a fight again—not that I fought more than a half-dozen times over the next decade. Turns out you don't need your opponent to sign a permission slip to begin throwing.

The season felt like a junior hockey trial run—smaller crowds in smaller towns, still some players who weren't that great. By the playoffs, I had established a reputation and become a target, particularly of some violent slashes to the hands right off faceoffs. By Game Two, one of them got me and broke my thumb, which was followed by the stupidest series of hockey games I've ever tried to play. The thumb was broken, very obviously, but I had never missed games and didn't want to then. So it was taped up and injected and I switched to a heavy stick that vibrated less, and I tried to play basically one-handed. I was awful. We lost in the second round of the playoffs, and so with that behind me I set out on some legitimate training with the goal of moving on up that off-season.

With that campaign all said and done, the best-case scenario happened—the Junior A Vernon Vipers of the BCHL, some 45 minutes from Kelowna, offered to sign me to a "card," all but guaranteeing me a spot on their team in 2001–02. Vernon was a great organization, it was close to home, and it was about to get real for me. Thousands of fans went to those games, players made the NHL from that league, and my real education in life as a hockey player was about to begin.

VERNON VIPERS, 2001–03

Maybe my brain was always programmed to write, because between the ages 18 and 20 I did an extremely strange thing for a junior hockey player: I kept a nightly journal. That may invoke imagery of me lying on my stomach on my bed, twirling my hair with one hand, writing about some girl I had a crush on with the other, but it was far less that and far more anxiety-drenched musings on the likely roster permutations, and me talking myself into fighting to improve my odds (I never did work up the chutzpah in training camp). Here's a look at the first page, which is from exactly 20 years ago to the day, as I first write this.

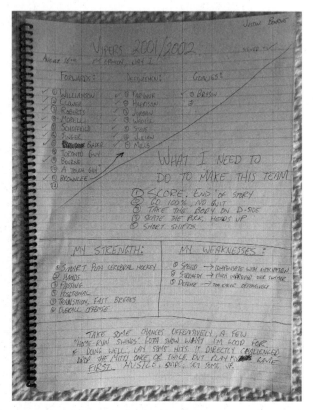

This is extremely embarrassing in retrospect, let's move on.

It started as me trying to figure out where I fit on the team, but it grew. As you may have guessed from the "2001–03" header above, I did fit on the team, and eventually quite well. I say "eventually," because initially it seemed more than likely they were going to punt me back to the KIJHL. (A good rule with leagues, at least when I was on the way up: the more letters in its abbreviation, the worse the league was. Five letters was . . . a lot.)

I got off to a slow start at camp, similar to how it had gone in Cowichan during my first kick at junior. It occurs to me now that I didn't really know how to get myself "camp ready" those first few junior hockey summers.

I had made the team (I surely wouldn't have if I hadn't already signed a card), but a couple weeks after the season began, I got the dreaded call to go to the coaches' office one night at 7 p.m. This was after the team was more or less set, and it was just a matter of a player or two who still might get cut or dealt. The office was a little rented place in a strip mall with a small reception area and a couple of back offices. But the call to an office away from the rink in off-hours, while a junior team is getting its roster settled— well, they usually don't call you in to say you're doing a great job.

What they called me in to tell me was, "You're getting sent down to our Junior B affiliate in Revelstoke," to which I offered the salient counterpoint, "No, I'm not." They wanted me to sign an "affiliate player" card that would let them call me up and send me down at their discretion; otherwise, they were just going to cut me loose outright. I still don't know if the way the next hour unfolded played out legitimately or if it was staged to scare or motivate me, but regardless, it still baffles me to this day. It may be the only time in my life I made the case for myself loudly and clearly. I hadn't been given a fair shot in a role that suited my skills, I absolutely *was* capable of being effective at that level, and they were making a mistake sending me down. It was all true, which helped me say it with my chest.

I was supposed to score, and I hadn't scored in camp, so I guess they had seen enough. I stepped out of the coaches' office and called my mom from the phone at the by-then-gone receptionist's desk to decide, well, what to do with the entirety of my life going forward. The conversation I had just had with the coaches was a serious rebuff of our whole "get a college scholarship" plan, given that I would turn 19 during the season and was still just hoping to make the BCHL as a rookie. In a phone call that lasted just a few minutes, one that may or may not have involved some tears (and a growing anger), we basically decided I would play out one more season of junior hockey while ramping up my online college workload in Junior B, and just see where that took me.

Vernon's coaches had spoken with my mom in the lead-up to that season, and so she spoke to the coaches then for clarity as well. That "clarity," I believe, included her making the point quite clearly that they had jerked me around and that she was very displeased with how this whole thing had gone. It's not as if I had lacked options after my previous run in Junior B. I spoke to the coaches yet again (reiterating my earlier points), and before I left their office that second time, they asked me to sit outside while they conferred.

The conclusion they reached was baffling: they weren't going to send me down after all. They had changed their mind, they said.

Has anyone ever gotten unfired just by saying they shouldn't be fired?

It was a last-minute pardon, something I'd never heard of before or since in hockey team building. Crazier still is that it wasn't even a halfway hedge, like some promise to play half the games, or to come up after Christmas, just . . . "OK, we have another plan. We aren't going to cut you after all." I'm sure that came at the cost of someone else, but I couldn't feel bad about that. I hadn't done anything nefarious, and this wasn't house league hockey anymore. Whatever happened that night bought me another chance.

I suppose the lesson here is to advocate for yourself when the time comes. Or maybe my mom threatened their lives—I don't know. (She claims she didn't, and she seems trustworthy enough.)

———

I realize the story so far is a bit of a wrinkle for everyone who assumes any portion of my success in hockey came from my dad. Maybe they think he knew someone who gave me a roster spot as a favour or something. As you can see, I might have had a parental advantage, but not the one most people assume.

The Vipers were fresh off a three-game road trip where I had played intermittently up and down the lineup, putting up a total of one goal and no assists with a dash-one. We lost all three games by a combined total of 20–6, and our record dropped to 1–4 to start the season. The coaches knew the team needed shaking up.

The day after those meetings, I was on the right wing with David Morelli (he earned a full-ride scholarship to University of Nebraska–Omaha), who had six of the team's 12 goals so far that season, and Chad Murray (who was bound for the University of Niagara), a dynamite skilled and physical player the team had just traded for. We embarked on another three-game road trip the next day, where the team put up a 2–0–1 record. I banked three goals and two assists and was plus-five playing with those guys.

I wouldn't have different linemates for the rest of season, and I ended the year with 55 points in 60 games, scoring 26 times.

The head coach in Vernon was Mike Vandekamp, and Vandy was unlike any other coach I'd had—and unlike anyone I'd ever met, in a variety of ways. Mostly in that he was junior hockey embodied in one person, and I don't mean that in a derogatory way. I don't think I would have ever gotten to the point in my career where I could pull on an NHL jersey—even just for a single exhibition game—if I hadn't ended up with Mike as my junior coach.

Oh, and I should mention that I flat-out *struggled* just about every second I played for him.

These days, I vacillate when I consider the best ways to motivate and teach players, and people in general, because I'll admit it:

Mike was manipulative and occasionally flat-out mean, yet . . . it made me better. Today there's a movement, and one I support wholeheartedly for the good of mental health, that says everyone is best taught with kindness and care. Big picture, life picture, that's the best way to operate, and one that comes much more naturally to me on the coaching (and parenting) side. Even if people fall short of their goals, at least they'll be in a better place.

But.

But I cannot pretend that I wasn't a guy who needed a kick in the ass, and that being handled with kid gloves simply would not have been the best way to get the most out of me, full stop. I had no idea how to work hard and didn't even know what my body was capable of on the ice. Maybe having someone who kicks you in the ass and challenges you can help certain people achieve their greater goals, which is, in the end, better for their mental condition. (There is, of course, the sweet spot of the hyper-motivating types who do it without cruelty—it's just a tough balance to strike.)

My journal from those years is littered with jokes about Mike being "psycho" and being labelled "Snapdekamp" for his short fuse. It's full of tough reminders of the unease that came with my life hanging on the opinion of this one man, though for junior hockey players that particular vibe was not unique to my relationship with Mike. I know there are countless thousands of players who've been on the wrong end of that dynamic, where the coach just didn't like them and their careers got submarined. Mike liked me, though, and by the time it was all said and done, I liked Mike, too.

The guys who make the NHL are not preordained. They are all good, but not everyone was the best player on their teams growing up. Most players need to have people in their corner.

The game of hockey itself involves a ton of luck over a sixty-minute span. You'd think a 15-to-20-year climb to the league would iron out much of the luck involved, but it still plays a great part in who fills out the bottom of the league's rosters. A coach's feelings about a kid at that age can change everything.

My education started in practice. I skated harder than I'd had to before, because we skated more than I ever had before, and if I didn't, I would've found myself behind the group and worried about my job. I hadn't previously been on a team where each day held the fear of losing what I had. But I found that my body kept working even when short on wind and with heavy legs. That was some epiphany. We bag skated at least once a week, and I learned how to push through discomfort and still use my brain when my body flagged. This is something I'm still grateful for today when I go to the gym or find myself doing anything physical. I see most non-athletes start to feel winded and take a break, but I was given the gift of learning just how much of pushing yourself is mental, knowing that your body isn't actually going to quit.

"You can do it" back pats and positive reinforcement would not have been as helpful as "do it or your life goals are in jeopardy." Over time the hard work got easier. I started with "survive" and aimed for "thrive," all to keep my hopes for ice time alive.

The "psycho" stuff, though—which I realize isn't a PC way to phrase this behaviour now—we should talk about that. Some days, it drifted into the farcical.

We were up a couple goals one intermission, and one of our best players, Chad Clower, asked our trainer what was happening on the rink during the intermission. There was always some entertainment before the Zamboni did its thing—a shot from centre ice to win a car, or fans racing in sumo gear, or whatever it might be—and knowing what it was helped us anticipate just how much time we had to kill in the room.

Vandekamp heard Chad asking a question that seemed unrelated to the hockey game at hand, stormed in and grabbed the first thing he could reach: a bag of oranges. With both feet set and a release point that alternated between Nolan Ryan and Dennis Eckersley, he hurled one orange after another at Clower, who was left playing high-stakes dodgeball. It was exactly as ridiculous as it sounds, yet executed without so much as a hint of humour.

That type of outburst became expected. We went through all the junior hockey clichés. We got on the bus directly after a bad loss in our wet gear and dress shoes for the ride home. We drove home late into the night, and rather than unpacking our gear into our stalls, we put it back on and went out onto the rink for a bag skate. When not everyone had running shoes on hand after one particular loss, we ran the stairs in the lower half of our gear—and, once again, dress shoes. We bag skated and bag skated and bag skated some more, and it was awful, only . . . nobody could touch us in the third period of any of our games. Our team was in immaculate shape and worked impossibly hard. (Maybe this kind of pushing is only possible with junior hockey kids, who have zero leverage.) We were in such superior condition that it wasn't even a fair fight late in games, and the confidence that came with knowing that didn't hurt, either.

A Vandy staple was that when we skated, we didn't just skate to the lines, we skated one foot *past* them. Every team does some version of "ladder" skates (or mountains, or lines, or whatever your coach calls them), and so to gain an edge (more mental than physical) on everyone, we went at least one foot past every line all year, and were told how many more miles we'd have skated than our opposition come the end of the year. Whether it made a physical difference or not didn't matter, because we believed we had that big advantage in our back pocket. We had done more.

If it feels like I'm coming off as overly positive about a scenario that was surely emotionally manipulative in a way that certainly wouldn't go over well today, I am aware it wasn't awesome then, and that the years have probably softened my view of some of it. Fortunately, I don't know anyone who thought it was too much to handle, because while hard, it was usually at least fair. (I say "usually" 'cause I'm not sure a barrage of oranges would be an accepted motivational tactic, for example.)

There also might be some Stockholm syndrome here, as I fully bought into what we were doing then. We won constantly and I got better and achieved my personal goals, and so it feels easy to look at what we went through as the type of struggles you have to overcome to succeed. Were the results worse, maybe it would've all held less meaning. There *was* a purpose, though, and so I look at all this affectionately now, the way scaling a mountain isn't easy while you're doing it, but afterward the work feels worth it.

And so it went, with the team operating under two guiding principles: When the puck dropped, we were told to "fuck, fight or hold the light," which simply meant get out there and do *something*. I don't hate the theory, even if the delivery is a little rough. The other core tenet that has stuck with me all this time was from a Vince Lombardi quote that ran in roughly three-billion-point type around the top of the dressing room: ANY MAN'S FINEST HOUR, THE GREATEST FULFILLMENT OF ALL THAT HE HOLDS DEAR, IS THAT MOMENT WHEN HE HAS WORKED HIS

HEART OUT IN A GOOD CAUSE AND LIES EXHAUSTED ON THE
FIELD OF BATTLE—VICTORIOUS.

Any time you prioritize—or should I say "obsess over"—
winning the way we did, you can lose track of what's reasonable.

The Chilliwack Chiefs of the BCHL in 2001–02 were the
single most intimidating hockey team I've ever had the bad
luck to face, in terms of both talent and brawn. They played in
an arena with rock-hard boards that turned more collarbones
to rubble than Scott Stevens. And those boards came up to
the usual dasher height, then gave way to . . . more boards
(before the eventual glass). It felt like you played in a hole
beneath the fans.

My first season with the Vipers, we drew Chilliwack in the
league final, and trying to describe the series is like recounting
the events of a rollover car accident. *I barely remember anything
except it was noisy. I think I blacked out at one point. All I know is
the condition in which I ended up.* We somehow handled our
business at home in Games One and Two, going up two games
to none before heading to their hellbox of a rink. Then they
took care of us in Games Three and Four, and the series shifted
back to our barn for Game Five.

Unfortunately, things got away from us quickly in that fifth
game, and we gave up a couple of goals early. The series was at
a pivotal moment. But a compounding factor was that somehow the opposing team's mascot had not only come to the
game in our rink, but had brought the big drum he liked to
bang in the quieter moments. He sat there, banging that damn
thing (without his mascot head, though he wore face paint).
The thing was, he wasn't just "in the building," he had miraculously procured seats *directly behind our bench and directly on
the glass.*

I mention face paint and point out that times were different, because the mascot's name was Chief Wannawin, and up till 2017 he was at every game, culminating in his retirement.

Yeah, good call, fella.

Even without the problematic mascot head, though, the guy was an unwelcome sight. Tension was through the roof, as we were down a couple goals in a huge game at home, and now there was a racially insensitive percussion factory who was all over a fringed drum directly behind our bench. Vandy was *fuming*. This scenario had no chance of not ending in conflict. Maybe you think, *Good for the mascot, who got himself in the right spot to be effective*, but that depends on how much you think said mascot valued having all his teeth intact.

Vandy was great at using early time outs to quell momentum against us, and he clearly wanted to in that moment, but he was certain we weren't going to be able to hear anything during a time out, given the banging in the background. So before calling it, he conferred with some staff on the bench.

I'm not saying he ordered the "code red," and you could never pin it on him even if I did. But I can confirm that conversations were had.

Vandy called time out, and we all came to the bench to regroup. It's not as though time outs in the first period are crucial from a strategy perspective, but they are good for taking a step back from the momentum that's piling up against you, taking some deep breaths, and starting anew.

But Vandy still wanted to talk, and as he tried, the drummer stood up to make that task harder.

And then it happened.

The evening news described it as "one type of drumming becoming another," as our barrel-chested trainer, Trevor McEachnie, reached over the glass, caught hold of him like a fox nabbing a fleeing rabbit, and went over the top of the glass with the agility of Jackie Chan. I'm convinced the mascot's attempt to run away actually pulled Trevor over, like a fish pulling a fisherman into the water.

There we were, players in a moment of seeking calm, watching our trainer look like he was trying to start a lawn mower with his right hand on top of Chief Wannawin, who in the assault case would say he received a broken tooth, a concussion and injuries to his head and neck.

I distinctly remember thinking about how, just a few years earlier, I was showing up to bantam hockey tryouts in unsharpened skates, and how quickly things had changed to have me in an environment like that. As a fairly composed guy, a theme I returned to during my career's violent and chaotic moments was the fleeting thought: *What the hell am I even doing here?*

No team composure was gained, there was no fresh start, and the only positive in the moment was that Chief Wannawin was kicked out of the game along with McEachnie, which you could argue accomplished his goal. The $35,000 in damages he'd be asked to pay, though, probably made that trade-off a tough one to swallow.

We did not win said hockey match, nor the next one. That's my enduring memory of the end of the 2001–02 season.

It was the most fitting possible ending for a season that started with impossible-feeling highs and lows and included no shortage of "The hell just happened here?" moments.

My two junior seasons in Vernon have blended together in my brain. The brawl where we met the opposing team in the hallway behind the benches, and someone threw a metal barricade into the opposition—was that year one or year two? Which year did Vandy shimmy across the dividing glass to get to the opposing coach for a fight? The time I got a suicide pass from my D-man so late that I tried to fight him on the bench after getting blown up on the rink . . . that was year two, yeah?

Whenever it all was, we were even better the second season, thanks to a heavy focus on defence. Our back end was loaded for a Junior A team, with all of our top six going on to play university hockey. We had good goaltending, too, and I was elevated to a top offensive role, finishing second on the team in goals and points, ending up in the league's top 20 in both categories as well. There were nights with that team where it wasn't a particularly fair fight. In the playoffs, we started with a bye week after finishing first in the regular season, then went sweep, sweep, before drawing Chilliwack again in the final.

This time, we promptly swept Chilliwack as well, getting our vengeance and winning the BCHL championship, and vindicating two full years of emotional swings in the process. It's one thing to be the better team. It's another to execute three consecutive sweeps, which speaks to how prepared we consistently were.

Junior hockey, particularly when you go further back, has a reputation for being a gong show. And while it was at times (see above), it wasn't in the way I expected. I wasn't hazed or forced to power drink on the weekends to fit in. The bad choices are available to anyone who wants to make them, but my life had become built around a full commitment to the sport itself, as the environment around me required. I imagine it would've been easier to go astray with a team less focused on having the most success we possibly could on the ice. The culture might have worn away some naïveté and brought me some much-needed edge, but I never felt forced down a bad path. My understanding of a life truly lived in the spin cycle of the game had only just begun.

During that second season it became clear I was, in fact, going to earn that much sought-after college scholarship. I started getting school packages in the mail early that second year, and the odd recruiter would pull me out of the dressing room after games to chat along the way. I heard from dozens of schools by the time it was all said and done. Eventually, I flew down to the University of New Hampshire and Niagara University, and was in contact about doing the same with Colorado College before getting flown *up* to the University of Alaska Anchorage, which had a few things going for it the others didn't.

For one, they offered me a full ride. That was huge financially: tuition, books, room and board for four years, all paid for. The offer also spoke to their commitment to me and how they'd use me. A full ride had been the goal all along, and it hadn't come from the other schools, who had discussed partial packages. Second to that, they played in the Western Collegiate Hockey Association, the best conference in the NCAA at the time. The national champion came from the WCHA five straight years, from 2002 to 2006, and I was making this decision in the summer of 2003. And as I said, I was going to matter there. Like the choice to try out in Cowichan, I decided to go where I thought I'd be wanted (I still believe this is a pretty decent life credo).

UAA had a pretty clear strategy: they weren't going to get the future stars that a University of North Dakota or University of Minnesota would attract, so they recruited older players, the still-talented late bloomers not pegged as future stars, and hoped to stay competitive with these lower-ceiling (i.e., older) players. In theory, that was me. (You, humble reader, may be able to ascertain that I was never going to be better than Jonathan Toews in the big picture. But the 23-year-old version of me would at least be able to hang with the 18-year-old version of him in college.) Finally, I thought Alaska would be a cool experience. On my trip there, I saw the northern lights, I saw moose and gigantic mountains and ate great seafood, and I saw the chance to just do something different. I loved the assistant coach who spent the time recruiting me, Jack Kowal, and that was all my mom and I needed to give it the green light.

I had done it. I had put in the work from midget hockey to Cowichan, to the Rockets, to the Heat and eventually the Vipers. I had survived Vandekamp and the bag skates and emotional swings and nearly getting cut. I had found out I could be a pretty good player by putting in the work on and off the ice.

I had earned a full-ride NCAA Division I scholarship.

That meant something beyond accomplishing a goal for my career. I now had four years locked in somewhere to actually get better, get bigger, and get used to playing against some of the best players inevitably bound for The Show. I was at a level that mattered without the fear of getting cut every waking moment. And y'know what? Some of the kids I had just played against got drafted, and they weren't that great compared to where I felt I was at. For the first time, I looked at hockey as a path to the future and thought, *I'm not gonna rule anything out just yet.*

Hockey aside, it also marked the start of a new chapter for me off the ice. In junior, the sport had been all-consuming, just games and practices and travel. There wasn't much in the way of personal development. But moving to a place that was a four-hour flight from home, and going back to school while only playing 35 or 40 games a year, was going to force me to better get to know the person I really was.

I mostly like that person. But I do hedge with "mostly" for a reason.

4

PERSONAL GROWTH, FOR BETTER AND WORSE

UNIVERSITY OF ALASKA ANCHORAGE SEAWOLVES

I committed to UAA fairly early in the 2002–03 season, roughly around the time the Seawolves won an out-of-conference game against rival Fairbanks and lost a couple of regular-season contests. After the first week of November, they were 1–3–2, and let me tell you, they'd go on to lose a few more. For the sake of accuracy, *they never won again*, going 1–28–7 for the season.

Ideally, as a freshman looking for real opportunity, you'd like for there to be some team flaws, and thereby some roster openings. But you don't want to be playing for the expansion Atlanta Thrashers, either. I didn't expect the team to be good, but Jesus.

The way junior had played out—with challenges presented and overcome, resulting in a league championship—I had built a loyalty to that Vipers logo that was so deep in my heart and sincere it was really hard to pull on the sweater of a new team that was, frankly, coming off such a disgraceful season. As junior organizations went, the Vipers, run by Duncan Wray, were the cream of the crop, and that aura went to our heads in the way you'd want it to for players. It felt like we had an advantage over everyone we played. Sports—and maybe contact sports in particular—have this way of forming legitimate bonds between players who have been through the same battles together. I had felt it in minor hockey, on our way to the provincial title, and after two years in Vernon, I had come to feel I'd do anything for that team, and that group. Playing NCAA hockey had been my goal going back three seasons, so I was legitimately surprised by what I felt as I started searching for that new connection.

The Seawolves, well, they weren't held in quite the same regard that the Vipers had been. I think this affects players more than they'd ever say—when you go to an organization that was a punchline the year before, and you don't have that pride and belief in what it is your side is doing, it's hard to puff your chest out and play with the confidence that goes miles in competitive sports. I'll never forget looking around the locker room as a freshman and thinking (and hoping) my allegiance to the logo would grow, because early on the brand was one to be overcome, not aspired to.

I'm proud to report that perspective would change, and change quickly.

My freshman year, the team went a much more respectable 14–23–4 and drew the University of Wisconsin in playoffs (featuring future NHLers Ryan Suter, Rene Bourque, Adam Burish, Tom Gilbert, Jake Dowell, college superstar Robbie Earl and goaltender Brian Elliott). All three games of the series were played in Madison, Wisconsin, and in a colossal upset, we took them down two games to one, going to the WCHA Final Five. We played great there, but eventually lost to a loaded University of North Dakota squad in a semifinal game (one I'd argue we deserved to win) to end our season. What I found built my love of the logo was the us-against-the-world pride that comes with playing in front of up to 15,000 people who are chanting, "What's a Sea Wolf (*clap-clap-clapclapclap*)." (Imagine cheering for a team named like, the Gophers, and chirping a mythical creature of the fearsome sea—you absolute fools.) I found freedom in the underdog status, and I enjoyed when teams would take us lightly and we could land an uppercut.

University was intimidating, thanks to the sheer volume of newness. There's a whole flock of new teammates and staff to get to know, but there's also figuring out what the competitive level looks like on the ice and in the gym. There's making sense of the social order and how to behave within your team (guys are generally around for four years, which changes things), not knowing who'd done what outside of the best players in the year preceding.

In retrospect, the dynamic is unlike hockey at any other level, where cliques are heavily influenced by geographic upbringing. In college, it's less "the Swedes are all going to dinner" and more "what are the sophomores up to tonight?" The older guys have contacts through the booster clubs, know which palms in town are pre-greased, and have a sense of how to best navigate life away from the rink. These things aren't exactly relevant on the ice, but given the lack of actual games in college, "on the ice" feels like a small fraction of your much sought-after time.

Compared to junior, it's just so *busy* when you aren't in the gym or on the ice. There was taking on a full course load, finding classes, and just figuring out what university schooling was all about. There's living in dorms and parties and being away from your family, and there's some studying (in theory)—it's all just a *lot*. But it's also thrilling, and since I was a 20-year-old freshman and someone who liked to learn, it was everywhere I wanted to be.

The most important thing, though, was my schooling.

KIDDING!

Of course I'm kidding.

The most important thing was stepping on the ice and seeing if I could hang at that level of hockey. Personally, I don't know any student-athlete who felt school was actually the priority, even though "'Student' comes first for a reason!" as everyone in the NCAA lyingly lies.

One thing becomes very clear on a university team: because there aren't going to be cuts or trades, your greatest hurdles to finding success are the names directly above you on the depth chart. If you fall into the wrong spot, you're stuck for years. I was a right winger, and UAA had about five of those, so it became cut and dried early: before I could worry about the quality of the league, I had to find my way into at least the top two or three of that group, or it would never matter.

Every year in the off-season, it wasn't my opposition that motivated me, and it wasn't thinking about the next rungs on the hockey ladder. No, when I tried to bust out that one more rep of something heavy in the gym, I was thinking about a teammate who, come the time for fitness testing at the start of the next year, I needed to be better than. (The individual motivations of players are probably what is missed most by fans and media at all levels of hockey. Before you can know anything about players, you need to assess their end goals.)

The other thing you can't count on is the players ahead of you simply graduating out of those roles, because each year the freshman class brings the new and exciting toys the coaching staff have just recruited, and they're going to get some opportunity to show what they can do, too. So, in that first year or two, you have to grab a significant spot, or you can be destined to four years of never playing the type of minutes that give you a fair shot at success.

That rookie season, it would become clear that there was one spot available for a right winger in the top six, and that the team had brought in three right wingers. The math there wasn't great. The player most similar to myself in every conceivable hockey sense was Brett Arcand-Kootenay. We were a month apart in age and similar in build, and we were coming off seasons where we'd put up point totals of 74 and 76 in the same league. I was on the right side in terms of size and points, but barely, and I'd give him the nod when it came to raw tools.

I had a real strength that helped me, though: I was coming in from a culture of buying into the team and pursuing the betterment of the group. It became the only way I knew. At that point in my life, I still didn't drink (with the odd exception, like the "mandatory" absinthe I'd agreed to at the rookie party because my decision not to drink wasn't some moral stance), I was in a long-term relationship, got decent grades, and generally fit the template of student-athlete who gave the coaching staff no worries. Hockey was my focus, and while we might not have been on the top line, I found immediate chemistry with a mishmash of humans who made up my favourite line of any I've ever played on. At centre was my fellow rookie and roommate, six-foot four-inch Charlie Kronschnabel (great handle there, I know), and five-foot six-inch senior Dallas Steward on the left side. One of them loved the Bible and didn't swear, while Charlie was also on the line.

I'm not sure if I even had other linemates that year, and with stability and consistency I managed 17 points in 40 games on an eighth-place team in a very good conference, which was a pretty good start. College points are sneaky-tough to come by (particularly on a bottom-ranked team), save for those superstars you can see are bound directly for stardom in The Show.

———

It was common to hear that if you scored 20 goals in the WCHA, you'd play in the NHL. That was the benchmark. Sure enough, the only teammate I had over my four years who scored 20 in a year was Curtis Glencross, who did it once, and he played a decade in the NHL. We were a lower-scoring team, given that we were, um, comparably bad, but still—outside of the biggest names who lit it up, even point-per-game players had a good shot at the NHL.

Kootenay put up 11 points as a freshman, and our roster slots were far from guaranteed heading into the next season. We were due to lose a winger when Glencross signed a deal with Anaheim that earned him a signing bonus of $750,000, a concept that just about vapourized my college brain. I mean, that buys a lot of Kraft Dinner. I so rarely considered the NHL as a real thing that seeing a teammate—one who was very good, obviously, but not consistently dominant or anything— earn a quick three-quarters of a million dollars was just a reminder of how much these games mattered. There was a time when I pretended ice cream sandwiches were "good luck" on game day, simply because I wanted to eat them, and in retrospect, maybe I could've used that contract as a reminder of what was really at stake.

We were also losing winger Chris Fournier, who as a sophomore (who'd been redshirted for a season) had finished with 32 points in 38 games, just two behind Glenner. Fourny, who was just about the most talented teammate I ever had, hadn't exactly been the "school" type, and he was going to try his hand in the minors, where it was less about practising and GPAs and more about pure hockey. That meant there were spots available up the lineup for any wingers who wanted to take them. Heading into camp, the stage was set for Kootenay and myself to jockey for time on the first power-play unit and the top line.

I don't remember all the details that led to the day, but early in that next season, Kootenay and I both had great starts. Off the ice, though, he ran into a couple of issues with punctuality, and, compounded with some frustration stemming from the year before, things finally boiled over. Our captain, Lee Green, was so sick of what he perceived as a lack of team-first attitude that he and the staff agreed Koots needed a punishment run . . . at six o'clock the next morning, in the cold Alaskan winter.

Green agreed to be there himself to enforce it, and being there that next morning, waiting in the cold for Kootenay—whom he never did see—clearly got his blood running hot.

It was early in the season—the day we weighed in and got measured and posed for our team pictures. We got to the dressing room, changed into our workout gear and awaited our instructions, but one thing was different: Green was sitting in Kootenay's stall. He hadn't arrived yet.

It's important to note that Lee Green is not just *from* Alaska, he's Alaskan through and through, and that means something. Remember the Alaskan guy who punched me to pieces in Junior B? Yeah, he was *Alaskan*. The guy who ate apples at intermission in Vernon by lopping off pieces with a Buck knife, stabbing and eating them? That was my guy Jake Wilkens, also Alaskan. Like them, Green was hardened and tough and not the type to take shit from anyone, and that morning had been a personal "fuck you" to him. And so the logical plan was, apparently, to fight Kootenay.

Kootenay surely would've known that not only had he been in trouble the day before, he had no-showed Lee Green at six o'clock in the cold, dark morning, and there would be hell to pay whenever he walked into that locker room. Nobody walked into that room by surprise, either—there was a loud keypad at the door that beeped clearly when each code number was entered, so you always knew when someone was coming in. With each set of beeps, all eyes were on the door.

In time the beeps came and Lee stood up, and the punch sounded like someone throwing a T-bone steak against a stainless-steel fridge. Along with the fleshy sound that comes with all punches was the unmistakable thud of something more solid within. It was like Vladdy Guerrero Jr. had barrelled up a fastball with a pork-wrapped bat. It wasn't long before our captain would appear on the evening news in an orange jumpsuit, facing assault charges, less than two years after I saw my junior hockey trainer go through the same process. It was an awful outcome for everyone involved, the team included.

Kootenay's jaw was broken and his mouth was wired shut. I remember seeing him on the couch at a team booster's house later that week, uncomfortably pushing a pill beyond his back molars to a space where he could swallow it down. It looked awful, and I vividly recall thinking that whatever happened to me in hockey, I hoped I never had to deal with *that*.

I played right wing on the top line that sophomore season (and for the rest of my college career), and grew more comfortable and confident while starting to seriously consider that hockey as a profession might be an option.

I've been left to reflect on where my life went from then on, because even as I get older, I ponder more questions and find fewer answers.

How much of my ending up in that favourable roster spot was the product of random luck, and how much of it was earned by keeping my nose clean? Was the growth of my hockey ability just genetic luck, a product of putting in the work, a product of circumstances? Or, more likely, how much of each of those things had taken me to a level where I suddenly seemed to have a future in the game?

Are we capable of grasping the circumstances that shape our life, and how much credit or blame we deserve for the outcomes?

Off the ice, I had a nascent relationship with the bottle that was, at that time, harmless. In the end, it wasn't. If I'm going to take credit for the growing on-ice successes, am I to blame for the backward steps I took off the ice at the same time? Were *those* just random circumstances, genetics, or some combination?

Life happened for me then as all life does, the results produced by some confluence of my actions, circumstances and random genetic luck, an idea we should probably talk about before we address how my career came to a split in the road and I forked myself over.

ALCOHOL AND ME

One thing I've barely touched on during my junior hockey years was partying, namely because I did expressly none of it. And while others did some, it certainly wasn't anywhere close to what I had expected from the junior hockey lifestyle. A lot of that is owed to the Vandy-led Vipers being a Very Serious Organization, one where those who wanted to party were quickly dismissed to organizations with less lofty aspirations. When we did have team parties, they usually came at obvious times (say, a Saturday at home with days off following) and with team-imposed curfews, and we legitimately did get calls to our billet houses to make sure we were back in time for said curfews. There are exceptions to every rule, of course—some guys found other windows and had their fun—but as a team we never had any major incidents that I was aware of.

Part of what shaped my decision not to drink then, and before, was that I recognized that my home life was already challenging for my mom and brother. Mom had two boys, which is never easy while working full-time as a single mother, but having a child with the challenges that come with being disabled is another complication, and I just didn't want to add to the pile. Along the way, Jeff had rods inserted in his spine to attempt to straighten it and increase his odds of walking one day, and to oversimplify, the procedure didn't take. That meant countless follow-ups with doctors and tests and procedures, and with the added appointments and stresses and just the time it takes to get ready for every day, Mom and Jeff—and to a lesser extent, myself—went through a lot. It never felt like it was too much for Mom, but it was certainly *a lot* some days. I can't for the life of me remember seeing my mom sit down outside dinner hours, or maybe just before bed. She worked hard for our family, and so the last thing I wanted was to be an additional problem.

Still, I was popular enough, and went to parties, and occasionally even had a beer (gasp!), but it always just made me a little uncomfortable. I think I self-identified then as "a good kid," and that was "bad." As I climbed the ranks in junior, I didn't even realize I was passing kids thanks to clean living (though in hindsight I definitely was). There was another teammate of mine in Vernon who didn't drink, and while it sounds hardcore that we would take turns bringing Coke to the party, we were legitimately just drinking cola. I suppose that would be stereotypically "uncool," but neither of us had any issue with friends or girls or anything really, so it rarely came up beyond some light needling. Hell, from where I sat, it made us stand out for not being like every other hockey guy. At the rookie party, I mostly skulked about in the corners and only accepted the random "mandatory" shot or two to get the more vocal meatheads to shut up. I ended up watching other rookies wind up naked and singing songs at the party (I believe the singing part was heavily suggested, the nudity just cheered along). Even if I wasn't super "in" with the drinkers then, I hadn't felt I wanted to be—many of them weren't that interesting.

University, though, came with a complete separation from family, meaning the odds of disappointing anyone other than myself with some drinking incident seemed significantly smaller. My rookie year, I lived in a "dorm," which was more like an apartment with four separate bedrooms, with three other players on the team—the aforementioned Kronschnabel, Nick Lowe and Brandon Segal (and, in future years, Chad Anderson). It was like winning the lottery that my life brought me into the same place as those guys, who are some of my best friends to this day. And while they were better versed in going out and getting a little liquored, they were also guys who could pick their spots and rein it in. They weren't "drinking as an identity" types, they just liked a good time. For a non-drinker without any real moral opposition to it, it felt like a safe space to dabble a bit more.

Until that point, I had never given much thought to drinking or the impact of alcohol. I had an arm's-length wariness based on my mom's stories about her father's drinking, and was aware of the issues of an uncle on my dad's side. Until my teen years, I never thought about Dad's drinking because, in front of my brother and me, it had never been a *direct* problem. As much as it might have contributed to some of the decisions that led to his leaving, I never recognized it as a contributing factor until I was older. We didn't live in the same house for much of my life. As the years went by and his problem added bulk muscle, I usually saw him at events where drinking made sense—a weekend dinner at his place, a day out golfing, or lunch at a local pub. It never felt like it was about going somewhere for the express purpose of drinking, although as I got older and my literal thirst grew stronger, I'd push for those venues as much as him. Funny how we never struggled to figure out where to meet up.

When I think back to my decision to not drink at a younger age, a lot of it came from how alcohol had been framed in my life. I knew we had some family members for whom drinking was a problem. Dad, who liked to drink, was then just a small part of that. And alcohol was a non-factor in my upbringing in the days post-Dad. I guess in general I had just come up with a sense that it wasn't good.

On New Year's Eve of 2004, I was in my freshman dorm when our coach sent out the notice of an 11:30 p.m. curfew. I had been pretty good about obeying authority figures up to that point, but at some point you can recognize when someone in a position of power should go kick rocks, right?

Even though I obeyed again, the repeated late unveilings of curfews on nights that most young people look forward to enjoying was one of the reasons I was glad to be done with hockey when I hung the skates up, inconsequential as that issue sounds. Early on, hockey players surrender control over certain areas of their lives (which I'm convinced is partially why so many struggle to make good decisions when they're handed back the controls and have no experience making their own choices). This happened at every level like clockwork. We were in Madison, Wisconsin, for Halloween one year, and after the final buzzer we had a curfew dropped on us of . . . 90 minutes after the game ended. By the time we showered and got out of the rink, we had an hour. For a college-aged kid, that's like taking a child to

Disneyland with 20 total dollars in your wallet. Every game I ever played in Vegas came with an early curfew. Your family's in town? *Doesn't matter, team curfew.* Not being able to make my own choices made me crazy.

That first New Year's Eve, I remember all of us in our separate rooms, full-on moping at our computers and having a Jack Daniel's and Coke to sip before coming out for a midnight cheers with my roommates. We were in a safe space and it was delicious, and suddenly I wasn't so bothered by the whole curfew thing. I felt pretty good, actually.

Really good?

It's crazy how clean the line is here, but that next morning was the start of 2004, which would prove to be a great year for me. It wasn't three weeks since I'd turned 21, meaning I was then legal drinking age in the US and could go to all the local establishments. I'd just truly enjoyed a drink for the first time and intended to do that with the fellas more often in the months ahead. To put it mildly, it *began*. It began as a gentle ripple, not some tidal wave, but if anyone consumed more alcohol than I did in the 15 years between that day and February 16, 2019, I would straight-faced bet they're either badly sick and/or broke and/or have gone through rehab themselves—or worse, are dead. By the time I hit that 2019 date, I *was* sick and broke and legitimately on my way to dead. It took a slow five years to get from the first day of 2004 to the end of my playing career, and it was then that I'd begin the decade-long intake level where I helped make some executives at Skyy Vodka, Absolut Vodka and Muskoka Brewing very rich.

For a while, booze made all the adjustments to my brain that I wish could be permanent. It quieted and calmed the ever-running background presence of anxiety and worry. It made me the happy version of myself I always want to be. It brought me out of my shell a bit, and it seemed like people responded well when I was more involved in the conversation. Also, I thought it was cool and I was getting started in college. Who doesn't want to be cool?

It's easy to not worry about what family will think when drinking is pretty ubiquitous around the world, and my early results were pretty positive. I was in control and happy, at first.

One thing I came to learn about myself the alcoholic was that booze didn't seem to affect me all that differently than the next person when I was drinking. I was a low-key drunk, for the most part, never the guy standing on the bar or looking for a fight. I just loved drinking, but I guess other people love drinking, too. For them, though, I imagine they love it the way I love ice cream. I love it, and love when I have an excuse to eat it and look forward to it very much. But I do not think about it as I'm brushing my teeth in the morning, nor do I *need* to keep eating it once I've started. I can wait to start, and I can capably stop. Not so much with booze.

It's important for alcoholics to remember that it's our sober brains that get us drunk. You have to decide to take the first sip from a 0.0 blood alcohol level (when it's able to get there). My sober brain is alcoholic, and it's the one I've had to learn to contend with.

Long before I got sober, I suspected I'd end up writing something like this. I used to write it in my head as I walked back from my son's daycare after dropping him off at 8 a.m., some two hours after I'd had my first drink of the day. I figured I'd lay out the insanity of how I drank—drink by daily drink—because truly, it was insane. I wanted to convey in those unwritten columns just how bad the 24-hour-a-day drinking was, how pathetic I knew it was, and how I knew even then that my behaviour was, again, insane. By the end, my wife would tell me I was "deranged," and she was spot on.

But also, envisioning sharing my real story allowed me to imagine a world where people were a part of my intimate world again instead of at arm's length. Alcoholics work at protecting their secret, keeping friends and family at distance, the way a hockey player practises protecting the puck. Priority number one becomes protecting the very thing that kills us. Isolation (and the dishonesty necessary to preserve it) is near the core of most alcoholic lives, by necessity. With isolation comes loneliness. Alcoholics can be lonely in a crowd because they'll still feel like they are the only person around who truly knows them through and through.

Stopping, however, was absolutely not an option—in part because of shakes and physical withdrawals, but mostly because I'd lost the ability to even consider it. So, back I'd trudge from the daycare drop-off to my couch and my self-labelled "shame bag" (usually McDonald's, numerous empty tall cans, and maybe a wine or vodka bottle to boot) to keep living what was then just a story I'd write in these fantasies I had where I was able to stop living in shame.

Whatever energy I had that wasn't used to acquire and consume booze went solely to retaining my job and family; I was fortunate that, in both cases, it would've been a huge hassle to get rid of me. I'm certain the potential inconvenience of doing so bought me time. It showed on both fronts, though (to say nothing of what bled through to Twitter, I'm sure). The whole charade was draining for a single day, let alone for the last and worst years that I blindly trundled through. I piled up a reputation as "flaky," making plans (when drunk) and bailing on them (when

sober-ish) as easily as breathing. By the end, I was microscopi-
cally exhausted, down to my last fritzing neuron. I couldn't get
out of this loop that always started when that godforsaken *want*
showed up. The second I had a flittering thought of a half-want
for something alcoholic, it immediately became a *need*, which
swallowed every aspect of my being until I swallowed what gave
me life for a minute and death by the day.

After all those mental rough drafts, I concluded that sharing
the specifics of how I drank while in the worst grips of my addiction isn't overly helpful (though those details are coming anyway).
But the more general insight into the mindset of an alcoholic may
help someone struggling with this issue. They need to know that
others like them have existed and made it through to the other
side. I was like so many people still out there, faking it and feeling
phony and existing just to get to the next drink. I would puff
myself up to be around people, then finally get to exhale and collapse back into a bottle when alone. I hid vodka around the house
and drank it at night to sleep, in the morning to steady myself, and
in the afternoon because I couldn't *not* drink. I built my routines
around my daily pints. I was absent even when present with my
family. I tried to jam my writing into windows where my blood
alcohol content was 0.00, but those windows became narrower
and less frequent, and so my work arrived sloppy and sporadically
as a result. My usual anxiety was badly exacerbated by the fact that
I always knew I was so far from my best, and much closer to my
worst. I was embarrassed by who I was, in light of who I believed
I could be. All of this combined to make me, a normally sweaty
guy, a puddle of a person when I was in the presence of others
outside my natural habitat of a bar.

The more that constant *want* became *need* and sucked the life
from me, the more I wanted off the spinning hamster wheel—at

least in theory, but not in actual practice. My drinking had gone through upward spikes before subtle declines at points in my past, and for an alcoholic, that's the easiest self-sell in the world. *Sure it's bad now, but it'll get better later, at some other time. I'll clean it up. It's just a rut; circumstances will change later.* "Later" turns out to be one of the few friends an alcoholic thinks they have (because nobody wants to make change *today*), only "later" isn't waiting with a salve, but a shiv. For true alcoholics, moments and days and weeks can get better, but if you zoom out, the "quality of life" line on the graph is almost always trending down in the big picture.

A couple years ago, when I was beaten into submission, that haunting *want* was leading to a new version of desperation: I wanted off the ride entirely, while other forces made it clear that it was to be my new *need*. My wife had threatened to leave and take our son with her. I received that news with my brain so fogged over from alcohol it could barely process English, but it pierced the fog like a lighthouse. It was in that fog that our relationship existed, as ships passing in the night—by my design—because if we tried to pass during the day, we'd crash.

And with that, my physical health was suffering, which manifested in myriad ways. One fall day, I was too hungover to go to work but had an article due, so I huddled up by an outlet in a restaurant called WVRST on King Street West in Toronto, to try to eat a sausage and drink some IPAs to get "better" while I wrote. I hadn't drunk at all that morning, though, as I hadn't stocked my hiding spots at home, and so I legitimately hadn't drunk in maybe a dozen hours. That's when I first noticed the hives that would, from then on, speckle my forearms whenever I'd try to get sober for any stretch, as if my body was rejecting being in that not-drunk state.

On those days, my brain would crackle like a dry static shock until I drank again, and I thought I could feel my liver push against my ribs as it tried to process the fresh ounces of alcohol. My health scared me (knowing that alcoholics who go dry are prone to seizures and strokes), which shoved my anxiety and self-loathing to the forefront. Alcoholics can lose track of their sanity, and I was on that track.

So, yeah: my brain had become my enemy. I was stunned by how many IQ points I was able to shear off from my best days. My frontal lobe was getting a shoddy dial-up connection at best. Worse than that, I had been entirely sapped of my empathy, my sense of humour, and my positive outlook, which I think my family would include amongst my defining characteristics. I had nothing left of myself for anyone; I was a shell that existed only in the most literal sense.

Gratefully, I'm what they call a "low-bottom" alcoholic, awful as the above may sound. I've been blessed with a loving and supportive wife and family and was lucky to avoid the law when I made my worst decisions. When I finally ended up in rehab in February of 2019—something we will get into in more depth shortly ahead—we were asked to list what alcohol had given to us and taken from us, and the discussion around the tables was jarring. One man, awaiting a jail sentence, mentioned losing his freedom. Almost everyone cited family members and other meaningful relationships. Jobs and money were nearly unanimous answers. Specific stories were more tragic, with tangential deaths showing up on multiple occasions. Brains had become permanently damaged. Lives had been lost.

I say I'm a "low-bottom" alcoholic because there's a myth that, one day, something bad happens and you hit this grand concept of rock-bottom that somehow forces you to start getting better. The truth is that *you decide what your bottom is*, because—here's the bad news—there's always a lower point if you wanna keep digging. I made the (heavily assisted) decision to get help before I officially lost all I was coming close to losing (namely my family, health, and job), which is at least part of why I wanted to share my story. You don't have to wait until you lose *more* to justify the decision. In the early days of my recovery program, I was dying to see more people like myself in the rooms, more people who weren't driven there by some external force (whether the law, an employer or otherwise), but who just wanted to be better versions of themselves. (I eventually learned that those people do exist; they're just more likely to clean themselves up and not need to be at as many recovery meetings, valuable as they will always remain.)

My dry date is February 16, 2019. Shortly before that, I was crying when I called Rich Clune—a fellow hockey player, a fellow alcoholic and a fellow I grew to respect immensely while I was on the coaching staff of the Toronto Marlies and he was on the playing roster. Shortly before that call, I was crying to my wife, acknowledging my need for help. And before that, I was crying alone in a hotel room in downtown Toronto because my family didn't want me at home.

In March 2019, my then two-and-a-half-year-old was in a room at a Renascent facility near Bloor Street and Spadina Avenue in downtown Toronto, playing with bouncy balls I'd bought from a nearby Shoppers Drug Mart. He had been told I was on a "work trip" for a month. My "work" was trying to find the man I knew I could be. That same March, I found my sponsor through my uncle Ken, Glenn Vogelsang, a man who's become immeasurably important in my life.

Almost two years to the day after my dry date, my wife, son and one-year-old daughter moved into the first house we've ever owned, thanks to a big decision, the support of many and a few remarkable bits of financial fortune. (I was broke when I went into treatment but had stock in theScore from my five years there, and news of its coming sale in early 2021 drove up the value a great deal. And as I finally started to get ahead post-treatment, we bought some stock in tech companies like Zoom before the pandemic. It was insane luck that I was able to take advantage of because I finally had an operating brain.)

It's funny how much the conclusions of our experiences shade the memories of previously lived experiences. I had a lot of great years from 2004 to 2019, and many—most? all?—of them involved drinking with friends. In the wake of going to rehab and getting sober, I worried about so many of those experiences being cast in a negative light, that people would regret great times we had shared together. Would that great Jack and Coke on New Year's Eve of 2004 be seen as some negative trigger rather than just a positive shared experience? Would my pub friends view themselves as enablers rather than just some of my best friends? Would the sillier moments Bri and I had shared be seen as sombre? I badly dreaded doing that to so many good friends and memories. I felt I risked rendering important years of my life as wasted. These people still meant the world to me, and I was worried that admitting I had let things go too far would void it all.

Maybe when I first went to rehab that did become the case, for a while. Maybe my friends and loved ones had regrets about their being adjacent to my drinking. But I'm pleased to report that with my sobriety and stability—a new conclusion—those memories have been won back. Getting sober hadn't been a "conclusion" at all, but a change in direction. My friends from my heavy drinking days were supportive and remain close. The great times my wife and I had out at the bars remain great times we share in our memories. The parties I went to with my hockey buddies, the same.

The ability to colour those memories dark or keep them light remains in my own hands, with my own behaviour. With my own sobriety.

Like most people who go through what I went through, it had to get bad before it could get better.

Now, where were we again?

UAA, YEARS 2 THROUGH 4

Prior to that second year, when Lee Green threw that fateful punch—when I knew I faced competition for ice time at right wing—I had figured I should get myself in actual hockey player shape, something I had never really done before.

That off-season, I got downright strong, thanks in large part to my best friend and only workout partner ever, Dave Cunning. We didn't have some team-assigned program, but I knew I needed to be stronger literally everywhere, so we pushed each other and hoovered protein and went to the gym damn near every day and ran stairs and skated to go along with the weight training. (In retrospect, it makes sense that Cunning turned that summer into a career in hockey and personal training.) Yes, I had dabbled in drinking that freshman year, but I had a quiet life with a girlfriend in Kelowna and still didn't really drink, so I mostly stayed in and kept it tidy and committed myself to the task at hand.

My efforts were noticed. That next fall, I was back on campus and holding 75-pound dumbbells to do sets of military shoulder presses. One of our defencemen stopped to watch, giving me the

"Oooo, way to go tough guy" routine, which in retrospect was probably a little bit of concern about his own off-season progress. I had always been lean but came to camp that year with 10–15 pounds of new muscle and obliterated my fitness testing results from the previous season.

This was going to be a defining season. My long-distance relationship came to an end, my classes were relatively easy, and that year felt like it was just me and hockey.

By the time it was all said and done, I had upped my goal total from 4 goals in 40 games to 12 in 37 games, and my confidence was sky high. I had improved for a lot of years in a row and this was a major leap. I didn't really think about my career beyond the year at hand very often, but I felt that with continued improvement I had a shot at getting to that 20-goal milestone, and then we'd see where that left me for opportunities. The best players my age were already cashing an NHL paycheque, but I was a late bloomer, and I saw an outside shot at this whole hockey thing.

But, speaking of shots: one thing I did know was that it was the whole drinking thing with which I was suddenly quite taken. Combine that with being a single guy for the first time since I was about 15, and going out started to have a larger appeal.

The end of the college hockey season doesn't line up with the end of the school semester, so there's substantial time for players to attend classes like normal students. They can also go out when they want, and not have to be in workouts and practices. It is what scholars would describe as something between a "shitshow" and an "unmitigated disaster." I'm not sure I spent a day dry between the end of our last game and the day I headed back to Kelowna at year's end. Most guys drank—and drank excessively—during that window, but I think I kept myself in the top

10 per cent of players who didn't miss many nights, if any at all (that should probably read "bottom 10 per cent").

I usually took a few weeks off after the season to let my body refresh itself, to mentally recharge, and to get motivated to get back in the gym and get better. That off-season I was having too much fun to get back at it so quickly. (The hardest day to stop partying is always the day after you've been partying, I learned. Apparently it was much easier to plow on, in perpetuity.) I'd been at the hockey grind for years, it seemed, with just a few weeks away from the constant cycle each year. For the first time in maybe ever, I knew my place on the team I'd be playing with for the following year. I would be our top-line right winger, playing a ton of minutes and getting a ton of opportunities. Hell, even if it didn't go great, I had a buffer on the other side—a fourth season. Rather than sensing that a pro hockey career was getting close and pushing forward, though, it seemed I subconsciously pulled the 'chute on my forward momentum.

It's only now that I look back and wonder if I "got comfortable," or if this was the first time my alcoholism held me back.

If self-sabotage was a factor, it likely came from an embarrassing arrogance I had found. Up until that point, things had just got steadily better and better and better for me. As I was getting older, I was finding that wherever I really put my focus, I was able to have success— dating, hockey, school, friends. It was a good run of time. It's not impossible that I was curious to see just how little I could try and still have success.

I'm not proud of that, but I do believe it happened, at least to some extent. But I also think it really was the first time that the desire for alcohol started to control some of my decision making in a negative way. I wasn't your usual 21-year-old partying on the weekends. I was having rough mornings as often as sober ones.

I have vivid recollections of that summer, walking into the gym—as I always had—on autopilot, and rather than just buckling down and getting into it, turning around and leaving because I was too hungover from the night before. Sometimes I'd lie back on the incline bench, where I often started lifting, to try to work up the motivation—and fail. Sometimes I'd tell myself that a good stretching session would do the trick for the day. My commitment was to going out and chasing girls and a good buzz instead of going to the gym and chasing gains. I turned around on runs that felt overly ambitious, which was a dramatic change from the previous summer, when I was pushing beyond goals. I showed up to my next camp without that pride from showing the gains, instead just hoping I'd done enough not to lose ground.

If there's a reflection from that summer, compared to the ones previous, I'd say that the work you do at the *start* of the off-season is where the gains are made. I tried later in the summer, but it's not like cramming for a test. There is no playing catch-up in August—you can make a difference, but by then, deep gains are unattainable.

Whether by random chance or some stew of universal karmic circumstance, I caught a bad bounce to start that third year. After an evening of going out with friends, I had a guest back to the house. Having not continued drinking at home, I drove said friend home late in the night/early in the morning. I had had drinks earlier and was sure I was good to drive by then. After the drop-off, I was the sole driver on the road in my little toy-like Geo Tracker (co-owned with my roommate). Some of the roads in Alaska develop deep, track-like grooves, worn by the type of tough trucks necessary to navigate the Alaskan landscape. Since our deceptively named Tracker's wheelbase wasn't as wide as the "tracks," you would sometimes get out of the grooves and tossed for a swerve, which is exactly what happened just as an officer pulled up behind me.

Getting pulled over shouldn't have been a problem. I was sure I was sober, and pretty confident I'd be validated if tested. But I had some sense that I was in trouble the second I rolled the window down.

You see, during freshman year there had been a post-season party at our dorm, which was a "dry" location, that managed to attract the attention of the police. An officer showed up just as cases of beer were arriving, and he asked for the ID of my roommate (who was carrying the beer). My roommate had a fake ID, which worked, but his girlfriend who was under the drinking age of 21 did not, so he managed to get a ticket for *contributing* to the delinquency of a minor, even though he was actually himself a minor. That's a tough one for the courts to sort out, I learned.

When the officer kept returning to our dorm over the next several days (and then weeks) to get his hands on our roommate and clarify the issue, we consistently told the officer he wasn't home, which was occasionally untrue, and our uncooperative behaviour apparently grew frustrating. (I don't remember why we were telling the officer that story, but we obviously had some sort of garbage plan we had agreed to see through.)

Seeing this officer's face at 2 a.m.—and having him see mine—I knew I was in trouble. I walked the line as he asked and blew under the 0.08 limit, but the police in Alaska are able to use their discretion when you blow between 0.05 and 0.08. Suffice it to say, he remembered our previous interactions and was eager to use said discretion. He put me in handcuffs, threw me in the back of the squad car and charged me with impaired driving. By the time I blew back at the station, my BAC was around the 0.05 floor. The charges would eventually be dropped, but my life felt like it hung in the balance while I waited out those months, and the season got started on the wrong foot.

The year was different in a lot of ways. We had a new coach, Dave Shyiak, whom I hit it off with immediately, but one of the first things I had to do was let him know I'd spent the night at the police station, processing a DUI. I spent that first part of the season with that weighing heavily on my mind, while sorting through my poor summer training, getting used to a new coach on a team that had lost some decent players, and starting to handle upper-year classes that were more demanding. Our team struggled mightily, and even with more ice time, so did I. I'll be honest, for a stretch of games there, I was awful.

Maybe the police interaction had been "unlucky," but only an oblivious person couldn't see their role in it. Similar to when I had "good luck" in previous seasons, I had made my own "bad luck" that year.

It was the first year I started to lose my way, even if my drinking might have been viewed as normal by college standards. It became a fight to rein it in, though only I knew how much. My hockey motivations were renewed the summer before my senior season, though there was still a pattern of workout days becoming recovery days. Still, I managed to come back for my senior season stronger than ever (partly because by then I was getting, y'know, old), and while I likely left some potential gains on the table, I was far more prepared.

Our team was marginally better in my senior year, and a fresh start did me good. I put together my best statistical season yet, putting up 31 points in 37 games, a number that led our team by 7 points (as I've mentioned, points are not easy to come by on a bad team in a good conference). If nothing else, I can definitely say I was not awful.

So, when it was all said and done, I was the leading scorer on a team in the best NCAA conference. I was too old to be a prospect, but I wasn't some duster who couldn't play. Opportunities started knocking the second my senior year was over, and knowing what move to make—particularly without guidance—didn't come easy.

I was always proud of my dad, which may not have come across super clear so far. When I was a kid, the times when his name would come up and the people we were dealing with would immediately change their comportment . . . that was just about the coolest thing. If you were talking to someone familiar with hockey—and I ran in a lot of hockey circles—bringing him up made people light up, and it often made them open to certain acts of generosity toward our family. I thought it was cool that he seemed to have access to certain things the general public did not, whether it was tickets, memorabilia, a hidden table at the back of a crowded restaurant, whatever.

It was also cool that those who got to know him personally during his NHL years seemed to revere the guy he was off the ice as well. I always wanted for him to find contentment, and I knew that more of it could be gained if the Islanders did more to recognize his contributions.

And so, when I got that call at the beginning of my senior hockey season, telling me the Islanders were going to be inducting Dad into their Hall of Fame, I couldn't have been happier for him.

I was happy for me, too. I hadn't been back to Long Island in forever, and for as often as it came up in my life, I was excited to go back. To summarize, my initial thoughts on that were something like:

a) Much deserved, what a cool thing for Dad.

b) Hey, neat, I haven't been back to Long Island in forever. And,

c) I sure hope this goes off without any problems.

That last one always kinda hung around in those days, but that's the type of worry and uncertainty that just kinda existed then, so what could I really do? I committed to going, and let my team know I'd be missing some hockey practices.

It was gonna be a big deal. I had no idea that, in terms of my personal life, it would become a *huge* deal. The most important deal, really.

When the Islanders were setting me up with a hotel room, my dad called them off. There was no reason for me to sit in a hotel room alone when I could stay with our close family friends the Gillieses, I was told. Our families obviously had a history together—there was no shortage of pictures of their youngest daughter, Brianna, and me together, and I had some memories—so I said that sounded cool to me.

After I rang the bell, a giant black, 150-pound Newfoundland dog was first to greet me—one of the Gillieses' three at the time—and Hogan wasted zero time slobbering all over the left arm of my sweatshirt. Bri was next to the door, and handled the problem by rolling up her own sleeve to rub it in a little (that'll fix it), and . . . I loved her basically immediately. It was Thanksgiving in the United States, so it was doubly endearing that she was in sweatpants and nursing the standard hangover that's earned around the country as students return to their hometowns from college. It's one of the biggest party days of the year. The whole vibe at their place was just comfortable and enjoyable and natural. To top it all off, she was cute and down to earth and . . . in a relationship, so, um, forget I mentioned those other things.

Dad's induction week was unforgettable, and the Islanders fans were amazing. In those days, when people asked me about my dad and his career, they wouldn't have known just how little I really knew about it, aside from the big-picture talking points. Being at his induction and hearing all the stories gave me a window into his life before what I remembered. Countless people told me how well liked my dad was, how important he had been to those teams, and how cherished those years were for the fans. The hospitality seemed endless.

The Islanders had gone out of their way to schedule the event at a time when I could come. They had bought my brother a brand-new sled for sledge hockey. And they put together an event our whole family was proud to be a part of.

Throughout that week, Bri ferried me around for an experience that culminated in my dad's speech, a final night of drinks and a flight back to Alaska. I thought we had connected but again, boyfriend, so we left it at that. Er, *she* left it at that. Some months later, when Bri's online status changed to "single," my brother sent me a text message to update me on the news. (I *told* you he's my best friend.) That was followed by me sending Bri a text message, which led to us being in more regular contact, which led to her mentioning to her dad that she needed to get to Alaska. Without flinching, he obliged.

And within hours of that flight being booked, my roommates were sending me videos of Clark Gillies beating the high holy shit out of giant NHLers, just as a reminder of what I was getting myself into.

5

PRO HOCKEY AND AN NHL TRAINING CAMP

It's widely known by NHL watchers that when the college hockey season ends, the best players and free agents often poke their heads into the big leagues for a few games. It's probably less commonly known that American Hockey League teams also scour the NCAA for talent. It gives them a chance to add pieces to their own pursuit of a title, and it can give the players a taste of what to expect from pro hockey before they embark on a summer of preparation. If that player is a free agent, it's a little like calling "dibs" for the season ahead.

But players don't often leave college to play in the AHL, for one main reason: usually, the end of senior semester is when classes are toughest. Having put four years into their schooling, most seniors want to see those courses through and wrap up their degree—if the alternative is nothing more than to "get in some AHL games," it's not an attractive enough trade-off. It's doubly unlikely that you'll make the jump when you attend university in Alaska, where you'd have to walk away from your schooling entirely or find someone willing to shuttle you back and forth to a state that's not exactly conveniently located. It happened very rarely over my four years, and I wasn't presented with any options that seemed worth walking away from school for. In truth, though, I mostly wasn't willing to walk away from the final months of my university partying days. I also worried that, were I to accept an opportunity to play in the AHL, I might make a bad first impression, being weak after a season of lost muscle and already a few days into the post-season party. I had conversations with teams, but not about anything that made sense.

What I did have was a local ECHL team, the Alaska Aces, that was competitive and so eager to have me join that they were willing to make concessions. If I ever had to miss a game or practice for school, they'd have no problem. Better still, they wouldn't ask me to play road games until playoffs—that way, I could stay in Alaska and focus on my studies (or, in my mind, parties).

My biggest concern was that branding myself as an ECHL player might be a bad move, an instinct I wish I had listened to, because I don't think it was a good look as I headed into that summer after my senior year. Worse still, because it was the ECHL—a league I viewed at the time as below my aspirations and talent—I didn't take it particularly seriously. Don't get me wrong: I tried when I got in the games and grew to really care about the players and staff in a super-short period of time. I just never let the hockey schedule get in the way of my party schedule. And as it goes, my college teammates were going out at a clip of about seven nights per seven days.

Even though I was not expected to play road games, the Aces' first game after I signed was in Boise, Idaho, and I went for it anyway. I was eager to see what pro hockey was all about and to *appear* committed. I'm glad I went, because Boise is awesome, but also not glad—because Boise is awesome in a way that wasn't awesome for me personally. One of the bars sold dollar cans of Miller Lite, which was my preference at the time (the preference being paying a dollar for alcohol, that is, regardless of the brand). The next day, before my first pro hockey morning skate, I threw up cheap beer in my hotel room, brushed my teeth, and trudged to the bus, hoping their morning skates weren't overly strenuous. I had expected to be the 10th forward for my first game, given that I wasn't all that familiar with the systems, staff or players yet. They only dress 10 forwards in the ECHL, as it's a "developmental league," and apparently they want to "develop" your ability to play a thousand shifts a night the second there's a single injury, penalty, fight, ejection or whatever. I was as disappointed as I should've been excited when, at that morning skate, I found myself on the second line, with very good linemates indeed. That meant I'd get real ice time, and in turn, I felt real regret. I skated hard as I could that morning, coming off very little sleep, hoping to sweat it out and get some salvation from a long nap in the afternoon.

Salvation there was not, but there were absolutely dead legs and a lacklustre showing in my very near future.

My half-commitment made my time with the Aces a missed opportunity. They were a veteran group with loads of talent, helmed by a future NHL head coach in Davis Payne. I only had the privilege of playing 17 games for him as that season wound down, but I consider him the best coach I ever had. Early in my time there, he grabbed me before everyone left the ice to have a conversation about something he thought I could improve (off-hand one-timers), and he was absolutely right. Getting better at that over the summer helped me in the years ahead. It's pretty common to get an early read on whether a coach fits your style. Davis was organized and attentive, and our teams had the most thorough plan of any I had played on to that point. He had notes and printouts available for players if they needed anything clarified, and I read everything he posted. Having such a stellar coach heightened my inner conflict—I was excited to play for someone with the ability to get me to a higher level, but I wasn't able to let go of what was supposed to be, in my mind, my last real run of partying. I don't know if that was immaturity, alcoholism or being an immature alcoholic, I just know I regret it.

I knew I should have just declined the offer to play for them, but they had really pushed me and bent over backwards to basically say "just come play games," and I let myself believe I could play well without full commitment while getting some good experience heading into the following season. I should have listened to my gut, which said, "You don't want to do this, you want to party. Have some stones and just say no."

I've never been good at saying no to people when pushed.

This was one of those occasions I look back on and wish I had someone outside of my mom to lean on for hockey advice. Because surely anyone paying close attention to my climb from Bantam B rep hockey at 14 years old to NCAA Division I scorer would have advised, "Playing 17 ECHL games isn't going to do anything positive thing for your career at this point. Just finish your senior year and get back to the grind this summer."

As much as I authentically wish I had had advice, maybe that's passing the buck. I was the one who was paying the closest attention to my journey, and I was the one who should've been able to dig in and make that call.

My university team provided me with dozens of beautiful one-piece sticks throughout my years there, but when it was over, they didn't think it was financially prudent to send me to another organization with a ton of extras. That's a totally reasonable stance. The pro team could supply their own players, right? So I joined the Aces with two or three sticks from UAA, and immediately ran into stick issues: I broke one and the other was going "soft." I needed sticks. The problem: it was April, and to order custom sticks takes time, and convincing an organization that was nearing the end of the season to buy a bunch, not knowing how much runway we had left, was not going to happen.

So I did the thing that happens with most players who are with a new team and in need of sticks: I went through the cast-offs of players who were no longer with the organization, and those of similar players on the team who had extra sticks on hand. It was not my lucky year, though, as nothing was even close to my preferred pattern—something close to an off-the-rack Sakic curve with a square shaft and some grip, with a stiffer flex. (In retrospect, it was the wrong flex for me, but I shoot a lot with my hands and felt that the bit of lag that comes with increased flex didn't help me with the type of goals I typically scored, which were in around the net.)

There was nothing close to what I liked, but I did find this stick that I'll never forget: a long-bladed CCM Vector, which had a wildly unfamiliar curve to me, a wedge-like heel-curve thing with not much on the toe. If anything, I preferred more toe curve than even the Sakic, not less. I had loved the Vector (it was a square shaft with grip) in the past, and the variable results I got from this unfamiliar stick in practice convinced me I could make it work.

(Smart guy, hey? Starting my pro career with an unfamiliar stick I didn't like and not taking the job seriously off the ice? Fucking brilliant, magical, well done, you absolute dipshit Bourne.)

I convinced myself I could make the stick work because, when I leaned into a snapshot, like I *really* tried to rip one past a goalie, one of two things would happen: it would rocket past the goalie and in before either of us realized it was off my stick, seemingly by absolute magic—or I would weakly fail to raise the puck off the ice. The latter happened probably half the time, which, as you can probably guess, is unacceptable for a pro. I figured with more use I could cut out the misses and, similar to golfing with blade irons, my good shots might be even more precise, better than what I had been working with before. Maybe?

The other thing was that I liked the stick for non-shooting purposes—the minimal curve helped control passes (and even in the ECHL, the passing was consistently harder than in college) and I was familiar with big paddles.

A quick tangent on paddle-like sticks: when my dad was coaching with Utah, I was a first-year bantam hockey player who essentially didn't know what he liked in a hockey stick—only that he liked hockey sticks, period. As with all kids, it wasn't like Easton did a demo day and let me figure out what suited me best. I got the most medium-priced ones possible that were in my familiar pattern, and that was about it. So, with Dad coaching in the US, he saw a chance to eliminate the need to regularly purchase sticks for me, by sending up a batch that nobody on his team wanted to use. As luck would have it, that meant a dozen Mick Vukota trees were available, and I mean absolute trees. (The Grizzlies had ordered the sticks for Vukota, but then the Islanders called him back up.)

I am not joking when I say the paddles—not blades, *paddles*—were the absolute maximum allowable size. They were like goalie sticks, and it made sense: Vukota was a fighter, racking up over 2,000 penalty minutes in the NHL. Anything he did on the offensive side of the puck—tipping, digging for rebounds, catching passes, or just straight-up slashing—would've been aided by a large blade. If I had to guess the composition of those CCMs based on their weight, I'd say they were concrete-infused walnut, but I wasn't going to complain if I was a 13-year-old with a chance to get his hands on a dozen free sticks. I couldn't bend them a millimetre, but I also couldn't miss a pass, and I scored a lot with them (though roughly zero of those goals came on actual shots beyond a few feet). I got very accustomed to using them, somehow, going through 10 of the 12 over the next couple seasons. They never broke; they just chipped away around the bottom until I figured I might as well switch because I had so many. In time, I moved on to something that more closely resembled a hockey stick than an oar. If my childhood home ever goes up in flames, the last smouldering embers won't be from the house, but from one of those two remaining yule logs.

This came years after Dad set me up with something very few players know existed: aluminum Branches shafts that were less aluminum and more literal rebar. (It's no wonder I learned to score around the net rather than off shots from distance. Every stick I used during my formative years was as stiff as a Zdeno Chara stick, only a third the length.)

To bring this tangent back to the original point, I believed I could make this somewhat foreign blade work because I liked the CCM Vector and had figured out big blades in the past. I was even proficient with them, at least at the bantam level. More than anything, though, the last thing I wanted was to make a first impression with my new team as a "gear bitch."

You already know what a gear bitch is without me telling you. A gear bitch is someone who needs everything just so, or they whine and complain and make excuses. From my playing days, I can name zero teammates who were gear bitches who weren't also a little bit difficult to deal with more generally. This is an area of hockey that I believe has changed over the past 20 years, and even in the time since I stopped playing. What's changed is that it obviously makes sense to make sure you have the tools you need to succeed. Teams at the highest levels understand that and want to put players in positions to succeed. But things aren't always perfect, and there's an undeniable overlap between people more prone to say "I can make this work" and those who help teams win.

It's hockey culture in a nutshell—will you put your precise wants aside for the team (even though, in this case, your wants help the team)? Gear bitches aren't straight-up ostracized, but if you're a gear bitch *and* a bottom-end player, good luck sticking around. Equipment managers are like Willy Wonka in dressing rooms, in that they have all the power to give you everything you want, whenever you want it . . . provided *they* want to give it to you. And by the same token, they're connected enough, from the players themselves to the coaching staff, that they can get you ejected from the factory. Not directly, of course, but if it gets back to the coach's office that the equipment guys find you difficult, then it's likely assumed you're also a difficult person, and that becomes a mark in your "cons" column. You can outplay your cons, but as a fringe guy, keeping that cons column clean is integral.

And so, on I went with a stick I never should've considered using.

It wasn't long after that first game with the Aces that I got to experience the ECHL at its purest.

Two things happened early: first, I was caught off guard by the talent disparity from player to player. Early in my first game,

I grabbed the puck and exited our defensive zone, shaking some defender who bit on a fake like I was Patrick Kane. Easy league, eh? I relaxed my shoulders, got my head up and settled in to . . . immediately get caught from behind by someone much faster than me, who took the puck cleanly and headed back the other way.

More than anything, I'll remember seeing Jeremy Yablonski walking up the stairs after the Idaho Steelheads' morning skate while we took the ice, and wondering, "What the hell is one of those?" which was a general statement about his entirety. He was built like a WWE wrestler (he would eventually fight in mixed martial arts), and that morning his T-shirt had apparently been painted on. I didn't have a clue how that would affect me until we lined up beside one another that night.

How it affected me, it turns out, is that it turned me into a proper coward, which served me extremely well when I avoided his attempted tomahawk chop on my wrist the first time we lined up against one another. On March 21, 2007, I barely knew my teammates' names and found myself holding back our captain, Mike Scott, from jumping onto the ice—in retrospect, I may have saved his life—while Jablonski racked up a sizeable suspension for jumping from fight to fight, all of them against players completely uninterested in fighting him. His five-game penalty paled in comparison to the 22-gamer earned by his teammate Matt Nickerson during the same shitshow. Nickerson had also tried to fight multiple Aces via straight-up sucker punches. It's the old "everything's a nail to a hammer" line of logic. The game wasn't out of hand, and there wasn't much happening to ignite the fights, but they were out there trying to make the game relevant to their skill sets. Getting suspended for more than 20 games in the ECHL in the year 2007 was difficult if you didn't do something bordering on criminal, and we were right up against the line that night. College hockey it was not.

What was odd was that same Idaho team was fantastic despite some of the roster choices they were making in the regular season. They were coached by Derek Laxdal, who was an assistant coach with the Dallas Stars between 2019 and 2022. They had veteran players with NHL experience who were just playing out their careers somewhere nice, along with some prospects and some talented players who were equally terrifying. I'll never forget lining up at a faceoff and seeing Rich Clune prepping to take a draw with his mouth open and tongue stuck out like Gene Simmons of KISS, staring at whoever he was about to take it against, looking like he might do literally anything in the next 10 seconds. The scary part was that he didn't look like *he* knew what was coming next, either; he just knew he was up for it. He might jump the guy, he might score, he might blow someone up with a hit—everything was on the table, and all I knew was I didn't wanna be in the way of whatever it was he decided.

Given my first impression of Clune—that he was unpredictable and struck fear into his opposition—it would have been impossible to predict how my relationship with him would evolve over the next decade. But we'll get to that later.

My involvement in the Aces' playoff was eventful, but also peculiar. I didn't travel with them during the school year (save for the one Boise trip), so I never really felt a part of whatever "it" was. That team went to the conference finals and I chipped in along the way, getting in eight post-season games and scoring three times with another two assists. Those are decent numbers, considering that the quality of play in the ECHL ramps up significantly in the post-season, and I wasn't being inserted into the lineup to play minutes on the power play.

Still, it wasn't a focus. I was never all the way in with the team, and when we finally fell in the playoffs to that same Steelheads team I had started against, I was almost grateful. The beginning of the rest of my life after four years in Alaska had been looming, and this weird ECHL delay had dragged out the big moment forever.

So . . . now what? I guess I just wait and see which pro teams call? What if nobody does at all?

My uncle Ken had followed my career closely, and he put me in touch with an agent named Tim Hodgson, a great guy who had a few NHL clients. He agreed to help me out for the cost of zero dollars and no cents, with the idea being that if I ever earned any real money, we'd talk.

I've got a lot of guilt about how that played out for Tim. But he fielded some calls in the weeks that followed, and opportunities would come because of my collegiate career. There was no shortage of chances to play in the minors, but this time I wouldn't need much advice.

One opportunity stood head and shoulders above the rest.

NEW YORK ISLANDERS

At 24, I was too old to be considered a serious NHL prospect, at least one with the possibility of moving the needle in a significant way for a team. I wasn't oblivious to that. But I'd proved I could excel in a great college hockey conference, I was a legitimate late bloomer, and I felt I could help an AHL team. I figured that with enough runway, I could figure it out and play well—I had at every level before—and if you play well at that level for a while, hey, you never know.

Also . . . the Islanders? The Islanders. That was a fairly significant—and obviously not entirely coincidental—team to be calling. The only other NHL team I had heard from over the years was Montreal, and they hadn't offered the chance to go to their NHL camp, which the Islanders did.

It made some sense for them to roll the dice on me. They were looking to shore up their organizational depth, I had a familiar last name that would make for a nice story, and I was willing to accept a two-way AHL/ECHL contract (despite our angling for a one-way deal with other organizations) for the chance to be in the *Isles* system. I figured if any team would give me a fair (or better?) shot, it would be the Islanders, and I would be silly not to make use of every advantage I had.

Also, while AHL opportunities were available in a number of cities, the invite to the Islanders' main NHL camp really solidified things for me. It was the best option I could've hoped for. That may seem like a strangely practical way of looking at something that should've made my head spin.

Still, what was I left to do as a player in that situation? Weep tears of joy over the blue and orange? As much as I saw opportunity, I saw the risk of tarnishing the same family name that had been celebrated in front of a sold-out crowd only months earlier. I saw work to do.

In past seasons I had used an individual player as motivation in the gym, but that wasn't the case this off-season. Going to an NHL main camp was all the incentive I needed, as I desperately didn't want to be perceived as the kid at camp who was there because his dad had asked for a favour, and I recognized that there would be no pity for me on the ice if I couldn't keep up.

I got into the headspace I needed to be in. That headspace? Well, programs for alcohol recovery recognize that there is no geographic or situational *cure* for alcoholism. You can move cities and change jobs and circles of friends, but if you're an alcoholic, you'll eventually revert to that lifestyle. The thing is, those "situational" cures *can* help for a short period of time— like a few months—and that was all I needed that summer. The "situation" was *pressure*. I worked harder and got stronger than I ever had before. While I still went out, I didn't miss workouts. By the time camp rolled around, I was in the best shape of my life, as much as that's the cliché for every player at NHL training camps. Part of it was my age, maybe, but I finally got legitimately strong, and I don't think I'd ever considered myself that on the ice in the past.

I landed in Long Island to stay at the Gillies house—I was newly in a relationship with Brianna—a few weeks before camp began, and got prepared. I was in shape and focused and a proper hockey player when camp began. I don't think the Islanders staff had anticipated what came next: I played really well. During a couple of sessions I felt like one of the better players out there, watered down as the camp was in the early going. That kicked off the most memorable season of my hockey career.

The assumption is that because I have the last name Bourne, I would know my way around Nassau Coliseum, but really, why? I was three years old when my dad left the Islanders. I visited the Coliseum when my dad was inducted into the Isles Hall of Fame in 2005 and went to a few games throughout the years, but I didn't see anything over that time that provided me with some mental map of the bowels of the building. When I first showed up carrying my green and yellow UAA Seawolves bag, I took a few wrong turns before getting some help and ending up at the right place, where I had a stall with all the fun gear you get at the start of a training camp, and where I was to change into my undergear to kick off camp. I was early, as I'm wont to be.

When I walked into the room, I was greeted by a smaller, balding man who asked all about me. He pointed to the locker with my name bar, and I sat with my bag, eager to change and get to the actual dressing room, where I could hang up my equipment and take a look at what would be home for my first NHL training camp.

Pulling on blue and orange gear for the thousandth time in my life, but the first in my professional hockey career, left me in a rush to block out any thoughts or emotions for fear of getting overwhelmed. The same way a golfer standing over a three-foot putt to win a major can't focus on what will happen if it goes in, I had to concentrate on the task at hand and let the outcomes fall as they might.

So, I made a conscious effort not to think about all the layers that went into my being there. I tried not to think about my dad and his legacy and my childhood and what that organization had meant to our family. I thought about none of it explicitly, but it all existed in a place beneath the surface that I couldn't help but sense. I knew there'd be plenty of time for reflecting after the fact.

It all began in a simple way. It was the first day of fitness testing, and so, with my new Islanders undergear on—the first given to me with the express purpose of becoming an actual hockey player—I asked that same kind person in the change room where the actual locker room was so I could unpack my bag.

"You're in it," came the reply from the amiable fella, who I had assumed to be a PR guy or something. He then promptly sat down in the stall with the WADE DUBIELEWICZ nameplate to gear up, making me feel like a putz. There's a certain way you should talk to new teammates, and a certain way you should talk to players with a proven NHL history when you're a peon, as I was then. It's not like I hadn't been nice, but I certainly showed I was less interested in getting to know the guy than I would've been had I known it was Dubie himself. I mean, this was the guy who, just a few years before, had thrown out one of the greatest poke checks in Isles history to put them through to the playoffs.

I was also floored because because I couldn't stop thinking, *Oh my God, how is this the actual dressing room of an NHL team?* Having that experience was why, despite how great it was for the team on the ice, I never once suggested the Islanders should stay in the Coliseum, despite some fans' love for its, er, rugged appeal. You simply can't compete when your dressing room would be just about the worst in college hockey (where home dressing rooms can be immaculate) and barely up to AHL standards, which are surprisingly not that high. Free agents pick places to play for the next periods of their lives; restricted free agents decide how long they want to commit to organizations; and you spend a huge portion of those years in your team's facilities. If some places are offering brand new saunas and steam rooms and weight rooms with wide, cushy stalls, and the Islanders are offering a high school locker room, players just won't choose to be there.

On top of the Isles' facilities being old school, their fitness testing was just the same. We did push-ups and pull-ups to a metronome until we couldn't anymore, and we even did that bizarre old hamstring test where you just reach as far past your toes as you can, which was not kind to me. I knew it was archaic then, and that was 15 years ago.

Then there was the VO_2 max test, where you wear the Darth Vader mask and run (or bike) like hell; and for every more modern test, there were two tests as primitive as they come.

In one inexplicable event, we had to get on our knees, pick up a medicine ball against our chest, and simply push or throw it as far as we could. I remember thinking, *Imagine thinking this is a useful assessment tool.* Of course, everything mattered to me, given that I was dying to make a good impression in any way possible, but I wasn't surprised to see others take it less seriously. By "others," by the way, I mean Bill Guerin, who was the captain at the time, and a full-on entertainer at this camp. He knew how much those fitness tests mattered, which was not much at all. He took the medicine ball against his chest, made sure the athletic trainer was ready to measure his distance, then dropped it so close to his body he probably trapped some leg hair. In retrospect, maybe it didn't set an awesome tone, but this was the same guy who worked his ass off in the gym and on the ice. It was clear that the issue wasn't working hard; it was that some of the testing wasn't a great use of said effort. He made that statement clear as day.

Guerin was the natural leader in that dressing room, a guy with a great sense of humour and the confidence to be the star of the show. He's the kind of guy who was comfortable singing the theme song to the teen comedy *Lizzie McGuire* to Mike Comrie, since Comrie happened to be dating the show's star, Hilary Duff, at the time. And he's the team builder who would direct everyone to the bar for a two-beer minimum . . . the night before my first exhibition game in an Islanders jersey.

As I said, though, I was ready. During testing, I got the ball rolling by banging out a set of 82 push-ups, which would take me about 20 minutes to complete if I tried today. As good shape as I was in, though, nothing compared to the fittest people at that camp. Jeff Tambellini was a physical specimen. One of the tests was a forward plank across two medicine balls, elbows on the front one, toes on the back. They literally waited until you established the position, started the stopwatch, then waited until you couldn't do it anymore and clicked "stop." I made it into the middle of the pack there, somewhere around six minutes. Tambellini promptly doubled that, finishing with a top time around 12 minutes. He wasn't a physical player, but he was strong as hell.

Something you come to learn over years of fitness testing: it doesn't actually matter unless you're an outlier in either direction. They just want to know who's in the best shape, who's in the worst shape, and who's in the best or worst shape compared to their recent history. There's a quote that's often attributed to Gretzky, though I have no idea where it actually comes from: "You don't score any goals on the bench press." Once practices start and the front office has shaped how they feel about you physically, it all but gets forgotten. If you can't do a pull-up but can score, nobody cares if you can toss a medicine ball or spend a day in the plank position.

I had done enough to not be a negative outlier, which meant I got to turn my focus to the ice, which was a sigh of relief every season.

Here's where I began to experience being a "prospect" who wasn't actually a prospect. Nobody thought I was going to make the Islanders, but the staffs of each team in the organization are at the main camp, including the AHL and the ECHL affiliates. It's a player's chance to show where they fit into the bigger organizational picture before the NHL team thins the herd. But when you aren't an actual *prospect*, you're on an absolute island.

I'm not saying there's something wrong with this. It's not unfair, it's just different for the undrafted. When a team selects you from junior, people are invested in you. Your success reflects on them, so they do what they can to help you. The better young players had people in the locker room talking with them after skates, pulling them aside on the ice to explain what they wanted to see more or less of. They received extra attention after scrimmage shifts. The difference between drafted and undrafted is a lot like a hockey adage that's as true as ever today: big players have to prove they can't play, little guys have to prove they can. The undrafted have to prove they can too, and so I set out to do that.

It became clear that wasn't likely to happen. I wanted to stand out, so I reached into my bag of tricks for a shootout move I had worked on for years but never used in a game. While approaching the goalie, I set my feet to shoot, pulled the puck towards me with the toe of my blade and then intentionally fanned on a snapper, letting it slide through my feet. I then picked it up on the other side with my backhand, and while the goalie was still on his knees from the faked shot, I slid it in behind him.

Not a soul flinched. It was the type of goal that would've been a big deal in front of all the brass, for a player who mattered more.

The one person who was truly in my corner over the early few days of skates was Bryan Trottier. Trots is a long-time family friend (which is why I'll take the liberty of calling him "Trots" here), and while we hadn't seen each other in years, he worked with me. I was using a new stick that was a little more flexible, and they actually had a few that roughly met my specs, so suddenly I found the puck jumping off my stick without the glaring flubs that had come with the Aces. Trots was all over me to shoot it more. I was a career pass-first guy, but the combo of new muscle and a decent stick to go with my six-foot two-inch frame suddenly meant I had a tool in my kit that I'd spent years not using. I was shooting on pro goalies and shooting to score, and score I did.

By the time we got to the first intrasquad scrimmage, I found myself with good linemates and started having some success. At one point, I was on a team with Marc-André Bergeron, who if you don't recall was a smaller D-man who had an absolute rocket of a shot (which is how he scored 40 in junior one year). I moved the puck up to him from the offensive corner to the point, and then broke for the net. He absolutely bombed one that hit me in the wrist and dropped directly at my feet while my hand went numb. I managed to spin and whip it along the ice, and as goalie Rick DiPietro moved across along with my direction, it went back through his legs and in, putting Team Blue up on Team White, 1–0, with all the brass in the house—along with my dad—looking on.

By the second intermission, I was having one of those games where, even if nothing happened in the next 20 minutes, it was going to qualify as a wild, surprising success.

Oh, what I'd give to have had nothing happen.

The problem was, there were too many guys like me in camp. By "like me" I mean "definitely not NHLers," and one of them was a defenceman on my team. I hopped over the boards and onto the ice for my first shift of the period as the puck was dumped in deep, and I went after it. This was training camp, so I did what any player with half a brain trying to make an impression would do in that scenario: skate like mad after it and finish my check with a glass-rattler, even if it was a bit late.

The problem was, as I got close to the D-man who rimmed the puck around the boards, I realized I was barrelling in on a giant of a man, and it was too late to pull up. He got against the

boards and I bounced off Andy Sutton in cartoonish fashion—
a play that wouldn't be a big deal were Andy Sutton not an
established vet, and me a putz of a rookie running around
annoying people, trying to do something, anything. A pretty
good rule of thumb with established veterans is "maybe don't
take runs at them." They're just trying to get through camp
healthy, and in theory you're on the same team (or at least in
the same organization), so spare your fiercest competitive fire
for the players you're directly competing with for spots.

The puck went back to our zone and behind my net, and as a
winger, I had a good distance to get back and get low on my wall
to support the breakout, but I was busting my tail and got there
with plenty of time. As my Definitely Not an NHLer D-man
came around the net with the puck, I looked up: open ice ahead.

YEP! YEAH!

I didn't get the puck.

YEAH, YEAH!

He looked me off, a righty coming out the right side of the
net who was basically skating the puck to where I already was.
He looked across our slot for an option, thought about it, then
smartly decided not to pass. We were a lot of seconds into this
play now, which is an eternity in hockey.

I looked ahead and figured I'd still have time to get it and
chip it before pressure, then hopefully not die.

YAYAQUICKYA!

He took another look across the ice and decided to give it to
me. By then, the pass was more of a rugby lateral, as we were
nearly parallel and a few feet apart, maybe 10 feet inside our own
blue line.

Andy Sutton had skated the length of the ice with me in his
crosshairs, and moments later, I swear I saw literal stars and tweety

birds like in a cartoon. My visor had somehow wrapped itself under my chin with my helmet still in place, keeping my mouth shut as though I'd just had my plastic surgery on my jaw.

I don't entirely remember the minutes that followed, except that something happened that altered the flow of the lines, and I somehow ended up needing to go over the boards about 60 seconds later. I was asked if I was OK, I lied and said yes, and to this day I have no idea how the rest of the game went, though I'm certain I didn't score again, and I can't help but notice nobody offered me a one-way NHL deal after the final buzzer, so I'm guessing whatever happened wasn't awesome.

To this day, I don't have any concussions on the record, meaning I've either been extremely fortunate or "on the record" just means I don't know that I had one.

My dad, who had come to camp that week, was supportive along the way, as he always was when he was able to see me play. I think it was tough for him to give me advice for a few reasons, but certainly only seeing me a couple of times throughout my college years made it hard to know what my game and tendencies normally looked like. So he kind of trusted that I knew what I was doing, I think, and encouraged me along when he could.

After a few days, it was time to hop on the team charter to Moncton, New Brunswick (as well as Summerside, Prince Edward Island), for some exhibition hockey, and I felt ready, with some new-found confidence I'd earned over the early days of camp. They posted the groups that would be going, myself included, and then sent us to a room to gather what we'd need—namely our itineraries and per diem money. At that camp, the per diem cash (meant for meals) came in a generic white envelope (as opposed to the little yellow ones you see throughout hockey), and having not been prepared to receive any money, I barely knew how to handle myself in a professional manner.

Eventually I would learn that the per diem in the ECHL was $28, in the AHL it was roughly twice as much, and in the NHL it was around $100 (even more for those who were signed to NHL contracts). As is the case with NHL teams today, the Isles also provided two or three meals a day, so the money was essentially a small bonus, and coming straight from college, I swore I heard relevant-to-the-era rapper Jim Jones yell, "*Ballin'*" when I looked in that envelope. We were going for a week, and inside was just under $700 in US cash, most of it in $100 bills. That used to be my budget for a four-month semester's worth of food and entertainment in college.

That week was incredible. The locals hosted us for lobster suppers, we went to the beach, where they boiled other seafood for us, and the team organized nice dinners regularly. We flew in a chartered plane, they gave us boatloads of team gear, and while it was no big deal to the legitimate NHL players around me, the lifestyle was eye-opening.

Crazy, right? The kid with the NHL "pedigree" is supposed to know about all this, but visiting my dad in Texas of the Western Professional Hockey League had apparently left a stronger impression on me than the Islanders days of my infancy.

It's not hard to see how you become accustomed to treatment like that. Having your bag unpacked and ready for you in your stall becomes an expected luxury (and a monstrous pain when you have to do it yourself a few weeks later). That run of weeks felt surreal every time I walked into the dressing room before a game or scrimmage and saw my socks folded and my jersey hanging in my stall with the nameplate facing out.

I was determined to do my best in the few games I'd get to play there. In that first exhibition game for the New York Islanders, I almost teared up the moment I pulled the sweater, with that logo, over my head for a *real game*—not some road hockey game or an Islanders event for Dad. I remember thinking that even if I never did anything more with my career, getting to that point would have been an accomplishment to be proud of, and I'm glad I recognized it in the moment. There's a picture of me in an Isles jersey, and even though it's not like I was close to playing any regular-season games, having played well enough to get myself to *there* felt special, given that at 14 or 15 I still hadn't considered taking the sport all that seriously.

Hockey's a funny thing. It's a little like poker—particularly for a winger, who's asked to stay in a position and react to the game play—in that the great players become obvious over the long run, but sometimes, within a small sample, you're at the mercy of the cards you're dealt. Sometimes the play never comes your way, and sometimes the bounces go against you. Centremen can pursue the puck across all 200 feet, while D-men don't need much to happen for people to say they had a good day (some guys make a career of low-event hockey), but wingers are most at the mercy of the gameplay bouncing their way.

In that first game, nothing happened. I wasn't bad; I wasn't good. The puck was just always on a piece of rink far away from me, and I didn't get many touches despite my best efforts.

I was frustrated by the third period, when it finally happened. I went in on the forecheck after a dumped puck, and in a bid to do everything I could to get noticed, I finished a check pretty late. (Apparently the Sutton incident had taught me nothing.) That put me behind the play as the puck went in the other direction. I was the last guy back up the rink, but working hard. Their last guy up the rink ended up getting a pass back, which hopped his stick, and finally, I had a break. The problem was, I had worked hard to get up to backchecking speed and was now above the hash marks. I threw on the brakes and tried to get going the other way as the defenceman who'd missed the pass turned, and it became clear he would catch me in a heartbeat. I wouldn't be able to take the puck in on net, so the only option I had was to use what Trottier had encouraged me to do and shoot the damn thing.

And shoot one I did, snapping it as hard as I could, grunting like it was a Monica Seles backhand. I placed it perfectly, blew it by the goalie's blocker side, where it . . . hit the elbow of the post/crossbar with a thud, bounced back off the goalie's ass, and dropped on the goal line, where he promptly fell on it.

There's a really good chance nothing would've changed for me in that camp if the puck had gone in, but it would've been nice to find out. It was eerily reminiscent of the moment I had with the Kelowna Rockets many years earlier, almost scoring in an exhibition game and left wondering if anything would've changed had it gone in, given how hockey people overreact to goals. Maybe I'd have been given better linemates the next game, or a little PP time or an extra game of exhibition. But it didn't go in, nothing else happened for me, and that was that.

On the ice, the rest of the camp passed in similar fashion. While I played fine, I didn't accomplish anything noteworthy. To reuse the poker analogy, at some point you gotta do something with your hand, even if you ain't got the cards. I wasn't bluffing anyone. The teams for the exhibition games started to separate into the NHL group and the rest of us.

On the plane back from Moncton, I was called to the front to sit between Ted Nolan and Garth Snow, who told me what I still believe to be true: that I had played really well, surprised people and was at least on their radar. Not much more to say when I was never going to be on that team, right?

On that flight, the menu had three options for the main course: filet, sea bass or chicken à la something-or-other. I ate my steak on a chartered jet headed back to Long Island, the place where it really all began for my family, and I thought about the ferry ride that had taken me from Vancouver to the Cowichan Valley. For a kid who hadn't thought about hockey as a career until my mid-teens, I'd travelled a long way.

You may recall that, during my first year of junior, I had gone directly from a WHL camp to a Junior B version. I expected the shift from an NHL camp to an AHL version to be similar. It would be like going from the big time to a cozier feel where I would matter way more.

Narrator: *He did not matter more, not at all.*

It became clear early on that there was zero intent for me to start the year with the Islanders' top farm team in Bridgeport, nor was I "trying out" for anything. Whatever I'd built up in my head about being able to play at the AHL level was not shared by whoever planned the construction of that team. As a player, it's easy to figure out where you fit by considering who they play you with, what groups you're put in, and how much the coaches talk to you. And I couldn't see any way to swim against that current despite my best efforts. Any organizational headway I'd made at Islanders camp had clearly been with people still on the Island.

The Islanders camp had been an experience—it was long, and there was time to get to know people and surroundings—but it hadn't occurred to me that once they put the minor leaguers on the downhill slide, our momentum would accelerate and the season would suddenly rush up on us.

AHL teams try to strike a balance between winning and development, meaning there's usually room for (a) veteran players with no NHL intentions who can help a team win, and (b) prospects, almost always draft picks. It doesn't make sense to have much of anything else, and since I was neither of those things, I got dealt a level of opportunity and linemates that was a metaphorical two-seven off-suit. But as much as it was "unfair" in terms of being able to show what I could do, I still recognize it was perfectly logical. I was 24 years old and just entering pro hockey. What was my likely upside? Once the NHL season starts, the AHL kicks into overdrive to get going quickly, too, and so, with only a few practices and scrimmages, was I really a guy anybody wanted to see getting power-play time? It was clear that the idea was to start me in the ECHL and leave it up to me to prove I didn't belong there.

Did I feel like I was better than a number of players getting more opportunity? To be honest, not really. At the time, I was as convinced as anyone that drafted players must either be better than me or were going to be better than me, so I just kind of rolled with the punches. It wasn't until much later that year I got confident enough to believe I deserved more and started playing in kind.

Maybe there's some irony in how I was living those early days of the 2007–08 season: 24 hours at a time. I don't mean that in an alcoholic sense, because this was one of the cleaner periods of my life since college. As I mentioned, they say there's no geographic cure for alcoholism (moving cities or jobs isn't going to fix anyone's alcohol issues in the long term), but this short-term fix of tryouts and pressure kept me motivated to be the best version of myself. So, one day at a time, I'd read the itinerary, be where I was told and be a pretty good me on the ice until my role on the organizational depth chart became clearly defined. I still had enough control to not drink when something meant enough to me.

Bridgeport would end up being my home for a good part of that season, but out of the starting gate, it wasn't meant to be. I wasn't put in any exhibition games and I was sent to Utah post-haste. There, training camp consisted of a few practices, getting to know where I'd fit in on the team and launching headlong into the season. I went from Long Island to Salt Lake City, touching Bridgeport the way a home-run hitter touches the bags on their way by.

There was a group of us on two-way AHL/ECHL deals, which meant we were guaranteed at least five AHL games at some point in the season, and that group of us just happened to hit it off. I ended up living with Jordie Hart (whose dad also played with the Isles back in the day) and Keith Johnson, a graduate of Maine who in theory was my direct competition (a right winger on an AHL/ECHL two-way deal). Even though he and I were battling for the same opportunity, he was such an easy-going guy that we genuinely rooted for one another.

That's a tough situation to explain to someone, but I believe it's real in sports. Obviously I wanted to do better than KJ, but I was aware that I was either good enough to play in the AHL or I wasn't, and if one right winger is enough to keep you out of the league, spoiler alert: you're not good enough. I never felt that crazy competitive push where I wanted him to make mistakes (I also had this positive vibe with my roommate and fellow right-winger in college, Nick Lowe).

There's definitely something about being in the ECHL that's a blow to the pride, or at least there is when you start the season with higher aspirations. It's a collection of flawed hockey players, and it forces you to accept that status. Players in the AHL are often on the way up or down, but there's still some lingering interaction with the whole "up" direction. The "Coast," as it was, meant something different. It was out of the spotlight and away from analysis, with players climbing all over one another for the few available spots above. I would grow to love a lot about the league and the life, but part of that was because Salt Lake City had a great rink and was a beautiful place to live. I couldn't believe people did the same in some of the cities that had teams.

Zoomed-out reflections on the whole circle of life thing regularly washed over my thoughts. There I was, off to the very place my dad had coached and I had hung around as a boy. I remember filling up a cup of "juice"—again, the brandless sports drink mix made from dry powder—and chewing the same Dubble Bubble that had been around when I was a boy, and tripping on the realities of time. Those moments brought a touch of pride. As much as being "down" in the ECHL wasn't cool, it helped if I remembered that, to a kid, and to many others, the ECHL seemed like a place that was "up."

Maybe the fact that I was in Utah, in the Islanders organization, wasn't all that random, but the team Utah assembled in 2007–08 sure as hell was. We existed at the crossroads of drinking, drugs and talent, and we were good, and for the third time in my hockey story, an event would lead to the arrest of a teammate (as well as that of another staff member) by the authorities.

While I was still in the Islanders camp, I'd turned my focus to the next one: that of the Bridgeport Sound Tigers, the team with whom I'd signed a two-way minor league deal, with whom I'd had little contact over my time at Islanders camp. My contract was for $70,000 a year in the AHL, and $650 a week in the ECHL. It was actually a decent deal at the time, or so I learned after seeing what my teammates in the ECHL made—the league minimum was around $350 a week. Between your per diem on the road, the team paying for rent and utilities, and how busy you were with hockey, that was enough money to actually save over the course of the season.

Not *much*, of course, given my growing penchant for drinking and my fundamental misunderstanding of fiscal responsibility, but some nonetheless.

UTAH GRIZZLIES

We needed the win badly, and it was reflected by that night's "money on the board" list. Before a pro hockey game, it's common to see jersey numbers written up on the whiteboard, each with a dollar amount beside it that varies greatly depending on the level (ECHL, AHL, NHL, whatever). The whiteboard usually includes some strategic diagram by a coach, a note about meeting times—and then, in the bottom left-hand corner, something like this:

8—$50
23—$100
12—$75
19—$100—TR
92—$50 GWG

The numbers on the left are the jersey numbers of players who've voluntarily committed a dollar amount to the team kitty—money that will eventually go towards a team dinner and/or party (depending on the league). The last player on that list, number 92, is committing an extra 50 bucks to the guy who scores the game winner. Ol' number 19 is going to give $100 to the training staff if the team wins (maybe not the best for motivation, but good for team morale). These pledges are usually collected by an assigned team treasurer, often on per diem day, when everyone has cash. They're collected along with team fines, which are set up before the season and exist for petty things like being late or not living up to the dress code or the team finding out you belong to a K-pop fan club or whatever (what's deemed fine-worthy is based on the whims of the day, and definitely depend on who committed the "infraction"). When the outstanding amounts get too big, time will be set aside at the end of a team meeting for a collections chat, with a deadline set after which unpaid fines and commitments will double.

As boring as that part sounds, money on the board is a fun and voluntary activity, and you'll see players add to it during games. It's meant as a motivational tactic. Guys will go up at intermission and throw $100 at the guy who scores the game-tying or game-winning goal if they feel the boys need an extra push for a win. Does it actually make a difference? Who cares? The players think it does, and it's fun.

This particular matchup I'm referring to was a road game, and we were facing something rare for a team that flew to more than half our road games: a long bus ride after the final buzzer. With that in mind, money on the board that day (tweaked for ECHL values in 2008) looked something like the above, but with this addition:

8—$25
23—$50
12—$50
19—$25
92—2 TECs

For those of you not familiar, Percocet is an opioid used to relieve pain—and during the long grind of a physical hockey season, they can be as present as rolls of sock tape, provided you're keeping the right (er, wrong) company. Percosets have the letters "TEC" on the back.

It's tough to quantify the value of a couple of "percs," which enable you to melt into your seat and smile and enjoy the ride home after a tough game. For players at that level, on that particular team, in the mid-season depths of a long winter? That player might as well have been offering a thousand dollars, given the pills' value around that room and the corresponding *oooohhh* that went up from the boys when it was written on the board before the warm-up.

A little kick in the pants to get everyone going before puck drop. And probably a bad reflection on collective priorities.

If this sounds weird, it's because it *is* weird. That Grizzlies team existed under a cloud of drugs, which shaped a wildly different year from any other I'd experienced or have since.

It's not like the year began and pill bottles were opened and everyone decided to dig in. For those people who've done drugs, you likely know that it starts with a small group of people who exist in their own bubble. It's a little shared secret among a group of friends (some might say that's part of the fun), and that group existed on most teams I've been a part of, whether I was only aware of it from the fringes or, later in my career, more involved with it.

Painkillers are one of those open secrets on hockey teams, and in my experience, their presence is directly tied to the training staff (team doctors included) and their willingness to dole them out. Another ECHL team I would be a part of down the road (the Idaho Steelheads) had a staff that simply wouldn't prescribe them unless it was absolutely necessary, instead offering large doses of ibuprofen. This Utah team, though . . . whoa, buddy.

For that small bubble of people on the Grizzlies, Percocet was their drug of choice, as it was for many in sports then (I say "then" somewhat charitably for those reading now). That reality is partially why the hockey crowd so gravitated to the Marco Belchior character in the movie *Goon*, who delivers this line to a new player walking into the dressing room: "Two rules, man: stay away from my fuckin' Percocets, and do you have any fucking Percocets, man?"

The pills became prevalent early in the season after a couple of players with minor injuries were prescribed them and there were some leftovers, which meant extras for travel days.

Our team physician was named Oscar Johnson, and the rumours of his willingness to prescribe pain pills spread quickly through the dressing room. The asks evolved from "Just say you got cross-checked and your back hurts and it's keeping you up at night" to "Just ask for some."

Years later, Dr. Johnson would be arrested and charged with possessing and distributing oxycodone. He received three years of supervised release and "time served" in prison, which was 47 days at the time of his trial.

The following information is from a story on *Oregon Live* in 2019 (Johnson's trial was conducted in the state of Oregon). It's full of crucial details from events that were launched into motion during that 2007–08 hockey season.

> Oscar Johnson, 64, had worked as a health care provider for the Utah Grizzlies and began prescribing pills to help player Jordan Hart with a shoulder injury between 2007 and 2009.
>
> When Hart left the team and moved to New York, he called Johnson about three weeks later and asked if Johnson could send him additional prescriptions because he had no

job or health insurance, according to Johnson's lawyer, Nathan Crane.

"That started the slippery slope," Crane said.

Johnson continued to send Hart prescriptions for pills for the next two years without treating or examining him, according to prosecutors.

Johnson mailed Hart prescriptions for 100 to 120 Percocet pills on 26 separate occasions between July 23, 2009, and July 5, 2011, allowing Hart to obtain 2,920 Percocet pills.

Hart, in turn, distributed the painkillers to NHL star Derek Boogaard, who died at age 28 of an apparent overdose just two weeks after buying pills from Hart. Boogaard, a New York Rangers enforcer, was found dead in his Minneapolis apartment on May 13, 2011.

At first, the government suspected the pills Johnson prescribed played a role in that oxycodone-alcohol overdose death, however prosecutors have conceded there is no direct evidence connecting either Johnson or Hart to Boogard's death.

In 2016, Hart—son of long-time NHL player Gerry Hart—was sentenced in federal court in New York to one year of probation and 100 hours of community service after he pleaded guilty to possession of oxycodone.

Boogaard died over three years after I left Utah, but the connection with the team was jarring. I thought the players I knew had escaped those years without issues. It was a naive notion, but at the time, the pill use seemed light and harmless. Guys weren't slipping in and out of consciousness after handfuls of pills; to my knowledge, they had just been taking a couple here and there to relax. Looking back at it, there was obviously true danger there. My understanding of addiction changed greatly as I got older and was more exposed to the havoc it can wreak.

By the end of that hockey season, well over a dozen players on the team would have a reliable supply of pills at home. I sustained some legitimate damage that season, and the second I had a reason to ask, I was no different. Between my roommates and me, at some point our house had full bottles of Percocet, Ambien, Xanax and Soma (a muscle relaxant).

By the time we got well into the season, nights in our home city without a game scheduled the next day usually involved what was deemed "proper relaxing," which was a far cry from how other teams partied. These were quiet hangouts, more like melt parties for a handful of teammates. We'd get ice cream from Cold Stone Creamery and some Percocet, put hockey on the TV and drink a little red wine. Those experiences provided positive reinforcement for what were obviously unsafe decisions—you could get hooked trying to chase down that simple feel-good feeling. I don't know how the rest of my teammates fared after that season, in terms of leaving the pills alone. Had I not been called up for weeks at a time, during which my supply would dry up, I'm not sure how *I* would've fared.

When I look back at that season, I see the transition I made from a party drinker to someone who realized he could get the same enjoyment from drinks by himself. It wasn't that I drank alone then; we played so many games and travelled so much, and lived in Utah (where bars close early), so much of the drinking we did was at home, on the couch, which . . . I enjoyed immensely. I realized it wasn't the party I loved as much as the booze itself.

On the ice, though, the season started with me making a good play in my first game, and getting really lucky as a result. I feel like those things go hand in hand, and account for how things even out for good and bad players over the course of a larger sample.

The puck was in the offensive zone at the right point, and I'm a right-hand shot. I was standing in the mid-slot, looking for a high tip. With no lane to the net, our D-man tried to rim a puck hard to a teammate behind the net, but the puck was moving too fast and snuck by its intended target. I raced to the left wall to recover it, beating anyone else to the puck by 5 or 10 feet, meeting it on my backhand at about the hash marks. I feigned obliviousness to the opposing winger coming down to challenge me, hoping to set him up to get to my favourite soft spot. I quickly pulled it off the wall with the toe of my backhand and cut hard just under that winger, who had tried to take the body. As you can imagine, his being out of position left an ocean of ice in the upper part of the zone. I took some steps to the middle and fired. A shot from there, unscreened, should almost never go in. I was above the faceoff dot and nearly as wide, taking a simple snapshot because I didn't feel I had enough momentum to get somewhere more dangerous. It always made sense to me to get off a shot with some force on it rather than to push it that extra foot and get your attempt tipped up into the netting. At every level above the ECHL, the goalie catches my shot there, but it hit the bar by his ear and dropped in for my first goal of the season.

One goal, one game, and I assured myself of some goodwill and opportunity from the coaching staff going forward. And thank God I did, because nothing went right for me for a while after that. By the time I checked the stat sheet after game 21, I still had just the one goal, and the coaches weren't exactly sure why. I had been creating chances, but my confidence began to drop by about the 10th game, and I just couldn't convince myself to show any sort of composure with the puck.

It was a strange thing, how that season started for me. I wasn't on our top line, but it was the ECHL—there are only three lines (you dress 10 forwards), so I played more than enough to contribute. I couldn't figure out the league, and once I started to press, that didn't help, either.

I had played some ECHL games at the end of the previous season, but the hockey just felt so different from what I had played in college, and it took me a while to figure out where players and teams could be exploited. I think because my strengths were never raw or overpowering and were more between the ears, it just took a while to get my head where it needed to be. I started to create more chances as the games went on, but it just wouldn't go in the damn net.

In game 22, I was lined up to take a quick one-timer off a right-side draw (I was a right-shooting winger lined up towards the middle of the ice). Our centre won the draw, but to my backhand side, so I had to make a quick adjustment to stop it from going past me and out of the zone. With the opposing D stepping up to check me, I went into default mode and threw a weak backhander at the net, which is never a bad option. It may be the worst shot I ever scored on in my entire career. It landed before it ever got to the crease and somehow trickled through the goalie's legs.

I didn't raise my arms but instead looked to the heavens, feeling the weight of the world lift off my shoulders. It shouldn't have, of course—stats aren't everything—but they're not nothing, either. I had my second goal of the year—and neither of them should ever have gone in.

Sometimes, though, that's all it takes—the slump buster. You can talk to me all you want about analytics and what's *supposed* to happen and luck. But the mental side of hockey is a massive part of it all, and slump busters are extremely real. It's not just some cluster of results, like a dozen straight roulette spins coming up black. I felt freer immediately, didn't feel as desperate, and the rest of the game felt *fun*, rather than a misery.

If I had to describe what playing poorly in pro sports feels like, I'd say it feels like you've just accidentally farted in public and you're constantly looking around to see if anybody noticed, praying they don't. *If I can just get away with it this one time, it'll never happen again.* Maybe they don't (*phew!*); maybe they do, and they're pretending they don't for your sake (quietly awkward); maybe they do and they're forcing you to admit it (outwardly awkward). You just pray it's only "this one time" and not over and over and over.

After that goal, I could look up without panic, and would you look at that, I made a few nice plays down the stretch of that game. I left that game feeling better, and approached the coming games in a good headspace.

From then on, I scored 30 points over my final 30 games, including 15 goals, made the ECHL All-Star team and became an entirely different player. For whatever reason, it just clicked for me after that, and a big part of that was confidence. Once I got results for a few games in a row, I believed I was good enough to get results, and I started playing as such. And once you get to a point where you become not just confident in your own abilities but skeptical of those on the other side of the puck, you begin to challenge them directly, and expose them.

That was another big takeaway from playing professionally: you don't always have to dangle like Datsyuk or bomb it like

Ovechkin to create something; sometimes you just have to challenge the guy across from you over and over. On a one-on-one, can that D-man keep pace and pivot if you hit top speed wide and cut in? If you can get a pass that's away from the net and really hit a one-timer, is the goalie good enough to get across and stop it? You've got to ask the question of the guy across from you over and over again: *Are YOU good enough?* And sometimes the answer comes back no. (This is a much better strategy in the ECHL than the NHL, I should note. But there are flawed players in the top league, too.)

I mentioned having grown up with using Mick Vukota logs and aluminum Branches shafts, but somewhere along the way, it turns out I learned how to shoot. Trottier had really helped my confidence there. My skating had improved, too, and it was like, all at once, I figured out I had tools at my disposal. College had gotten rote, and I needed a new style of hockey to find new ways to be effective.

After Christmas, I got my first call-up to the AHL. By then, I believed I was good enough to play in the AHL. But I had to be good when I got there. Now I just needed a fair chance to be that.

BRIDGEPORT, PART DEUX

Something about Bridgeport was more intimidating than being around the Islanders. That may be in part because I had the Bourne name, which was worth a shred of attention on Long Island. Not having much of a chance to actually make the Islanders had taken some pressure off, too. I had also played well, and it was the start of the year, when everyone was shaking hands and getting to know each other, so all in all, I had felt included.

Not the case in Bridgeport.

I realize years later how important feeling like part of a team had mattered to me on my way up. Our great midget team full of high school friends, my successful junior team that bought in hard to the logo, and four years with a college team had built a belief in me about the importance of *team*. The minor leagues of professional hockey, for obvious reasons, are not about team at all, as much as those involved will try to tell you otherwise. It was a sharp learning curve, one that was steepest at the level closest to the NHL. To players in the AHL, call-ups aren't like college freshmen joining the team for the next four years. They're upstart competitors, like young apes working up to challenge the big incumbent leader of the troop, there to be smacked back down to their appropriate place as soon as possible.

I think they liked me fine as a player, but there was not really any situation where I was a *priority*, let alone a concern. Combine that with my near obsession with being an easy guy to have around (a trait generally smiled upon by Hockey People), and I just sort of existed during my first call-up. I slept in the black car all the way from LaGuardia Airport to Bridgeport before my first game, and arrived at the arena about three hours before any-body else did for the 10 o'clock morning skate. And off I went from there, feeling awful from the get-go.

Simply "existing" was probably okay because my first games were against good AHL teams. Not getting embarrassed felt like a win. Ask players who've played AHL and NHL games, and they'll tell you the biggest difference is not so much the speed of the game, but the speed of particular areas (passing, decision making, consistency, finishing, and on and on). Ask those who've played in both the AHL and the ECHL, and they'll tell you that raw speed is unequivocally the biggest difference. The best skaters are in the NHL, but the AHL is packed full of NHL-level skaters with some other deficiency. Some guys will tell you the NHL is actually an easier game to process mentally because guys are more likely to be where they're supposed to be. In turn, the AHL ends up being fast as hell but more chaotic, and when you play the more talented teams, it can be tough to process the hockey.

It was a tough spot to make an impression. I wasn't going to be in their top six, given the other names on the team. Kyle Okposo, Jeff Tambellini and Frans Nielsen were at the top of the group of forwards. Jeremy Colliton, who went on to be named coach of the Chicago Blackhawks after his playing career, was there, too, as were long-time NHLers Blake Comeau and Micheal Haley. They had good grinders like Tim Jackman, and talented players who would see NHL time, like Trevor Smith, Ben Walter and Steve Regier. So I drew lower-line duty, and that wasn't really something I'd ever done. I didn't really have the tool kit to play some other version of my game, so I saw minimal minutes, worked hard in practice, and finally had a decent showing in my third game with the team.

I cannot think of a better way to explain how my first call-up played out than to talk about the way it ended: in line at a Tim Hortons. Our bus had stopped on the way back from a road game, and the boys piled off and into some poor, unsuspecting Tim Hortons. I don't know what Tim Hortons pays, but it's not enough for the task of serving 30 members of the brotherhood of the travelling track pants. The line was set up like an airport check-in, in that it zigzagged back and forth, and Jack Capuano—the team's head coach—was in line ahead of me by a few spots. As the line cut back and we were about to be face to face (which is a personal nightmare for someone like me just hoping to stick around as long as possible), it happened. He looked up, saw me, and said in his thick Rhode Island accent, "Boahney! Good job yesterday. Hey, been meaning to tell you you're going to the ECHL All-Star Game tomorrow."

That was a lot to process in a single sentence, because (a) we, as in Bridgeport, had a game the next day; (b) the ECHL All-Star Game was on the other side of the continent, and to get there by the next day I'd need to leave basically immediately; and (c) there was no mention of where I'd be returning to *after* said game, which was not overly promising.

"Been meaning to tell you"? How long had he known?

I've never been one for comedy that's rooted in awkwardness, but me having about 20 questions yet not the gumption to ask them, combined with the line weaving back and forth a couple more times before forcing us back face to face, and me still saying nothing . . . that's some footage I'd like to look back at for a laugh.

My alarm went off somewhere between three and four o'clock the next morning, after which a black car took me from Connecticut to LaGuardia, where I would eventually board a flight to Oakland, where a vehicle would take me to beautiful Stockton, California, for the skills contest.

That next night, I arrived at the rink with my bag at about 6:45 and rushed into a dressing room of fully dressed "team-mates" whom I didn't know, where someone from the skills contest found me dropping my bag in my stall. The news wasn't great: I was in the first event—the skating/agility contest—and was first up. And it was just about that time. That meant the first thing I'd have to do was a full sprint down the rink, followed by tight turns and pylon dangling on the way back. There was no attempt by the organizers to push my time slot back or soften the blow. I was taping my shin pads when I heard my name announced out on the ice, and as of this very moment, I cannot tell you how I did, except that I'm certain I did not win my head-to-head race. I know I didn't fall, but we're talking about clearing a pretty low bar here.

After the All-Star Game, I was returned not to Bridgeport, but Utah, where I went and played some of my best hockey of the season, resulting in another call-up about two weeks later.

At this point, I hadn't seen Brianna since the beginning of October, and we were a new couple in that madly-in-love phase that can be a little overpowering. The text messages, they were a-plenty. A few months apart took us to Christmas, when I had flown home to BC to be with my family, which took us into January and eventually February, when we *finally* had a trip on the books. During her reading break, Bri was going to fly from LaGuardia to Salt Lake City for Valentine's Day. The day mercifully arrived, and she called from the airport, boarded the plane and sent that final "See you soon, eeek!" text . . . just moments before the phone rang.

It was Bridgeport. They wanted me to come play for them in a little over 48 hours, and wanted to know if I had time to get to the rink to get my gear before boarding the flight that left Utah in three hours.

I *did* have time to get to the rink and to the airport, but what the hell was I going to do? I had been playing great and was dying to get called back up, but if I left on that flight, there was a chance Bri would land in Salt Lake City and I would already be in the air on the way to New York. After everything a player goes through to get a call-up, could I possibly *decline* one and miss AHL games? Of course I couldn't.

And so I set out to do some finagling. There was a red-eye that would take us to LaGuardia later that evening, which would not be awesome for my sleep, but what was I to do? They got me booked on that overnight flight, and I used just about every penny

I had in my meagre bank account to buy Bri—who was still in the sky and unaware—a return trip back to New York along with me.

That's how she saw me for the first time in nearly four months: with a suitcase, hockey bag and hockey sticks in tow, ready to drop the (mostly bad) news on her. We settled in to spend a few hours at the airport, awaiting our trip to the very place she had just left.

The things you endure for love.

The good news for both of us was that the team seemed more committed to my presence this time around. People knew who I was, which helped my comfort level. I imagine they recognized that I wasn't some guy who intended to come in and be a major disruptor (maybe it would've gone better if I were), and so some mutual trust had started to build. I found my way to greater relevance within the team thanks to a combination of injuries and taking advantage of those opportunities. I'd also be a healthy scratch for as many games as I played (16 of each in total), but being around the team from early February into late March, earning the bigger paycheque and being near my eventual wife made it impossible to be mad about the scratches. Those were great days.

On the ice, what really changed were my linemates and my confidence. The two go hand in hand. I had a game in Albany where I just had "it." My legs and brain and drive all worked together to make me effective every time I got thrown over the boards, and it resulted in my first AHL goal off a loose puck in the slot that I didn't hesitate to fire, half-slapping it in over the goalie's blocker.

Playing better and getting more chances exposed me to something else for the first time: elite goaltending. My college league had plenty of good goalies who went on to NHL success, including Brian Elliott. But even then, we're talking about younger versions of eventual NHLers, still with holes in their games. In the American League, they were big, grown men who were athletic and positional—and, for the first time, some of my usual tricks didn't work.

I had that moment in the NHL exhibition game where I wondered if my shot off the post would've done more for me had it gone in. I had it in a WHL exhibition game. This one in the AHL, this one I'm sure would've helped me work my way into greater opportunity. A game or two after my first AHL goal, I found myself on a line with Micheal Haley, whom many people know as an NHL tough guy, and rightfully so. But the guy has great hands and good vision, which is why he stuck around the NHL as long as he did. Haley was on a rush up the ice, a one-on-two, when my change came to the bench and I hopped over the boards. One of the two defenders was a covering forward—those are never of very much use—and each of them thought they had Haley on their own, so both guys went to him. He curled just inside the blue line and held on to it as I saw a wide-open lane from the bench to the net and started sprinting. He left a beauty of a spot pass in the middle of the ice for me as the two defenders got to him, and I was in alone with the back-checking D-man at my heels.

I was coming from the right side of the ice, and I did everything I could to sell that I was coming across the net to make an attempt on my backhand. As a forward, you know when you've sold a move well or not, and I got this one right before cutting back to my fore-hand, leaving the goalie sliding across hard to his blocker side.

In junior, in college and in the ECHL, I would surely have done enough to pull the goalie out of position. This time, I got casual with my finish and set myself up to slide it across the line. In the AHL, against a goalie with NHL experience in Yann

Danis, it turns out the puck isn't in until it's in, and he dug in, pushed back across the net, managed to kick his left leg out just enough, and my finish left the puck wedged between the post and his toe. If he had slid across just an inch further . . . *if, if, if.*

As my junior coach Vandy used to say, "If ifs and buts were candies and nuts, every day would be Christmas."

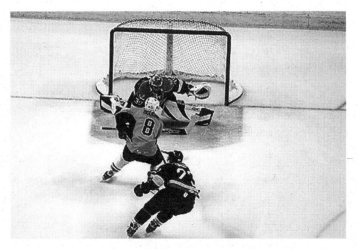

JB dekes right as the goalie slides left.

In retrospect, it may have been one of *those* moments for the coaching staff: if I'm supposed to be a handsy offensive producer and I can't finish here, what use am I? If I put that away, do I magically morph into a guy who, from their vantage point, seems to be finding himself and his confidence and maybe just needs more opportunity? It all sounds like Uncle Rico from *Napoleon Dynamite* reliving meaningless moments, but I think it speaks to a broader concept about the little moments in sports and how they can have butterfly effect–like impacts on the careers of players at the fringes. (And if you want to extrapolate that beyond sports, it's hard not to wonder how the little moments in life affect what comes next. Things that happen in a blink can have profound, lasting effects.)

As I settled in at that level, I found ways to be involved in a couple of scoring chances per game, and I'd score again and tally a few assists, ending the year with a simple AHL stat line of 16 games played, with two goals and three assists for five points. I was with the team for around 30 games and two months by the time it was all said and done, but I wasn't allowed to finish the year without one more "almost" moment that still haunts me.

During those days in Bridgeport, I struggled with the same issue that had cropped up with the Alaska Aces. It was the Utah Grizzlies who had ordered my custom sticks, and with the few I'd brought with me now broken, I was into the Sound Tigers' stash, which was vaster than the Aces' but still didn't have anything near what I was looking for. I tried an old Eric Boguniecki model; I tried sticks from some of my right-handed teammates; I even tried a misordered batch of Kyle Okposos, which the team had set aside because nobody wanted them. (Fun fact: I was the last guy there one day and the equipment guy put all 12 in my vehicle. I mostly gave them away back home during the off-season. Thanks, Kyle!)

I had brought some other sticks along with me that I'd been using over the past year, just in case they didn't have any to my liking. The obvious answer to the problem of "no sticks I liked" would've been just to go to the local sporting goods store and buy a couple and submit the receipts or something, but again, I badly wanted not to be a pain in the ass.

And that's how I came to use that all-or-nothing stick from the Alaska Aces with the big paddle that resulted in either super shots or total flubs. You know where this is going.

This is a picture of me as the puck carrier on a two-on-one in a close game at home, having faked a pass, trying to absolutely rip one high on the glove side from my sweet spot. I'm not proud of how closed my eyes are here, but I'm telling you, I've never tried to put more mustard on a shot, hoping to really showcase how I could fire the puck, planning on releasing one of the good ones from that big, challenging blade. I don't know what your worst feeling in sports is—getting jammed on an inside fastball, or releasing an air ball you know is short of the basket the second it's off your fingertips—but for me, the feeling of trying to fire a high shot that comes off low gives me the shivers. This could not have hit the goaltender more squarely in the crest, an awful shot by every measure from a spot I had learned to make my weapon.

This is a picture of the worst shot of my life.

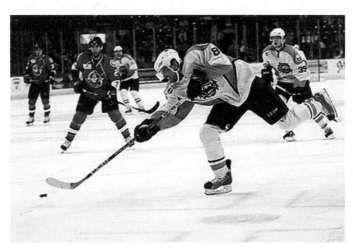

JB shooting, poorly.

Pathetic. Haunting. Please burn this page.

In the end, jamming pucks against the post and hitting goaltenders in the crest wasn't enough to keep me in the American

League for the Sound Tigers' playoff push, so with Utah's post-season looming on the horizon, back down I went.

I was a different player by this time, mostly with the puck. Certain players in the NHL have this ability that most rec players can't fathom, and for a short time in the ECHL, I got to feel what it must be like for those guys. It's that you've got so much confidence, you don't feel the need to move the puck unless someone *forces* you to, and you'd be surprised how rarely they actually do that if you just . . . hang on to it. It turns out a big part of defending is bluffing that you're going to go right at a guy in a bid to get him to move the puck, because if you do go all the way right at someone, that commitment often pulls you out of position. And so you're trying to force a dump, or force a pass, or just get the player to move the puck where you want. Having the confidence to hang on for that extra half-second allowed oceans of room to open up that I hadn't seen before.

I also felt more confident about my ability to play physically in a league with other fully grown men, and my willingness to whack someone back who whacked me was revealing, too. It turned out that some guys who whack you are mostly feeling out who they can bully, and pushing back makes life a little easier out there. I was learning piles of lessons (many of which would strongly influence the way I comment on skilled players in the media) and felt primed to tear apart the ECHL playoffs.

In the first round, it felt like that might happen. The Grizzlies were matched up with a physically tough opponent in the Fresno Falcons. The series was a grind. In the third game, we found ourselves in a battle that leaked into overtime—and when it was done, it would enter the record books as the sixth-longest game in ECHL history. (A few have since surpassed it.)

I know you've seen how the pace changes in games that make it into triple overtime in the Stanley Cup playoffs, but we're talking about a league that only dresses 10 forwards, where guys also skate much worse. Not to mention, nearly half the games see you lose at least someone over the course of the action, whether to ejection or injury or straight-up benching. The few fans who went the distance that night deserved, I dunno, free season tickets or a hot dog or a hug or *something*. The pace of play had slowed to a crawl, and chances became fewer and farther between.

In that third OT period, I managed to get myself to the crease, driving to the net without the puck, but whether by bad luck or sheer exhaustion, I ended up sliding into the net.

As I got myself together and started backchecking, I saw their puck carrier start to bobble it just as their last D-man back decided to jump up in the play. I slowed my backcheck immediately, reading that a turnover would leave me in a position for a pass with a clean breakaway back the other way. I was tired, but who doesn't have the energy for a breakaway?

The turnover came, and my man Keith Johnson got me the puck immediately.

I made essentially the same move that Yann Danis had stopped weeks earlier in the AHL, only I started it a little sooner and let the goalie come back to my forehand (as Danis had) before going back across to my backhand, and then tucked it in. I selected the "Ninja Turtle spin on back" celly, a decision I'm still very pleased with.

I'll never forget the elation and adrenalin in the dressing room afterwards. It's amazing to be on the winning end of a game like that, and to score the game winner felt better than anything I'd ingested away from the rink over the course of that season—it was an absolute high. I had scored two OT winners in university, one against our rivals in Fairbanks. I had scored an OT winner every year of junior hockey, too. But nothing came close to a triple-OT winner in playoffs.

Two days later, I'd be in the same dressing room seeking out painkillers, but for a different reason than on some other occasions. This time, I needed them. I had been covering for our centre low in our zone, battling for a puck as the opposing forwards went for a change. By the time I had dug the puck out of the corner, the player I was battling against had headed off for a change, and one of their players whose sole purpose was to smash players had jumped over the boards but was obscured from my view. He had a full head of steam from their bench, and I was stationary with the puck on my stick against the boards.

I swear to this day that he hit me so hard my shoulders touched in front of my body. My sternoclavicular joint was left so mangled that doing a bench press hurts to this day.

At the time of this injury, I had an unbelievable record going that nobody would've been aware of but myself: I hadn't missed a game because of injury since my first year of bantam hockey, meaning I'd gone 10 seasons without missing a single game, including the one that was just about to wrap up. I had played through all kinds of misery because, at every level for the past seven or eight of those years, I had been vying for ice time and trying to rise through the ranks, and the great adage that "the best ability is availability" remains true. The hockey season train stopped for no one, and I saw plenty of guys with iffy injuries get "Wally Pipped"—they probably needed a little rest, took that rest, and then were surpassed in the lineup by their replacements.

These were the playoffs, and I had no intention of missing a minute, so on we went. I took cortisone shots and tried to play, terrified of absorbing a hit and unwilling to throw one. It felt like I was full of bravery and valour at the time, but it was probably a selfish decision. I hurt our team going out there, but as long as they would play me, I wanted to play. On top of being bad for the group, it wasn't good for my career, as a post-season stat line that reads 13 games, two goals and no assists doesn't look great for a "goal scorer."

Despite my attempts to stay in the lineup, I did end up missing a game in the second round after a hit aggravated the injury. Our team took part in 14 playoff games that year, losing in the conference finals to the Las Vegas Wranglers. For me, it was the second year in a row losing in that round, though this time it had real meaning, as I'd come to care about that group. Prior to the playoffs, our captain, Travis Rycroft, had blown out his knee and couldn't play, and he teared up while talking to the team about it. Hockey relationships come and go quickly, but going through as much as you do in a season with guys like Rycroft, you really start to care.

That season had been a monotonous grind and a blur all at once, and as I set sail into yet another off-season, I found I was utterly, absolutely, entirely used up. It had started with a hard summer of training, led to the daily stress of an NHL camp in the Maritimes, and ended with a defeat to Las Vegas while in Salt Lake City, Utah. I found myself wondering if all pro hockey seasons were like the one I'd just completed.

The truth was, I was pretty sick of the whole machine, at least in part because I was tired of not getting to do what I wanted, when I wanted—and what I wanted to do was drink and not have to worry about my physical performance the following day. The previous summer, my mantra had been "Don't drink, because you don't want to embarrass yourself at New York Islanders camp." Then it was "Don't drink during AHL tryouts or ECHL camp, as the pecking order is being established." And then it was a million other things—games and travel and practices and workouts—that kept me from indulging the urge that had grown throughout the season from something I could manage to something that I felt in my bones I just needed to give in to for a while. I didn't know if I could pull out of it after that, but I knew I needed just a little time when I wasn't fighting back.

In the bigger picture, too, I was generally tired of grinding my way up the ladder. I was tired of curfews, I was tired of the constant puffing-up of the chest from guys in the room and on the ice. Nobody can just take days off work, but in many careers you can shift your work around to more optimal times. There's just no hiding in hockey, where your physical performance is judged nearly every single day, regardless of where your mind and body are at.

I was jealous of everyone I saw who got up and showered in the morning and went about their day looking decent, not living in increments between shower and sweat, which came both on the ice and on buses and planes. I felt chewed up and spat out, and I had two issues that would lead me where I went next: I was physically hurt and needed to take time to rest, and that beast inside me—the one that just wanted to drink and stop with the hockey grind—had only grown bigger and stronger through a challenging season with very few windows to let loose.

I hadn't hurt my stock in pro hockey, but I hadn't fully established myself as an AHL player, either, so that off-season I didn't get the one-way contract I had been hoping for. At my age, not taking a step after year one in the minors was basically a death knell for a career. I had numerous opportunities for another two-way AHL/ECHL deal, but I had decided that kind of deal wasn't the smartest thing to sign. The reason is that, as a right winger, you can play terrific in the ECHL but you're essentially vying for one of the four jobs at right wing on the AHL team above you. Barring injury, there just may not be a chance there. If you're on an ECHL one-way deal and you play well, anyone in the AHL who has an open spot at right wing can sign you. I remember the season before, watching a teammate on an ECHL-only deal get called up to a team riddled with injuries— a player I felt I was better than—and thinking, *Wait, why am I limiting myself to one team for call-ups?*

I was disappointed because I had thought the offer of a one-way with Bridgeport might come. Instead, I got offered the chance to come back to the Islanders' NHL camp and to sign the same two-way deal, which signalled that they weren't as enthusiastic about keeping me around as I had hoped. Still, the NHL camp experience had been great, and they knew me now, and it's very possible that, had I gone back into the same situation, I could've advanced to the next level. I thought about it and told them I wasn't sure—as late in the summer as August.

One of the bigger problems was that I had started the summer slowly because of my nagging injury and my growing issue with alcohol, and the clock simply ran out on me. It ran out at least in part because of the way I had started the summer, knowing I just needed to let go and stop fighting the pull of the bottle for a while. I had truly believed that if I gave in for a bit, maybe it would help me gather strength to do the right things again later in the summer—the training and preparation I knew were necessary. Before I knew it, it was August again. It's only now that I can look back and pinpoint that early-summer need and semi-conscious decision to "let go" as the beginning of the end of my playing days.

I had missed early summer training and hadn't regained the level of strength I had been at the previous summer. I was entering a season in worse shape than the year before. Mentally, I didn't know how to process that, and I was scared.

I remember scrolling my phone in bed, badly hungover, one morning when an email showed up that said the Islanders finally needed a hard answer—was I coming to training camp or not? Had I been in a different mental state in that moment, I might have answered differently. But I didn't know where I was as a player or a person, and I was openly worried about hurting the family name. That's where my brain was during that brief moment of processing—that I simply could not go back to Islanders camp and be *worse*, and embarrass us.

Long Island remained a place where my dad and his reputation, and in turn mine, were rock solid. I had been a positive surprise in my first year at camp, I was told, and I liked contributing to the positive way we were viewed there. My girlfriend's family still lived on the Island, and I would surely be spending serious time there in the future, including time around the Islanders. The last thing I wanted was to go out there and play like a dog and fall short of expectations.

That went hand in hand with my belief that the best thing for me was to start fresh at an AHL camp in a different organization. I knew I wasn't in good shape, but with the way I'd ended the ECHL season, I figured that even if I started in the Coast, I could show enough ability that an AHL team might want me back up fairly quickly. If that AHL team didn't want me, it would leave me with an open road ahead to play anywhere in the AHL if things went well, as I imagined they would.

Off the ice, my priorities had clearly shifted in other ways. Brianna was a year away from completing her master's degree in occupational therapy on Long Island, and we were sick of doing the long-distance relationship thing. As far as the ECHL went, I had my pick of teams, so I chose one that was as close as possible to her, the Reading Royals, strictly for that reason. Southern Pennsylvania wasn't exactly *close* close, but she could drive to see me and get there in a few hours, and that mattered to us.

I chose Hershey from the AHL tryouts I'd been offered, as it was also closer to Bri (roughly four hours by car) and the organization had (and has) such a wonderful reputation.

Strength-wise, I had gotten back to a decent level of muscle, but it was my cardio that was awful, so that was how I made myself feel better about the year ahead. I told myself if I could just get my legs under me at camp and get my wind back, I should get better as the season went on.

I remember a handful of things from that camp, but these are the ones that stand out: I got a flat tire driving between Long Island and Hershey and rolled into town on essentially a donut, a great metaphor for my level of mental commitment; we did a cardio test on the ice that was essentially "get down and back three times in 45 seconds" and I got exposed; and had I been in better shape, I might not have gotten hurt.

My play started to come around by about day four of camp, and I finally put together a great practice. Everything I shot went in. I was gassed, though, and at the end we did a three-on-three down-low battle drill, and I was out of steam. It was physical—which for the coaching staff was the point, I'm sure—and after a few hits, I got the puck and had a player charging at me.

I moved the puck and had time to get out of the way, but I was too tired to fully move, so I braced for contact. As I got hit, my skate stuck in a rut on the ice. I went over backwards, I felt a clean pop in my knee, and I knew. It didn't hurt, exactly, it just felt loose, and I skated myself off the ice without saying anything to anyone, hobbling my way to the training room.

With no argument from me, the doctors essentially told me I had best go to Reading, where I was to start the year, and I could start to work with the doctors down there, because my MCL was torn.

Before I had the chance to get back to a level I expected myself to be at, I was on the shelf, with one saving grace: the ECHL regular season didn't start for nearly a month. Players would be reporting there in 7 to 10 days, and then there was an exhibition season, so I had some time to get myself right before the real games began. In the interim, though, I was reporting to a new city and team, with just an hour of rehab to do every day, leaving me with what was slowly becoming my worst enemy: tons of free time. There wasn't a big staff in Reading to lean on me and push my recovery—I was just some guy they'd signed to play there—so they booked me appointments at a rehab clinic and I was in and out without much personal interaction. After setting up my new room, I got the biggest bottle of Absolut vodka they sold, made myself vodka-and-tonics on the couch, and waited for days to pass with nowhere to go and nothing to do. It's what anyone would've done in my shoes, I told myself, as I began fusing myself to the cushions.

As the team showed up, I started skating on the second sheet of the rink by myself, little by little, and tried to work my way back. I spent all that time rehabbing and waiting for the approval to skate with the team as I watched lines solidify and power-play units get constructed, and I started to worry about falling behind while I was ringing wristers past imaginary goalies on my lonely side of the arena. A day before the season, I got word: I could skate with the big group and was cleared for contact.

A day after my first practice—which went fine, I guess—we travelled to Elmira for the opening game of the season, and somewhat inexplicably, I was in the lineup. I'm sure I was asked if I could go and I said yes, but in retrospect, that was a horrible call by a whole host of people. I couldn't go upstairs without sucking wind, yet I was about to play a pro hockey game.

I played on our third line and I can remember one play, a three-on-two, where I turned the puck over at the offensive blue line while trying to saucer it over the stick of the defenceman. We lost and headed back to Reading with the roller coaster of a season officially under way. It was good to at least get a game under my belt—and come out alive.

Back home the next day, we practised, and as I was drying off after my shower, our coach told me to come see him in his office. I popped into his little room in my towel, and he said to come back when I was dressed. Y'know, it's never a good sign when the meeting is going to be longer than a quick exchange.

After I had chosen Reading to be close to my now-wife (which they knew), after they'd shipped my car out to get me there, after I'd rehabbed a torn MCL to skate in one practice and one game, head coach Jason Nobili told me he and GM Gordon Kaye had traded me to Boise, Idaho—across the country, really. The Steelheads and their coach, Derek Laxdal, had tried hard to get me to go there after university, and had seen me with the Aces and Grizzlies after that, and there we were. It's one thing to get traded in the NHL, or even in the minors, for some sort of reasonable cause, but this was a cruel misery inflicted without care or thought. Apparently some NHL deal had happened, and that pushed an extra player into the organization and pushed someone—me—out.

I can report with great joy that that Reading Royals team finished DFL—that's "dead fucking last"—in the 22-team league that season.

So, yeah, Idaho.

Idaho? What the hell do I do now?

I felt more than lost. I went to the Gillieses' in Long Island to decide whether I was going to report to Idaho or not. I spent time considering deals overseas and had an offer in the Netherlands (The Hague) that paid about 750 euros a week with all expenses paid and a car provided, and that was a major consideration for me. God, how I wish I had done it. But that would've meant saying bye-bye to Bri for the full winter, and that was just too much to handle.

In the end, my knowledge of Boise—good rink, good city, good team—and some prodding on their end convinced me to go. It was undeniably the end of the road for me in North America after that season (I was mentally making plans for a future in Europe as this unfolded), but I wasn't ready to just pack it in. It sucked all the start-of-the-year excitement out of me, but I'd played while feeling thoroughly unexcited before. And while I knew I wasn't where I needed to be as a player, I'm an optimistic guy when it comes to big-picture things. Maybe this was happening for a positive reason? I'm a fan of the Chinese parable about how to react when things go badly.

A farmer and his son had a stallion that they relied on to earn their living. Bad news: one day, the horse ran away, which made the farmer's neighbours express their sympathy: "That's awful, sorry that happened, just terrible luck."

The farmer replied, "Maybe so, maybe not, we'll see." (The farmer was probably an annoying neighbour, given that "Yeah, no kidding" is the easier response there.)

The next day, the stallion came back, leading a few wild mares, which was great news, and so his neighbours said as much. "Hey, the big guy's back with reinforcements. That's amazing luck!"

The farmer went back to the well with "Maybe so, maybe not, we'll see."

Sure enough, the next day, the farmer's son is working on breaking the mares, and he falls off one in the process, breaking his leg. "That's bummer luck," noted the neighbours, to which the farmer of course replied, "Maybe so, maybe not, we'll see."

It *was* bad, of course, but the next day the national army came through, looking for able-bodied young men to go fight in a war, and so the recently injured son avoided being conscripted. To which the neighbours noted, "Jesus, man, can we at least acknowledge that your son's not going off to die in some random war is good luck?" And the farmer said, "*Never! We'll never know if anything is actually good or not.*"

The greater point of the story, as much of a pain in the ass as the farmer seems to be, is that big life events change so many things, it's impossible to judge whether everything will have been for the greater good or made things worse. I could see a world where I showed up to play for a team that had wanted me for years, got myself back in good shape, and it became the best thing to ever happen to me.

When I got to Boise, I had hope. The medical staff was great, and the strength and conditioning coach was Brad Jellis, who's been with the Dallas Stars for years now. He got me on a better rehab program for my MCL, and it helped. I liked the apartments, and they had some deal with a beverage provider that let players take home four drinks per day, which sounds like nothing, but in the ECHL, free cold-brew Starbucks drinks, Powerade and iced teas felt like the big time.

I was impatient, though, and was away from my girlfriend and family. I was the new guy on the team, my car was stuck in Pennsylvania, and I had had one real practice and one game under my belt before taking a week off while deciding whether to show up or not. I was just generally off, so you will not be shocked to hear I did not come out of the gates hot. I started to get better as I got back in shape, and finally scored an ever-loving goal after about eight games with the Steelheads.

I was integrating nicely into the team, getting along easily with some pretty great guys, seeing my stock grow in terms of linemates and PP opportunities and all those good indicators. Before my 10th game of the season, I was feeling pretty good. As I always did, I was warming up playing two-touch with the boys, before my more formal warm-up and stretch.

Two-touch, for the uninitiated, is simply hacky sack with a soccer ball, but if you're the cause of the end of the rally with a bad touch, you're out. Players are eliminated until there's one man standing, and it all culminates in a big final game as pre-game meetings get closer.

Of course, it's not just like keeping a balloon airborne with a child; to win, you need your teammates to mess up. It's amiable and fun, but at some point, someone will decide to "sewer" a teammate (some call the game "sewer ball") by giving them an intentionally bad ball, maybe with way too much pace or in a place they can't do much with it.

I'm okay for a North American player (the Euros are always better), but it's hard to win with 10 guys, and so I was taking it at least one per cent too seriously when I found myself one of the final two guys, trying to win that last game. A pass came my way but was going to fall short—though still in my "territory." If a player is deemed to have chosen to let a ball drop when he could've got to it, that player is out, not the person who touched it last, so I overextended myself. Bad. My MCL popped again, as did any notion of getting my season back on track. I was right back where I'd started some six weeks prior.

Here's the funny part: injuries that aren't hockey-related aren't covered by the team, and being in the US, you just never know how that's gonna go. I was nervous about how pre-game two-touch would be labelled (is that a hockey injury?), and so I did something that seemed ridiculous: I put on my gear and dressed for the warm-up, hobbled onto the ice, and pretended to slip on a puck about 30 seconds into the warm-up, just to make sure all bases were covered. Not quite "Slippin' Jimmy" from *Better Call Saul*—I was legitimately hurt—but it still seems laughable now.

No questions were asked on the spot, which was good, but now I was in a position where I went back to my apartment to wonder, *What now?*

Being injured is a lonely experience in pro hockey, as teams often have players come to the training room at staggered times so they don't bog down the staff. And so, mostly alone in the middle of Idaho, with my career heading in the wrong direction, I began to see how some players suffer with their mental health in-season.

As the team went on road trips and I resumed my half-assed one-legged squats on a Bosu ball, I also resumed buying a large bottle of vodka for the house to keep me company at night. I made drinks every evening, working my way through a bottle here and there at a pace that seemed acceptable enough.

OK, maybe I'd make one more than would've been acceptable. Two on special nights when I was really feeling it.

Soon, I'd need another bottle.

The good news was, it turned out that aggravating the injury wasn't as bad as the initial tear, and it was only a couple of weeks before I was willing to give it another try.

Were the farmer to find out about that bit of "good" news, he might have wisely offered, "We'll see."

I was able to return just in time to go on the Alaska road trip with the team, still having barely played all season, presumably still in bad shape, and on a knee I'd just be testing out. But it was Alaska, and I knew people and places there (shout-out to the F Street Station pub, the best place in Anchorage), and I was glad to be going.

Besides, it was all coming together for a nice story: my first game back would be in Alaska, and on my 26th birthday—surely the hockey gods would give me a favourable bounce. By that point of the season, and of my career, I knew I would not be playing in the NHL. All I could do was play well and see how the year would unfold. Maybe I'd go to Europe the season after, I thought.

That first night back, on my birthday, I felt surprisingly good. Sullivan Arena in Anchorage is an Olympic-sized ice sheet, and it has the best ice in North America. It's hard—like, garage-floor concrete hard—and fast. When I was in college and you stepped out on a freshly cut sheet of ice, you could send a puck the length of the ice with a half-assed kick.

I had a great first period, during which I was all over the net, so our line got the nod to start the second period. We carried on our good play, getting into the offensive zone, and I was about to create something immediately.

If you're looking at the net, the puck was in the left corner, and I got to it first, with a D-man charging after me. Other players created a bit of a scrum on the near side of the net. I had a direct passing lane to our D-man, so I didn't need to bank the puck; instead I went with a direct tape-to-tape play. Having some surprising pep in my legs that night (the muscles were certainly rested), I jumped around the defender, who halfway held me as I skated by, but I was getting to the net, where I would look up to see whether I could get my stick out to tip a point shot or needed to park in front to screen.

As I looked up and to the right to see what my teammate with the puck was up to, I turned into his unscreened, untipped slapshot, which connected cleanly with what had once been my jawline. I've seen a lot of guys get pucks in the face over the years, but they're almost all tipped or caroming off something else, which dials down the force of the impact a bit. I can't recall many instances of a guy getting all of a clean slapshot, where the very next thing the puck hits is bone.

I slid along the fast ice some 30 feet in a heap, and I knew immediately it was bad.

My most vivid memory of that moment was knowing I was in for a long recovery, running my tongue across where my teeth should have been, and saying out loud the word "OK." Like, "OK, here we go, time to buck up and get to the long rehab process, 'cause it's bad."

My teeth were tough to make sense of, because they were no longer in a neat little row, yet they were somehow still attached. A tornado might destroy a row of homes, splintering boards and scrambling their parts about the ground. An earthquake may just wholly displace them, leaving them at different elevations, leaning askew. This was all earthquake, no tornado. The tectonic plates—meaning my jawbone—below my molars had shifted, and where they had been previously, they would never be again.

I got up and skated straight off the ice, knowing my way through the bowels of that rink to the training room, where I encountered three relatively disinterested medical employees who I resent to this day. I was terrified of what lay ahead of me, and I basically had to beg for someone's attention as they were in the midst what was surely a gripping fishing story.

Having finally got one of them to look at me, I remember halfway saying, "Is it bad?"—the way you would if your mouth was full of novocaine and propped open with a dental dam. That person, seeing the two halves of my jaw move independently—the pressure of the impact on the side had also split it cleanly down the chin line—immediately began arranging to get me to the hospital.

The plastic surgeon was summoned, as this was apparently not the type of thing that could wait. I was in Alaska and headed to the ER to rebuild my jaw.

Naturally, I thought of my college teammate whose jaw had been broken. I also wondered if Alaska was the type of place you wanted to be when you needed your face rebuilt in the middle of the night. No disrespect to Alaska, but I imagine it's tougher to recruit the best surgeon in the US there over, say, New York City.

When the doctor arrived, I said just two things, which went like this:

ME: Just please don't wire my jaw shut.
DOCTOR (*bursting into outright, unrestrained laughter*): Oh, we're wiring it shut.
ME (*already heavily medicated*): OK, just make sure I look pretty.
DOCTOR: (*More laughter*)

Oh, we were having a blast, me and Doc. Despite my skepticism, he ended up being wonderful.

That's just about all I remember, aside from being holed up in an Alaskan hotel room for the next two days, waiting for our return flight. I was given liquid Percocet and cans of soup broth to heat up in the microwave, and my next journey began.

As I sit here today, writing about this, it's hard not to think about that farmer. It was awful, that moment, that year, and it would further contribute to more tough moments ahead. But it also stopped me from prolonging a career that wasn't going to result in anything on the ice, aside from merely existing within pro hockey and having "fun" for a few more years. It would've gotten unserious fast—maybe it already was?—and that moment forced me to start a life after hockey within a matter of months, which all leads to where I am today. Maybe my career, which I'm very happy with and proud of, would've happened some other way if I'd kept playing. *Maybe.* But it certainly wouldn't happen the way it has, or taken me where I am, which is somewhere I'm exceedingly happy. The jaw injury was a bad thing—unequivocally, it seemed.

But sometimes, y'know, there's value in "We'll see."

6

LIFE IN THE REAL WORLD

Hi, my name is Justin Bourne, and I'm an alcoholic. That's not remotely hard to say anymore, given that I *am* one, and I've said it thousands of times now. I never wanted that phrase to define me, but unfortunately, it wasn't a choice; it is a part of who I am. So, here we are.

But when exactly does one become an alcoholic? I'm of the belief that alcoholism is at least in part biological, but it's not like that switch was always turned on. Hell, I didn't drink until I was 21 or so, right? Is there a day where an alcoholic drinks to excess and it suddenly becomes like, *OK, now you're officially an alcoholic?* Was it a secret level I unlocked on my 100th drink?

I wonder, because I'm not sure I was an alcoholic at 26, with my jaw wired shut for nearly two months (thanks to infections and follow-up procedures). Others may argue that alcohol had affected my training during previous summers and was already a detriment, so I had qualified all the way back then.

I believed I had control over my drinking in those jaw-wired late hockey days, because, hey, if you throw up with your teeth wired shut, you can *die*, and throwing up was a possibility because I was on a variety of drugs. I drank liquid Percocet and an anti-nausea drug (on the streets you'd call it "lean"—promethazine with codeine) that was aimed at preventing the vomit death. I was also on antibiotics for runs of time while wired shut, and given that drinking limits their effectiveness, I maybe only had a few drinks over the next couple of months. (Fun fact about having your jaw wired shut: they have you carry around wire cutters in case you *do* get sick, because you'd rather mess up your last jaw surgery than choke on your own vomit.)

So, at this point in my life I'm not really drinking, nor am I eating, and I'm just on drugs and waiting to figure out what the hell to do with the rest of my life.

Being hit by a chin-high slapshot required me to get a 10-screw plate on the right side of my jaw to keep the various pieces of jawbone close enough together. In theory, they would join forces again, like Power Rangers, and become one super-bone (apparently, bones heal so that they end up stronger where they've been broken than they were before the injury). I also needed an X-shaped plate with four screws to hold the two halves of my chin together. That plate is still in there, while the 10-screw one on the side eventually had to be removed—sadly, the bone fragments turned out not to be Power Rangers, and pieces of the jawbone died.

My daily relief, liquid Percocet.

When it became infected, the signs weren't subtle.

My life in the aftermath of the "de-facing" looked like this: I would drink that liquid Percocet, following the guidelines on the bottle but applying a bit of "strategy" I'd developed in my previous experiences with Percocet: I'd try to take a little less per dose during the day so I could take extra in the evening and hopefully feel, for a rare moment on those days, "good." I was alone on the couch a lot.

The drugs had a profound impact on my mental state. I talked to Brianna on the phone the day after the damage, while I was still full of some variety of oxycodone (or maybe just morphine), and I probably came off like a televangelist. I vigorously explained how great it was that the injury happened, because I'd finally have more time to read. I could finally read the classics! I exclaimed.

I like to read, but like, man, relax.

I don't know how to describe liquid Percocet exactly, but the closest analogy I can think of is this: Have you ever taken a shot of alcohol and felt it all the way down into your stomach? Maybe normal people haven't consumed alcohol straight on an empty stomach before, but *phew*, if you do, sometimes you can feel the burn all the way down. With the Percocet, the farther it went down past my mouth, the farther *up* the sides of my smile went. Liquid or otherwise, Percs worked like a hug for my insides. Some people don't like painkillers, but I gotta tell you, they work for my particular brain in an extremely pleasing manner.

One thing I did conclude was that I had no interest in *playing* hockey again that season. On the couch where I spent those months in Boise, I very rarely even considered suiting up again. Even when I got back on the ice by myself as the team moved towards the playoffs, and they asked if I'd wear a full cage and get back out there for the team, I couldn't fathom it. With my wires finally off, I found I could barely open my mouth. I mean that quite literally: the muscles could barely do it. At the doctor's urging, I had to lay a Popsicle stick flat and slide it between my teeth, and each day stack another stick on top to slowly pry my mouth open, but not in a rushed way that damaged anything. I was months away from being able to confidently bite an apple,

I was in terrible shape (with my weight down from about 190 to the low 170s), and so the idea of going into the corner after a puck in a playoff hockey game was a complete non-starter.

This was the ECHL. I wasn't on some million-dollar deal. I'd played 11 games that season. The idea of putting myself at further risk—for what, exactly?

I ended up needing three procedures on the jaw in total, spending nearly two months in wires, bottoming out at a weight in the high 160s. I had spent a decade pushing myself down a path that no longer existed. Even the idea of pursuing hockey to Europe evoked a similar feeling in me then—for what? More hockey felt like putting off the inevitable.

When I realized what this all meant, I needed a moment, to be sure. It was over? That path was the only one I knew, and just about the only place I'd ever aimed my sights. I wasn't exactly young to be asking, "Wait, what do I want to do with my life?" Even during my best years, I had felt the constant immersion of "being a hockey player" in-season, and how it left few hours for anything else. Even during my worst summers of flaked workouts, the daily push to go and train wore on my brain. It was how I self-identified—I had become a Hockey Player, and I didn't know what I was without the sport.

There had always been a fringe hope in a place I rarely looked at directly, I think, of getting to where my dad had been. I never would've verbalized this, but I also liked being the guy who kept surprising people. I don't think anyone from my hometown would've had the young me pegged as a guy who would play pro hockey, and I think I wanted to at least get a taste of the top level to take that surprise to its logical conclusion. I say "I think" because these were never tangible, processed goals I wrote down in some dream diary to manifest. They were just feelings.

The realization that it was over was a reality check. Had I really thought I would play in the NHL after a college career in *Alaska* that saw me end up in the hockey mecca of *Boise, Idaho*? Had I really stared in the face the reality of where I had been in the pecking order of pro hockey? Had the whole thing been silly, naive?

As I saw it then, there really wasn't anyone to consult on the "decision." The sport seemed to have made the decision for me. I talked to my mom and Bri, of course, and was met with the support I expected. Same when I talked to my brother. Same when I talked to my dad. But those conversations were less "Should I be done playing hockey?" and more "I'm done playing hockey, what now?" There weren't options to choose from.

But those emotions passed in a relative blink, maybe over the course of a few days. What emerged, more than anything, was relief. Injuries had given me an out from something that seemed to be holding me back from what I thought was the life I wanted to live, from which I was being pulled. I didn't want to have to be at my physical best anymore, not every day.

Suddenly, new paths emerged, which I viewed like a dog sneaking behind a child about to open the front door, providing the puck-width crack of light I needed to nudge it open further and start running.

With no clear plan, I saw the chance to run to something different.

7

ARIZONA, BECOMING "MEDIA," AND COACHING WITH THE MARLIES

One of the cities that was desperate for occupational therapists had sent Bri an offer: *Move to Arizona to work, and we'll give you a $10,000 signing bonus.* Ten grand to a woman who was back living at home after seven years of university, who was dating an ECHL hockey player—well, that might as well have been a million. To go with it, Phoenix had a few things going for it. My mom and stepdad had recently bought a small place there for winter getaways, and I was sick of living in cold places. Family would occasionally be around. And better still, the Phoenix Roadrunners were still in the ECHL, and so a plan was formed: I would play one last year in the ECHL, and if anything happened (for instance, if I got traded or they just didn't want me), I'd quit.

I could contemplate continuing to play for one more year as a compromise of sorts, because my broken jaw had opened up an opportunity for me, just like the Chinese farmer's stallion had returned a few mares. I saw a way to play while transitioning to the next thing.

Maybe I had liquid Percocet to thank for that. Once the sides of my mouth would creep up past horizontal, I would turn on anything on TV that was tangentially related to sports (the Westminster Dog Show? Sure!) and play around on the internet, often trading emails with my uncle Ken, who had been a sportswriter for years. He had once been a member of a highly acclaimed group of Stan Fischler interns, a group of people who'd basically go on to run hockey (the NHL offices, team operations and broadcast networks are littered with former Fischler gofers).

By this time, Ken had a media relations and communications business based out of Saskatoon, which I found interesting, and we'd always been like-minded and as close as you can be with an uncle who lives in another province—and country. I had all the time in the world to respond to emails at length those days, and given the drugs, I was likely a little liberal with the word count.

Given that I had so much time and was watching and talking about sports and writing, he had a suggestion: Why not start a blog? They're free, and "other people would find these thoughts interesting." And, presumably, he wouldn't have to sort through my multi-thousand-word emails anymore. Clever.

So, jtbourne.wordpress.com was born before I ever got on Twitter, which I note because I'm not sure how anybody even knew my work existed in those days. I'd watch something sportsy, write my thoughts on it and publish, and then those words existed on the internet, waiting for people to find them. (Maybe they searched for "mass typos," which would have turned up those blogs early in Google's search results.) There was some link-exchanging among bloggers, as in "I'll list you in my blogroll on the side of my free blog if you do the same." Somehow, the blog got discovered—like a raw but talented player in some obscure beer league.

One of those early readers was Chris Botta, who was running *Islanders Point Blank*, a very successful Islanders blog at the time, and he offered to let me write the story of my relationship for his readers. Given the Bourne-Gillies connections, it was relevant to the blue and orange faithful.

That was my first exposure to a larger audience, and the return link to my blog helped garner some readers who were more than one degree removed from family. Someone from the *Hockey News* came across the article, and another opportunity arose.

In retrospect, I can see how a couple of opportunities popped up. The best players in the NHL are not going to waste their time writing about their experiences on the internet. They make too much money and are presumably too busy for such a thing. The *Players' Tribune*, which publishes first-person stories by pro athletes, didn't exist back then. And if any players had even wanted to do such a thing, it's a smaller group yet that would have committed themselves to writing well enough, often enough to build an audience. I have to work at it now, let alone 15 years ago, but because of the dearth of other athletes writing, some significant media outlets were interested in my work.

The *Hockey News* had me write a piece while I was still employed as an Idaho Steelhead, and we shortly reached an agreement whereby they'd pay me for one piece a week, at a whopping $15 per.

I was a paid and published author, baby! Look at me go!

I had a secret weapon in all this: my uncle Ken didn't so much aim me away from his inbox as he saw potential in what I was doing, and he ended up getting far more involved. For the next several years, he edited just about everything I wrote. His role as a mentor in my life really solidified then, with just about every big decision I've ever made involving his consultation at some point. We already had a relationship, but we became involved damn near every day after this.

His edits in those years allowed me to see patterns in my bad habits and learn from them. If, every time your editor edits your work, they delete the first two paragraphs, maybe you're taking too long to get to the point? It was stunning how consistently you could delete two or three paragraphs from my early work and lose nothing.

I checked the daily views on the website religiously and felt the first endorphin rushes of being an internet content creator when something succeeded. I didn't know what I wanted to do with my life then, but being done with hockey forever was on the table. Only one thing terrified me about that: if I walked away from hockey, I'd walk away from a life's education in the sport (and the love for it that hid beneath the surface at that point). It was the only venue in which I was a legitimate expert. I could find another job, I was sure, but I wanted to use my life-long knowledge of the game, and so I wondered if maybe I could make the writing thing work.

We flew down to Phoenix to see the area and consider our options while we stayed in my mom's place. Bri went for her interview and they offered her the position over the phone the moment we drove away from the hospital. We didn't bother conferring; we were so excited about being together in a new place, we just shared a quiet, happy nod and she said yes before the call was over, and that was that: we were moving to Arizona. It was the type of decision that only people without kids—or even possessions—can make.

Now cue the sad trombone: within a month of that decision, the Roadrunners folded.

We were pot committed, though, already deep in plans to move there. The fates had decided I was making the transition from hockey player to writer with no buffer year. I suppose I could've created my own "fate" and changed course here, but if you've got the vibe from where I was at in my playing career, it felt like the type of out I was looking for.

I wasn't surprised to find that I didn't miss hockey in the early going in Arizona, not at all. It was warm and everything was cheap and I was with Bri and finally taking a step away from the grind.

I *was* surprised to discover that at no point did I miss *being a hockey player*. I sometimes missed playing actual games, but not being caught up in the machinery of it all. Somehow, by being done as a player, I found my love for the sport again. The yearly cycle had wrung the joy out of me, and I was ready to take that back. I loved hockey in its purest form—free from the politics and the climb and the pressures—and wanted to rediscover that part (which I would eventually do by joining a beer league team).

Maybe the ease with which I moved on from playing the game was made possible by my upbringing. Not the part where I grew up in a hockey family and around the game, but the part where I never grew up with designs on being an NHL player. I wasn't letting go of a dream I'd had since I was a boy. I was just finding my way in life, and life hadn't taken me to the NHL—that much had become clear. And so I think I looked at it pragmatically: if I wasn't going to the NHL, it was better to move on sooner rather than later, and maybe I could still use all this knowledge to make a life within the game.

I love the game more now than I ever did when I was younger, maybe even more than when I played. A couple of factors led to some stretches of years where I didn't even consume NHL hockey. When I was in university, there was an NHL labour dispute, and worse, the league's best American TV deal offered one game a week on the Outdoor Life Network. Thanks to those people for helping prop up the league when it was down, and I don't mean any disrespect, but come on: the *Outdoor Life Network*?

We didn't have PVRs then, so unless you were in front of the TV between 7:07 and 9:40 on a Wednesday night (or whatever night it was), you hadn't seen an NHL game in six days and it was gonna be at least seven more before you got your next chance. I practised every day and played hockey and, obviously, grew my education within the game, but my knowledge of the NHL in those years could be generously described as thin. Further to that, as a player in the two seasons after university, I still lived in the US and was busy most nights playing. Hell, I lived in the US for three years after that, meaning that when I watched *SportsCenter* each day on ESPN, I ended up knowing more about Mark Sanchez and Rex Ryan's New York Jets than I did about the return of a Jets team to Winnipeg.

When we moved to Arizona, my wife made me a deal: I would take one year to focus on making a career out of being a writer, and if I couldn't make progress there, I'd move on to something different. We had no money, but we didn't need much, living in that state at that point in our lives.

I found a more consistent place in hockey's public conversation that year and found more freelance opportunities. *USA Today* had me contribute a piece once a week (I believe it was for $50 a piece the first year), and a website called *Hockey Primetime* solicited a piece a week as well and paid me best of all, somewhere around $100 a post. Between that, the *Hockey News*, and eventually some pieces at Yahoo! on the *Puck Daddy* blog, I might have been able to scrape together between $600 and $700 a month. We lived rent-free at my mom's place while we looked for our own, and with my wife on an entry-level salary, we managed to get by.

The bigger point was, you could actually read my work at a couple places where people read about hockey. It was the 2009–10 season, I was months removed from being a "player," even if I hadn't done much playing that last year, and I was a unique voice on the scene. Honestly, that I was able to make that much money was nearly impossible, given what freelancing generally paid then. Though I wasn't financially successful, I felt like I was having success.

And it was enough money for my wife and me to justify plowing ahead with this potential career. In year two, I started to grow comfortable in my writing skin, or as they say in the biz, I "found my voice." I wanted to write like I talked, more or less, which I hoped was "smart without taking it too seriously." At the same time, that type of voice was making real inroads on the sports scene. Bill Simmons had blown up and was writing must-read columns. I read *Can I Keep My Jersey?* by Paul Shirley, a player whose story isn't too dissimilar to mine, although he was actually good and played in the NBA. *Seemed Like a Good Idea at the Time* by David Goodwillie is an unbelievably good book, about a college player who played minor pro baseball before going on to more fascinating careers. While they weren't hockey players, I saw a template for success amongst athletes (and other bloggers), and I set out on that course.

After year two on the freelance blog beat, I got a call from Joe Ross at theScore, a company that has taken various forms over the years, all of them successful. It was a cable TV channel, then a digital media platform, then an app-focused company, and now an app with a sports-gambling bent. But back then, they were moving heavily into original online content, and they made me a great offer with a catch: I could do the job for one more year in Arizona, but after that, I'd have to move to Toronto.

Toronto?

It sounded extremely not-Arizona in terms of pace and cost and weather, but if I was going to make it in my industry, maybe it was necessary? My wife had a great job in Phoenix, though, and that was our basis for choosing the state. It didn't seem particularly fair to ask her to move to *Canada* for my less financially viable and more unstable career.

Things weren't great, though. They were great with us, don't get me wrong. We loved our time there together. Starting fresh without friends or family in that state allowed us the time we'd wanted together, and we became dependent on one another, in a positive way. We were all we had.

But I wrote in the mornings, and my work hours were done early since Toronto was in a later time zone, which meant I had begun spending afternoons at my local watering hole, playing on Twitter and drinking $1.75 gigantic mugs of Bud Light. My plan was to spend just $10 a day—three big-ass mugs of beer, plus a little tax and a tip—and then head home for dinner. It wasn't long before $10 wouldn't cut it, though—not even close.

When I talked about the opportunity at theScore with Bri, she was surprisingly amenable to uprooting the life we'd started building over a couple of years to that point. She saw the chance for me to have co-workers and an office and a purpose aside from typing some words alone, then burying pints. I'd say I was early down a bad path, but to her, the direction must have been clear. The farther down it I went, the worse it would get.

Bri not only agreed to it but pushed for it to happen, and did everything for us to facilitate the eventual move. She had been at the heart of why we were in Arizona, and in a roundabout way, it would be the bottle that drove us out of there. Yes, the opportunity for me was a good one, and it was my best chance at becoming something more in my field of interest. And no, we never explicitly said that booze was a root cause for the move. But it was an underlying contributor, at the very least.

I was insanely lucky. Lucky to have her, of course, and lucky that she'd allowed me to take a year in my mid-20s to just focus on hockey writing. We hear of athletes who "bet on themselves" in single seasons; this was that, but with more faith—*she* bet on me.

Having such a supportive partner was, and is, one thing. But the fact that theScore was creating what they were creating right as I was gaining prominence was extremely fortunate. It's not as though there were dozens of these places popping up online—at least, not ones that actually paid, and the $65,000 they offered was substantially more than the, oh, $6,500 I'd made the season before. That number would go up if I moved to Toronto—and I eventually would—instantly transforming me from a fringe freelance writer to someone with a hockey-writing livelihood.

TheScore wanted a network of league-specific blogs that were partially personality-driven, as were their team-specific blogs. Andrew Stoeten and his blog, *Drunk Jays Fans*, was a great example of how a personality could bring their followers with them, and he came to theScore. When the offer first came, *The Basketball Jones* (Tas Melas, J.E. Skeets, Trey Kerby, Leigh Ellis and their team) was still there, Drew Fairservice was covering MLB (with Dustin Parkes), Richard Whittall was on soccer, Sean Tomlinson was on the NFL and Scott Lewis was on basically all of them (doing a ton of great NHL work, too). It was an office packed with big personalities and talent, and an unbelievable place to develop my skills on the job while creating the NHL site. God, was it a fun work environment for a while.

It was also a trip. I was given a freelance budget, which was not something I'd experienced in the ECHL. My completely unconventional path to becoming a blog . . . editor? . . . led to some random ideas, which led to some neat work. Given the frequency of injury in sports, I managed to get Jo Innes—an actual doctor!—to write about recent injuries for the site. I called people *way* above the pay range I could offer, because I didn't know any better, and I was surprised when people showed interest—and some of them joined the site.

This definitely led to some of my more violent episodes of imposter syndrome, particularly when I tried to "edit" some pieces for content for the blog. Ellen Etchingham was a freelance writer for us, and this is someone with, I assume, a pile of degrees and a vocabulary to make both Merriam and Webster jealous. Meanwhile, in that first year, I would find myself with one eye open at 7 a.m., smelling like vodka and trying to figure out how someone would let me be in charge of anything, let alone people very clearly more qualified to write than myself.

Thank God I knew pucks and sticks well, I guess.

The freedom was almost intimidating (particularly in light of our mandate to produce so much content), which made for some big hits and bigger misses. Truth be told, nobody cared about the misses; I was just swinging at every pitch like Shohei Ohtani, with the homers justifying the strikeouts. I wrote a thousand-word breakdown of an outfit Jaromír Jágr once wore in the early '90s (a thick but loose-fitting quarter-zip sweater with no shirt underneath that was fully tucked into his jeans and topped off with a chain). It did great, and I measure "great" here by internet traffic compared to our usual amount. I checked the views on each article the way I used to go over my own stats, finding personal validation every time the site did something that garnered attention. It was engaging, finding something statistical to chase when I was a few years removed from chasing goals.

If, every time I tried a specific shot, I scored, you can imagine I'd have taken that shot a bunch. And so, when I debuted my Systems Analyst posts, where I'd take some screenshots and explain what had gone wrong on a play—something that came very easy to me—I found my sweet spot. People read it, engaged with it and wanted more.

It turned out that the mainstream hockey media hadn't done much play-breakdown work since Howie Meeker stopped saying, "Stop it right there," and there was a thirst for it.

It led to the strangest thing—at one point, this general manager in the Ontario Hockey League sent me a direct message, commenting on a play I'd broken down. Kyle Dubas must have shared the post with his head coach, Sheldon Keefe, who followed me on Twitter as a result. Some time later, Sheldon wrote me to refute some points I'd made in an article about the advantages of the NCAA route over playing major junior. For what it's worth, he was right, and I learned from the points he made, but it was representative of how my work was being perceived—as worth taking seriously. The Systems Analyst posts showed I wasn't just a guy posting Jágr-in-funny-pants pieces, but that I knew my stuff.

There was also validation for something I'd always felt as a player: I understand the Xs and Os stuff inherently, and I was baffled when teammates couldn't grasp basic concepts. And, dare I say it, I had a couple of coaches in whom I wasn't overly confident that they understood what they were trying to "teach," either. I had always wanted to ask questions like "You want me to stand here, OK, but why?" but the risk of seeming difficult didn't seem worth what I guessed would be the answer: "Because that's where we told you to stand."

But as I wrote from Arizona and found traction with *Backhand Shelf* on theScore, I was losing my footing in my personal life. Frankly, in what I now recognize as a fight against alcoholism, I was taking a beating.

My articles had been getting shorter and making more liberal use of subheads, as keeping a coherent stream of thought going through anything of significant length became impossible. Bri did everything necessary to get us ready to move, and I mean that literally, because by the end of year three in Arizona, I was incapable of organizing my thoughts in any meaningful manner.

Three years removed from playing professional hockey, I had gone from 190 pounds to 225 (eventually topping out at around 230). Light beer is only light if you don't drink, like, eight a day with chicken wings. My wife had to schedule our move and get certified to work in Canada and deal with citizenship issues and on and on. You can't just move cats into a country without paper-work, apparently.

Knowing we were leaving and how poorly I was doing, I just needed out of Arizona. I needed to get where we were going. Bri tasked me with one thing: "exporting" our car to Canada—and days before we left, I finally figured out I had misunderstood the assignment. I assumed they'd just let us take the car across the border, because I'd driven between the US and Canada plenty of times, and that's what they do.

When you're *visiting*.

It was brought to my attention in the days leading up to the move that you actually needed the title to bring a car into the country permanently, and to get that from Arizona, you had to own the car outright, which we did not. That meant we wouldn't be able to get the car into the country without paying the 10 grand or so we still owed on the 2009 Jetta I had bought used in 2010.

It was the perfect encapsulation of the secondary role I had come to play in our relationship. I hadn't done anything overtly bad, but I couldn't be counted on and needed so much support that I couldn't be a partner. I was more like a child. (In the end, we were fortunate to be able to borrow money from my mom, whom we paid off over the subsequent years.)

That first real wave of alcoholism in Arizona snuck up on me. I had been drinking those daily beers, but you know, your tolerance goes up. I got a little more efficient with my work, too, so I started going to the bar 15 or 20 minutes earlier here and there, and ordering a little sidecar of espresso vodka with my beers, to speed up the buzz without the need to drink so much bloating beer to get it.

Bri enjoyed Nate's Third Base, too, so she got why I liked it, and I always explained I just needed to get out of the house every day to talk to another human, which was true. It's true that it was *one* of the reasons I needed to get out of the house.

As I waited to leave for Toronto, I was starting to worry about myself, as it got harder to convince even me that my behaviour was normal. I knew I was struggling to talk to people, so I started to seek out therapists. I don't know if I just had bad luck there, but I was turned off by how quickly I was offered medication, including Prozac for depression, which blew my mind. I wasn't remotely unhappy; surely I didn't need to add meds to what I was already putting in my body (and which I had no intention of stopping putting in my body).

Those visits to Nate's used to get me to a nice buzz by the time I saw Bri at four o'clock. But Phoenix commutes aren't easy, and she started early, so she was in bed most nights by nine. That meant that if I had a couple drinks (and maybe snuck a couple more) between four and nine, I could keep that buzz going without crashing and have some nice, heavily imbibed couch time when she was in bed. The hiding to drink "extra" had begun.

I don't always know what I said on Twitter while watching hockey those nights, but I do know I was much more prone to take shots at people.

This whole alcoholism thing became a daily cycle. On my worst nights, I'd wake up and need a little help sleeping from the bar I kept in the house—usually just a good tug of vodka—which led to my worst nights becoming sloppy mornings.

After a run of bad days, I vowed to myself not to drink after a single morning pull of vodka to steady myself, the sober hero that I was. As the day went on, my voice grew weak and I'd get shaky. To avoid thinking about it, I went to bed early, but I couldn't come close to sleeping while sober. Hours later, as I started to drift, I started to sweat heavily (this became a theme of my life for years). And just as it felt like I was about to finally get to sleep, my body reacted as if I'd been hit with a taser. It was a full-body spasm that lasted maybe four seconds. I stood straight up out of bed and looked around—had someone done something to me?—fearful of what it meant about my health. There was no one in the room. Had I just had a seizure? Was this "delirium tremens," or DTs?

I walked out of the bedroom, grabbed the vodka and drank like it was a desert oasis. And with that, I managed to find what had become my body's version of "sleep," which never left me feeling overly refreshed.

Not long before we left Arizona for good, my wife came home and found me splayed out on the floor, too drunk in the middle of the day to stay conscious. She wanted to rush me to the hospital, worried I had gotten concussed playing beer league the night before. But she smelled the booze on me, and I tried to explain that the late game, and the drinks after, and the one I had at lunch, had just left me exhausted.

She grew worried about me.

We were in our first few years together, and she loved me, and I always had an excuse. But we had hope that a new life in a new place could be the answer. It was time to try to manage something that had gotten away from me, and it was time to see if I could control myself.

The move to Toronto, then, was to be a fresh start in all regards. Being around people would help for a variety of reasons, one of which was that I wouldn't be able to drink all day. I believed with my heart that I was capable of finding the person I had been only a few years earlier, someone who could be sharp and motivated and, at the very least, somewhat useful.

On the four-day drive from Arizona to Toronto, I'd fill a Dasani bottle with vodka and keep it in the wheel well of the trunk to take intermittent sips at rest stops—concealed from my wife as she took bathroom breaks—strictly to keep the shakes at bay. This wasn't drinking for fun, it was drinking to keep the physical symptoms of withdrawal away. I hated having to do that, I hated feeling like a prisoner to booze, but mostly I was sick of hiding my drinking from her, which was obviously a weird form of lying. I vowed to myself to get better, to get rid of the need and to move back from a habit to a hobby. I liked drinking, obviously, but was already aware I was going to have to fight to keep it at bay to have success in my daily life—for the rest of my life.

When we arrived in Toronto, that life *was* immediately different, and I'm not sure I fully processed what was ahead of us. Our monthly rent payment doubled, while the size of our place was cut to one-third of our Arizona condo. We moved directly above a great Irish bar on King Street West (this made me happy, dangerous though I knew it to be), and the city was *busy*. I hadn't been anywhere but home (quiet), my local pub (quiet) or a golf course (same) over the previous three years, and it had altered my ability to interact with the world. I hadn't had many face-to-face interactions, particularly sober, and I honestly didn't know anymore how to hold myself in those moments. Eye contact made me feel like I was under a microscope, and frankly, I'd become embarrassed by the man I presented. I was badly out of shape and all the liquid had eroded my once-sharp brain smooth.

It was a borderline identity crisis: I considered myself a smart guy, a hockey guy, and I had always been confident in my appearance, right or wrong. And here I was meeting people in what felt like a big metropolitan city, and I felt dumb and looked like I had the athletic prowess of a pug. Given that I didn't self-identify as pug-like, it led to a physical and mental contrast I didn't like.

The writing, though—I could still do that. I knew the game well enough to get by there, and I hadn't entirely lost my sense of humour, as much as my ability to process the nuance of jokes had dulled. Just as long as no one looked at me or talked to me, I was fine.

The first day I was to go to work at theScore's offices in Toronto, I was terrified.

I imagined they were expecting some fit, sharp hockey guy to roll in, and I've made it clear the sort of person I felt I had become. I was also worried because I had formed relationships with a lot of those people online. I was anxious about how many people I'd half-recognize but should know, whom I sort of had relationships with but didn't. I thought I'd be fine once it was no longer a big deal that I was showing up, but I had suspected that my first day might be treated as one.

The office was in the Hyatt Regency at King and Blue Jays Way, and I stood before the elevator that first day trying to press the button but couldn't. I tried and tried, but I couldn't manage it stone-cold sober. I went across the street to Wayne Gretzky's and drank a couple of pints, eating lunch afterward and then crushing mints to get ready to walk in there and not smell like beer. Gretzky's, just up the street from what I knew as the SkyDome as a kid, felt like the moon compared to Arizona. It would've been cool if I hadn't been so paralyzed by it all.

I didn't show up until after 11 a.m., and I sweated and sweated and sweated from anxiety (and being out of shape) while they got me set up in what was affectionately known as "Blog Jail" before it was lovingly rebranded "Ghoul Island," given the shared sense of humour and cynicism of the blog group they'd pulled together.

The best thing to happen to me was that this was a group that liked to go for pints, and the second I could get them into that setting, where I didn't have to worry about the booze on my breath and I could relax, I could be myself and get to know the guys.

Surprisingly, this arrangement became how I was able to wean myself off constantly having alcohol in my blood. I knew I had to show up in the mornings, and I was excited about doing that with the guys who were there. That excitement was the key—I was eager to be my best and contribute to the team, like in my best hockey days. I also knew the job had flexibility (hours were loose, so long as content was posted), so I'd be able to get out in the afternoon for a drink or three. And going with these guys I really liked meant that people were with me—and it wasn't normal to have shots with your beers in the middle of the day. So I went later and left earlier and gradually reduced my physical need for booze. Within a month or two, I stopped shaking when I didn't have a midday pint. I could eventually go whole days without, and sleep without, and felt like I had found myself again.

That's not to say I didn't drink copious volumes of alcohol, but at least the settings became more acceptable for a 30-year-old dude with some income: after work, with friends, and on the weekends most heavily, but no longer alone and in hiding. With no kids and myriad downtown options, those were great days for my wife and me. We regularly met up after work for a few drinks, and settled into a much more normal, healthier life. We were happy.

The Foggy Dew—or, more accurately, "The Dew"—became our outlet for fun. Bri and I acquired a group of friends from that pub below our house, people we value to this day. They became more than bar friends, as we shared our most special memories together—holiday meals, going to cottages, even travelling as a group of 12 to Mexico. We helped each other as friends do, and it was so much more than just drinking. They're our best friends in Toronto to this day.

I mention that because my drinking past doesn't *just* bring to mind the expected constant regret—which isn't always common among those who've gotten sober. Brianna kept me on the right side of awful in those days, as she always knew when we should call it a night. She knew when it was reasonable to go out, but think about that: what a huge burden for her. I *constantly* wanted to go and drink, and she had to manage us collectively because I couldn't manage myself, whether we spoke that truth or not. I'd have lived in the bar had she been cool with it, but fortunately, she was more important to me than the bottle.

In the early years in Toronto, the decision between whether to indulge the beast inside me and just drink, despite all advice, or to stick with her was never a challenge. The decision itself would never become one. But that beast grew stronger, and to satiate it, my choices would only grow worse. But when it was more manageable, we went as we went, together, and for the better.

Weeks existed as inconveniences between the great weekends we had with our closest friends, until the record-scratch moment came.

TheScore had decided to move away from original content in favour of becoming a purely news-based outlet, which meant the end of the original content department, which was mine. They laid off our team, yet somehow I managed to survive. *Backhand Shelf*, however, did not. I guess I had a big enough following that generated enough traffic that I was asked to continue writing original content for our NHL page, but it wasn't remotely the same. Ghoul Island was done, and the work was no longer satisfying. What I wrote was tossed into the news feed and bumped down and out of sight the second we carried the report "Capitals Third Line Left Winger Leaves Morning Skate Early." Our excellent freelancers were no longer around, and the heart of what it had been—particularly the fun and somewhat goofy podcast, with Jake Goldsbie, John Noon and Ryan Eligh—were dead and gone. The purpose I had found was gone, too.

I grew worried about my employment and worked to make myself relevant in other ways at theScore. I took over "brand integration," which essentially meant that as our sales department sold ads, I'd work on creating original content to pair with them. For Bacardi, I wrote a series of articles on great East Coast hockey players (did you know Bacardi is a big drink in the Maritimes?). For Rogaine, a top-10 list of the best flows in the

NHL. It was . . . not perfect, but it was employment, and I was still writing about hockey and collecting a decent paycheque.

Even though I plowed on and kept a job, I got lost at the-Score. Maybe it's more accurate to say I successfully managed to get lost. I was no longer a part of a team but on my own within the company, so nobody really knew who I was accountable to. Therefore, I became accountable to nobody, which for a while was pretty great. I started showing up after 9:30 and leaving by 2:30, sometimes far earlier.

The emails still came, and so I needed to be on my phone, which meant finding somewhere quiet I could drink those afternoons—somewhere far enough from work that people wouldn't be stopping in for lunch, but close enough that I could return if I needed to. I knew too many people at the Dew, and work was a 10-minute walk from my house, so I'd post up at the Wellington Pub for a couple of hours each afternoon before stopping into the Dew, before going home.

It was back to me and the IPAs and trying to keep that buzz going till Bri would go to sleep. You'd think a smart person would recognize the pitfalls of heading down that path again, but it was always a problem I pushed off until tomorrow, or when I would need to. "This isn't healthy, but I'll just have a couple before noon here and answer some emails" would become the start of a long day of drinks. I'd proved to myself I could manage the drinking, hadn't I? I'd improved the problem once before; surely I could do it again if I had to?

I lived in pubs in the west end, doing just enough to avoid trouble at work, skimping on time and effort with what I wrote (which had declined in volume from multiple pieces a day to a handful a week). There is no geographic cure for alcohol, and I found that out the hard way then. My wife would get up and go to work in the morning while I'd sleep in, given that I'd started drinking more after she had gone to bed in the evenings. It wasn't sustainable, and I once again began to think I had to fix myself, which I would assuredly do, tomorrow.

Tomorrow.

Tomorrow.

By this time it was 2015, and back home in Kelowna, Dad had some wayward struggles that mirrored my own.

He had launched the Hockey Greats Fantasy Camp with the financial backing of an old-time hockey fan who saw the chance to be a part of something awesome, with the hope of maybe turning a profit at some point.

The camp had provided Dad with a good, year-round salary to organize a four- or five-day event, and for a handful of years, the event was a massive success (albeit not financially). Players would pay four or five grand to spend the week at a beautiful resort in Kelowna in the summer and spend their time around a dozen former NHLers, usually half of whom were Hall of Famers. They'd have a hockey practice in the morning (run by Dale Hawerchuk or Bryan Trottier, usually), they'd golf one day, go on a houseboat another, and have a hot stove session on another. There were dinners, and it was sponsored by Okanagan Spring Brewery, so they were drinking from wake-up to bedtime. It was an extremely loose event, as the organizers—OK, mostly my dad and I—participated in the all-day drinking as well.

For Dad, though, I think it was the culmination of the beast I had been fighting, only his had been growing for years before.

Whether on the Legends Tour or doing the fantasy camp, life had largely been one drinking event or another, until that's all that was left.

We spent more time together in those years than during any other part of my life, as we sat in pubs and planned the event—or didn't plan the event and just sat in pubs—while I was home visiting. He had been down to Arizona, and those trips went like they did with my college roommates. On one trip, we won a Super Bowl pool, went back to the bar to collect the hundreds of dollars we'd won, and returned home in an embarrassing fashion with no dollars and zero cents.

The fantasy camp had at least seemed to give Dad a purpose, but it wasn't enough of one, I worried. I guess I hadn't yet processed that no "purpose" was going to change the issue at hand.

In those days, I saw how it obviously affected him, and the moments it led to, and I swore to myself that I'd find a way to drink without letting it get away from me.

I'd be lying if I said I didn't see some of those NHLers who came through our fantasy camp and think, *They might be on the spectrum of alcoholism too* (which was a thing I'd apparently made up in my mind), *but they seem to do it the right way.* I became convinced there was a *way* to suffer the awful pull to the bottle that I felt, but manage it in a way that society found acceptable. I thought I saw it in a few of those men, and wanted that secret. I figured there were probably more people like that than I had ever realized.

Or maybe I was just seeing them on vacation and they could actually stop? I'm not sure why I never considered that an option at the time.

Those sloppy times in Arizona only got worse when we moved to Toronto and Dad made a couple of visits. (You may recall the one I mentioned at the beginning of this book.) Nobody ends up in rehab without moments they regret, and these were the Regret Years. At one point I ran into him in Toronto, days after he'd "left" after visiting us. It turned out he had actually stayed, having made some plans during one of our pub sessions, and had chosen not to tell us. There was just no trust left.

Back home in Kelowna, he had moved in with my brother. The fantasy camp didn't become financially sustainable, the backer was upset with how it had all gone down, and those days were over. Things had mostly fallen apart for my dad, and finally there was no more denying what was at the root of the mounting problems. After one last blowout at Jeff's house, he recognized it was time to get help.

I remember the great irony of the moment when Dad called from rehab—God, was I happy he was finally going to get clean—and we had a powerful moment. Partially because of the infrequency of our visits (with us in separate cities most of my life), a lot had gone unsaid over the years.

My brother and I were asked by his counsellors to tell him directly how his drinking had affected us, and so we did. We told him how heartbreaking it was to see someone who had started with hero status disappoint us. He listened, and we cried, and he cried.

I took the call in a park just outside Bar Wellington in downtown Toronto, a handful of pints deep and with my tab still open in the middle of the workday. Everything I'd said and felt that day was real, but I knew how hypocritical it was to get into it when I was down that path myself. Knowing that did make me more compassionate, though; at least I understood how it could get so bad.

By then, I knew I was an alcoholic, full stop. But I also knew I really liked drinking and didn't want to *not* be an alcoholic. Maintaining my status quo was just about the clearest objective I had in those days. I wanted to be an alcoholic who could live a normal life and reap all the benefits of a sober existence, aiming to have my cake and eat it, too. Maybe I could outsmart my problem? I thought it was possible, or at least worth a try.

There's something to be learned about alcoholism here that started with me believing that I was a "different" alcoholic. In books and movies, you hear that "admitting you have a problem is the first step," and so on. I'd admitted it to myself years before, way back in Arizona. I wasn't in denial; I was into obstructing my truth from others. I didn't see drinking as a problem, then. I saw the opposite—being forced to live a life of *not* drinking—as the big problem. And so, even after "admitting it," I set out to live my life within those parameters. I don't know this for sure, but I suspect other alcoholics out there have done the same thing. Is anyone hiding vodka bottles under laundry at the back of their closet while telling themselves they don't have a problem? I was trying to manage it because the last thing I wanted was someone to tell me I couldn't drink anymore.

So, while that moment was drenched in irony, it didn't faze me. I was an alcoholic like him, only I was hoping to do a better job of keeping it from derailing my life. As mentioned, I saw older men in the hockey world who I viewed as having issues with alcohol yet they seemed to have happy, complete lives. How delightfully well-rounded.

It's also why I was likely more sympathetic to my dad than many in my life would've preferred. The disappointments came, but I was quick to write off incidents without ascribing much individual blame, because I *got* it, I *got* what he was going through.

Whether I actually did or didn't, I *felt* like I did. The pursuit of alcohol in the brain of an alcoholic is just all-consuming; nothing in your life matters but that next drink, and I just kept believing his heart was pure and he'd find a way to his happy ending before all was said and done. I've always believed in happy endings, and to this day I have a hard time believing there isn't still one waiting for him. Maybe that's not life, which teaches many people some cold, hard lessons without the fairy-tale finish. Maybe. But I'd rather believe in that and be proven wrong than not believe and be proven right.

8

HANGING ON IN THE MINORS, YET AGAIN

I was in the midst of a rare window when my wife was out of town, and so, after some days of getting my work done, I had cut loose and spent the previous night in the Dew with some buddies. The next morning, I woke up from an extremely short sleep mentally damaged, and I mean *severely* damaged, to a ringing phone.

It was Toronto Maple Leafs head coach Mike Babcock.

"Bournie. What're your thoughts on Matt Beleskey?"

I had never thought about Matt Beleskey in my entire life. He was an NHL winger at the time.

At least, I didn't *think* I had thought about him.

I assure you there is no more confusing question to handle two seconds into consciousness after a hard night of drinking, particularly when you're under the pressure of answering someone you badly want to impress. Matt Beleskey? Wait, do I have an opinion on him? I ran the search function on my brain and honestly, I don't know what I came up with, but I surely said something. I'm not sure there was ever a point in my life when I could've answered that in a meaningful way clear-headed. To this moment, I truly don't know what I might have said. And just like that, he hung up. Moments after, I wasn't even sure if it had really happened—like, what could my input possibly have changed for anyone? I rubbed my eyes and stared at the ceiling from the couch, where I had apparently passed out the night before.

In retrospect, Matt Beleskey did not end up a Leaf, and given that I *think* I said good things about him, I don't think they valued my opinion all that much. But it was a trip for a guy just writing about hockey from the outside to have Mike Babcock call him for an opinion at all.

Mike was calling because I was in my second summer of cutting off-season video for the Maple Leafs, and Mike would've assumed I had watched a few games' worth of Beleskey's shifts while clipping them for more important people to go over. This was a pattern I saw quickly in Babcock's behaviour—he solicited opinions from everyone who had a pair of eyes, which in this case was me, bleary as they might have been.

It started around the time the Toronto Maple Leafs were taken over by Brendan Shanahan, a period that kicked off with him conducting a one-year assessment of the organization. Just as I needed change to find a better version of myself (again), they needed some, too. When management realized the team's massive issues, the Big Purge happened. They fired much of the staff and aimed to start anew, which included hiring Kyle Dubas.

I mentioned that in the years prior, Kyle was one of the people who'd reached out to me about my Systems Analyst posts. We shared some thoughts back and forth on those. I think we had a mutual respect, and so the lines of communication seemed open. After the big purge, I saw an opening—while drinking on the couch one evening, of course—and took a flyer. I asked if there was anything I could do for the organization while they tried to fill all their job openings, saying I was eager to help. Which I was.

The universe works in funny ways, and my timing was beyond good. His response: "You messaged at a perfect time. We are looking for video help for Draft and after Agency Prep right now. What's your email?"

Chalk one up for shooting your shot.

It wasn't so much that they needed a hockey brain, just someone to help them cut video. My previous work had included screenshots and GIFs, so they were correct in assuming I was computer-capable, and that I had at least enough hockey awareness to know where to look to find what they wanted. I was handed off to Adam Jancelewicz, who's been at the helm of the Leafs' video department for over a decade.

It was 2015, with technology well behind what's available now, and they wanted shifts cut together so that, when they watched individual players, they didn't have to sift through full games to find where and when they were involved. I was taught how to use basic software that would clip out the parts of the game they didn't need and spotlight the player in question for a few seconds.

It was pretty rote work, but still, it felt like a big deal. I worked out of the Leafs dressing room, with its shining silver logo looming on the wall, in what had been the assistant coaches' office. I developed an understanding of who they were considering as draft picks from the players I was asked to clip together (and which ones they wanted to see more of). I heard internal conversations as if I were a houseplant (and I chose to say as much as one), and was in rooms with rough draft lists. I soaked it all in but obviously couldn't use any of that information professionally, aside from the odd throwaway comment ("Y'know, I'm not sure they really like Player X all that much," I'd knowingly muse in a radio interview.) I added enough value that they added unrestricted free agents to my plate, too, and so I began pulling together shifts of potential targets for the front office to sit down and watch.

It was a strange time in Leafland. I was in the assistant coaches' office when the Leafs brought Guy Boucher through, and they were legitimately discussing remodelling the office to suit his desires at the time. (He wanted it less secluded from the players.) Shortly after that, the Leafs signed Babcock. Boucher was out and a new course for the Leafs was set.

It was a bizarre turn of events for me, because I already had a loose tie to Babs. My aforementioned Uncle Ken had gone to high school and played baseball with Mike, and they were buddies. When I was working for theScore, Ken put us in touch and I interviewed Mike about his strategy of using the front of the net to relieve pressure from opposing forechecks (it was unusual then, not so much now). It was a bit of a family "in," so when Babs first showed up in the dressing room, he treated me like I wasn't a complete stranger.

That was a trait of Mike's that I came to learn and respect. He listened to everyone's opinion. Not to say that he valued those takes equally, but he certainly wanted to hear from everyone. One day I was cutting video of some Finnish junior, and Mike asked me what I thought. I gave him my input, and he said, "Let's see about that," pulled out his phone and dialled a name with many consecutive *ii*'s and *aa*'s and got their input. He'd make snap calls like that for feedback regularly, calls that ended before they hit the one-minute mark but got him the information he was after.

There's always been some big discussion about whether Babs wanted to draft Mitch Marner or Noah Hanifin, and I was in the room for several conversations on that. Sometimes I hear people suggest that Mike didn't want Marner, and that couldn't have been further from the truth. At that time he had concerns about Hanifin's ability to think at a top-pair level, whereas with Marner, he just wanted to see enough to believe he could be valuable when he wasn't creating offence. I think they saw it and set out to refine that part of his game, which likely laid the foundation for Marner getting Selke Trophy votes (for best defensive forward) now that he's in his NHL prime.

That second summer, I saw another coach walk into the dressing room: Sheldon Keefe was being considered as coach of the Leafs' AHL team, the Toronto Marlies. There were discussions about Sheldon being Babcock's assistant coach for a year before taking over the Marlies, so that he could learn how Babs liked guys to play and could develop players just the way the big club wanted them, which was both smart and original thinking. The plan was for Babcock to be The Guy there for a long time. But that introduces a whole host of other complications. (For example, would it have been good for minor-league players' development to have a temporary head coach for a season?) They set out to teach Sheldon during the summer and refine that relationship. Given that Keefe and I had interacted online through direct messages in relation to articles I'd written, we said a quick hello as he went into private rooms for some of the more important meetings of his career.

The timing was working out perfectly. The 2015–16 season would be Sheldon's first as the head coach of the Marlies, and Babs's first with the Leafs. I was in the Leafs room before either of them walked in, which I think gave me a small slice of credibility. Luck is a huge, huge factor in life, and the bounces I got that summer aren't the type you can replicate with any sort of planning.

In the early going, one thing Babcock set out to do was to use the organization's financial clout to its advantage, something the Leafs hadn't been doing as well as they could. They'd committed big dough to Mike, and the last thing that made sense was to deny him the tools he wanted. He wanted to use a different video program, so a switch was made. They'd go to XOs rather than Pucks, an organizational change that I believe to be a six-figure undertaking. But mostly, as that first awful season got under way, he found he wanted another set of eyes on all the video they were able to get their hands on. He had Andrew Brewer, a guy who had been at his side for years in Detroit and at the Olympics, but it's a huge job. Any team with just one guy is leaving answers on the table. The most obvious name for that new role was Ryan Ward, who had been the Marlies' video guy at the time. That would mean the AHL would need to find a new guy in-season, which certainly wouldn't be easy.

Unless . . .

Unless someone who had some video capability, who could use a computer and knew the game well, who happened to live in the city was available?

Kyle asked me to head down to the Ford Performance Centre in Etobicoke (then the Mastercard Centre), where the Marlies practised, to meet with Sheldon and see if we vibed enough to think there could be a partnership. A video coach and head coach are inseparable throughout the season, so that's important.

There were a few real problems for me: one was that, at that point, the daily cycle of alcohol dependence had tightened its grip on me. I believed myself to be physically dependent again, but hadn't had to dry out long enough to find out. Another issue was that I had become socially anxious again, basically only existing comfortably in bars, given how little time I was spending in the office (and without a real department to work within when I was there). And I had recently gotten into a Twitter pissing match with Rich Clune, who was on the team, and whom I was already terrified of from my playing days. (The disagreement wasn't about anything huge—I had basically said Nashville goalie Carter Hutton was no Pekka Rinne, and Clune told me I didn't know what I was talking about—a fair point. But it was at least a small day-one concern for me.)

The meeting with Keefe went well, with me managing not to sweat all over myself long enough for him to agree to have me, and honestly it was a pretty insane life switch, *immediately*. When we were done Sheldon asked, "Can you start tomorrow?" and within a matter of days I was thrust onto a treadmill moving full speed, with the Marlies a month into their season and me not having a clue what I was doing (this was no small source of stress, given that I knew my brain was as useful as unsharpened skates). The contract provided a small raise over what I'd been making with theScore, only there'd never be time to spend a dime again.

My ability to process hockey had brought me to a unique opportunity I knew I was perfectly suited to excel at, were I able to win the battle against myself first.

And for a while, I won. I was too busy not to, and while it felt physically awful for some time, my alcohol intake and mental condition improved markedly.

So, the job helped me temper the drinking problem, acting as the heroic hand saving me as I dangled from a cliff, just as my arrival in Toronto had done the same. I went from what had become working alone to working shoulder to shoulder with people, so I was accountable and busy—too busy to be day drunk or badly hungover. Within a month, I was able to go whole days without a drink, sometimes even consecutive ones. My brain came back online a little, which was a treat. Food tastes far better when your brain isn't swollen and numb.

Even though I was home considerably less because of all the travel, the job was good for my relationship with Bri. We missed each other when I was gone, but I also think she saw me being productive and focused—the sharper version of the guy she loved.

That booze stuff was my personal fight, though, and it largely existed in the shadows. The professional dimension was a much more public challenge. I had the hockey expertise, but not the technology background, to be the most useful person in a highly technical role. An old dog can learn new tricks, provided the tricks aren't double back handsprings.

There were five coaches with computers: Sheldon Keefe, A.J. MacLean (assistant coach, forwards and power-play unit), Gord Dineen (assistant coach, defencemen and penalty killers), Piero Greco (goalies) and me (all things video). There was a computer dock (where laptops would plug in to link up to the server) in the dressing room of the practice rink in Etobicoke, and in two places in the Marlies' home arena—then known as the Ricoh Coliseum, now the Coca-Cola Coliseum.

Each computer had a dock in both arenas as well at our respective work stations, and was wired to a server that allowed each to be on a shared internal network. That server went everywhere with us and was my baby, my life, our crown jewel. Those five computers and the related docks had to be functioning or I was in trouble, and I am *not* an IT guy. Maple Leaf Sports and Entertainment has IT guys, but they're not hanging around hockey rinks, waiting for things to go wrong. When disasters struck, they were days away.

As mentioned, the server was the most important object in my world for two years. It held everything everyone did, everyone's video packages, and all the media (the raw game footage) necessary for those clips to run on their respective computers. It held everything Keefe used to teach.

Further to all this, there were projectors, and iPads to upload player shifts on, and a travel printer and walkie-talkies, and just dozens of pieces of technology that had to be working on any given day, all of which moved from arena to arena, city to city, on a near-daily basis, often stowed away in the bottoms of buses and planes.

I'm tech-capable and smart enough, so it's not like this part of the job was impossible to learn. But it was that I had to learn on the fly, in-season, while forming relationships and hopefully not just doing the job, but doing a *good* job, in a high-pressure environment. To say that at times I looked a little frazzled in the early days would be an understatement. On my worst days I felt people's pity, which is not the emotional reaction you're hoping to elicit from co-workers in professional sports.

Maybe it didn't seem all that unlikely to some that Sheldon would get to the heights he's achieved, but let's not forget that his reputation in hockey in the early 2010s was more than a speed bump on his road to the NHL. Like most people, I was superficially aware of his background—his ties to the controversial junior coach and player agent David Frost—but Sheldon rarely had a drink, so it's not like we found ourselves in any late-night heart-to-hearts where I could ask him about any of it.

All I knew was that coaching the Marlies was a huge opportunity for him, and he didn't need to be hampered by some technological noob who was sweating through two shirts a day. As much as he might have felt for me in the early going, he wasn't about to accept anything less than work of the utmost quality, which reminded me of my junior days with Mike Vandekamp. In both instances, we were *grinding*.

It was just before 5 p.m., moments before I was supposed to have the six sheets posted in the dressing room for the players who were already arriving for the 7 p.m. game. It was one of my first weeks on the job. Each game, I posted the opposing team's systems, drawn and explained, with the way we would counter them diagrammed. There was the player scout sheet (or "pre-scout," as it's redundantly known) that listed the strengths and weaknesses of the opposing team (and special notes for how to counter some guys); our lineup; the opposing team's lineup; and two sheets detailing the two teams' special teams. (Do all the players read these sheets? Hard no. But the information needs to be there for those who care to prepare.)

As I left the coaches' office to post them, Keefe stopped me to go over what I was posting one last time—and which we had already been over once. He circled a couple of commas he didn't want in there on the systems sheet and told me to reprint it. *Commas?* I wasn't exactly sure if he was messing with me or not—*seriously, am I actually supposed to do that, or are we having a laugh here?*—but didn't quite have a read on him yet. In retrospect, I'm glad I didn't. I fired up the computer and reopened the document. I learned that Keefe believed everything we brought to players had to be perfect, as it reflected on us as a staff, and you'd best show a professional level of preparation if you expect it from others. I absolutely agreed—I mean, who wouldn't? The problem was, we just had different standards for what merited the term *professional* in those early days. "Good enough" absolutely was not. As a result, there were many days when I found myself baffled at having to spend 20 extra minutes ironing out some tiny detail under his watchful eye, while still feeling incapable of executing anything quickly enough. It was a long time before I felt I had time to do anything *well*.

In the hour between 4 p.m. and 5 p.m. on game days that first year, I was never not full-on frazzled. And given that it was crunch time for the staff and their personal meetings with the players, anything resembling pity dried up then, because they had jobs to do, too. There were moments in those early days where I questioned my ability to do the job—and frankly, whether or not this new boss of mine was sane or not.

I mentioned Vandekamp, and similarly, I resisted being pushed so hard at first, but eventually I grew to adopt the same standard, and in time I became grateful for finding an off-ice level of work ethic I didn't realize I had been missing.

One question I have for myself in the aftermath of my time there is: How much of the pressure I felt was I actually responsible for? My brain was still cloudy from the heavy drinking I had done before I started there. My ability to retain information and stay focused was still so weak, and I had so little mental stamina, that I wonder if a clearer-headed version of myself could have handled it better.

Whatever the case there may be—I'll never know—it was just about the coolest opportunity I could've had at that moment in my life. I still worked my ass off to meet the team's requirements. I just wish I had more to give when I left the rink, during the time when extra work could've been done, but which I had otherwise reserved.

If anything makes me feel like I let them down, and let myself down, it was that when I left the arena, I was all the way out on thinking about the Marlies. I thought about drinks and my wife and my friends and getting away from the daily pressure. I didn't think about picking through video to find things that could've helped us, or about ideas for us to try, both of which I could've provided were I fully sober.

If my regrets are about my time away from the rink, I do feel like I was good for the work environment, because I think my comportment is generally relaxed (outside that 4 p.m.–5 p.m. panic window), and I think that worked well with Sheldon, who is not one to leave a stone unturned. I'm not sure he spent more than a few minutes not thinking about the team while I was there, for two years straight. A calmer presence was probably good for him then.

My job kept me tied to his hip. He would prepare for his many video-review meetings using the XOs Thundercloud platform and download everything to the server, and I would get them up and running in the dressing room. I "drove," using the clicker to skip back and ahead through the footage as he talked, learning his cues and timing. Beyond those meetings, I basically existed to make sure he had what he needed to assemble his meetings, both team and individual, which often meant going into our previous games and mining them for "the perfect clip," which rarely existed. He constantly had questions about our team and wanted to know more, and I did my best to accommodate.

As it goes with technology, I learned the hard way. Sometimes, things have to go wrong and get solved for you to figure out how to solve them the next time, which is a terrible journey to go through in front of a bunch of athletes in their 20s. The dressing room is a snark-tastically judgy place, one where I fit right in as a player. But it's amazing how quickly things can change.

In 2008–09, I had been strong by pro hockey standards, though notoriously on the skinny side. After my jaw was wired shut that season, I went from 190 pounds to the high 160s and had trouble putting the weight back on. Seven years later and a video coach, I was about 220 pounds of decidedly not-muscle, so I did not look the part, which is undeniably part of fitting in with that group. It's a room full of athletes, and you want to be taken seriously athletically, but these guys wouldn't have believed I could jump from the road to the curb without toe-picking, let alone that I could play hockey. I was round, clean-shaven as per the directive of Leafs general manager Lou Lamoriello, and always shiny as a result of those two things. I constantly had my nose in a computer, dealing with servers and *bleep–bleep, blorp–blorp* technology.

There, I felt decidedly uncool.

It's tough to reconcile how others view you with how you feel inside. I still felt hockey-young and cool, partly because I liked to have a good time (read: drink) in my downtime. Even as a member of the media, I had been "the player who wrote" rather than a true hockey writer guy, which at least left me with notes of coolness and undertones of difference from the norm.

These years were my first exposure to not being "in" in the dressing room, or at least not feeling cool within it. None of this mattered, logically, and part of why I wasn't "in" was because I was a part of the coaching staff. There was *supposed* to be a separation there. What I'm really talking about here is my own perception of myself, and figuring out who the hell I was at that point. Had I been in decent shape (being bigger definitely changed my self-perception, rightly or wrongly) and had my wits about me, I would've been in a unique position to really bond with the players, and likely could've helped our staff more by being more in tune with the guys. But because I felt the way

I did about myself, I was always something near embarrassed, and often got out of the room as quickly as I could.

As I got more established with the team and figured out how to keep the technology functioning as everyone needed, I started to find my niche. A big part of the job was live-marking games (I think video coaches call it "coding" games, which sounds fancier), which means watching our game unfold in real time on my computer monitor and tagging events by hitting certain keys as they happened. To give you a very basic example, I'd hit the *B* key whenever a breakout occurred, and every time I did, the software would grab the 10 seconds of video before and after the keystroke and put it into a "Breakouts" folder, so that the coaches could come in at the intermission and watch all our breakouts from a given period.

After games, we'd have each folder sorted to dig through, and the staff divided up which categories and game states were their responsibility to review. Obviously, tagging the game correctly was integral, but as I got better, I learned how to go from just tagging the game to doing it in my own unique way, one I hoped would make me more valuable than the next video coach. When I first started, I was logging between 600 and 700 events a game. By the end, it was closer to 900, and occasionally more. There were the standard keys—forechecks and faceoffs and neutral-zone forechecks and regroups and on and on. You're hitting a key every few seconds. But there was also a "coach's comment" button, which would bring up a comment field, where I could enter notes that the program would group together and sort, as it did with the other buttons. By the end of my time with the Marlies, I was making upwards of 30 notes per game in my own words for the staff to review, and Sheldon eventually began to review these first thing after each game. I've been a home-row, eyes-on-the-screen typist for as long as I can remember, but those days took my typing ability to new heights as I quickly typed out a sentence on something I saw in real time.

I learned how to crib my observations into little packages to show the staff after games, I started speaking up more in the office, and eventually, I was handed more responsibility. At the start of year two, when the other assistant coaches were assigned teams to specialize in, I was handed a few myself, to go along with reviewing faceoffs after every game and putting together a package of any trends that might have developed. I was asked to present my findings to the team, but I still wasn't comfortable speaking in front of anyone, let alone a hockey team, so I declined.

This whole "fear of speaking" in that situation was ridiculous, but it was rooted in what was basically an identity crisis. I felt that the team would see me as the IT computer nerd guy, whereas less than a decade ago I had been *them*, watching the video on the other side as an actual hockey player. I was still self-conscious, still feeling inexperienced with the technology, and let's face it, hockey players can be ruthless. I just wasn't ready to put myself out there yet, because God forbid something should go wrong.

Sheldon, like my college coach Dave Shyiak, assured me that eventually I'd have to get comfortable speaking in front of people, to which I always replied something like "Counterpoint, no, I don't."

Many times since, I wish I'd had the courage to try earlier.

In the year leading up to my employment with the Marlies, my wife and I had been trying to have a baby, but with no luck. I was, as I've noted, not remotely healthy around that time. About a month after I joined the Marlies (and found myself not reliant on alcohol for the first time in forever), we broke through. It was not a coincidence (the same thing would happen the next time I had to clean up my lifestyle). After the Boxing Day game at the ACC, we came home and my wife had two presents for me, "to express appreciation for me taking on a new job that was an accomplishment to land and so all-consuming": a hockey-stick tie clip and . . . a soother.

Charlie Jeffrey was—wait for it—Bourne the following August (we gave him his middle name after my brother), and the next Marlies season was upon us shortly thereafter. With my mom and family out west in Kelowna, and my wife's in New York, she was handed a pretty heavy burden, given the travel commitments of a pro hockey team. I was often gone for weeks at a time that next year, and she was asked to plow on with Charlie on her own.

One of Lou Lamoriello's greatest beliefs as a GM is to make the AHL staff feel included and looked after, too, meaning we got the NHL per diem (somewhere around $100 US a day) on the road and we stayed in nice hotel rooms. There were numerous nights when we were taken out to some beautiful steakhouse on the road (above and beyond the per diem) and would return to our own hotel rooms with king-sized beds, and I'd get a text from my wife suggesting she might sleep in "the goddamned car" because Charlie would not stop crying all night.

Needless to say, the lifestyle was not great for starting out a new family.

Lou Lamoriello has had great success in the past and has proven capable of changing the perception of organizations. He's a respected guy for a reason, and he certainly has my respect. Still, the experience of working for him then was wild. He took care of staff, but some of his requirements had similarities to the old "Mattingly, cut your sideburns" bit that Mr. Burns demanded of the pro ball players he assembled on *The Simpsons*. Lamoriello was so secretive that when he got to Toronto, he insisted that his fax machine be "encrypted." Nobody knew what that meant exactly, so I'm told they switched a wire from blue to red and told him the job had been done.

Lou had a strict "no facial hair" policy, although it was monitored a little less strictly with the AHL team because Lou wasn't around. Going into my second season with the team, Mike Babcock and Andrew Brewer were at the World Cup of Hockey, and so I was with the Leafs along with Sheldon Keefe. There was a pre-season game in Buffalo and I had about four days' growth, which assistant coach D.J. Smith repeatedly warned me would not go over well.

I replied that after that game, I'd be off two weeks before Marlies camp, and that I was looking to get a head start on the beard I'm most comfortable wearing. And also that, as the AHL video coach, I would huddle in the corner and Lou wouldn't even notice me. I'd be a ghost. A shadow.

A 5 o'clock shadow?

Moments after that exchange, Lou walked into the coaches' office and said loudly, to everyone, "Can somebody please lend me five fucking dollars so I can buy this guy a fucking razor?" I laughed, which was not well received. He approached me slowly and silently, getting really close, looking up at my eyes and saying, "Don't you laugh. This isn't funny." I mean, there is no good way to react after that. Okay? Sorry? Are you serious? You can't win, so I didn't try. He sent me away to shave my face with about an hour to go before game time.

Unfortunately we were in the bowels of Buffalo's arena, and I was left to walk around looking for shaving supplies when I came upon some stuff usually provided to the visiting team in some random dressing room. There was a razor, but no shaving cream. I ended up in a bathroom with a disposable razor, dry-scraping my facial hair off before a pre-season game (as a video coach in a room nobody would ever see) because Lou does not play around.

Lou and I had a good chat later in the game between periods about not cutting corners, and I appreciated that the man lived up to his reputation.

I grew more comfortable as part of the staff, though that may be misread as an overall positive. The Chinese farmer thinks not. Having a better sense of what the days would entail, I learned where I could save time on my duties. Getting more efficient, I managed to maximize my time after road practices, getting drunk in random cities around the East Coast. I was an anomaly for the rest of the staff, who probably thought I was a bit of a flake. They knew I liked to drink, but I rarely drank with everyone else, which was a strange combination. I'd usually go for a few drinks with them—I liked almost all of them a lot—but the truth was I wanted to stay judgment-free when I got blasted, and not risk damaging my reputation. Even those who went out drinking didn't drink quickly enough for me, and I didn't want to get singled out as the team drunk.

That part of alcoholism remains a defining characteristic for me: it requires isolation to truly embrace, which fosters loneliness even when you don't have to be alone. I had the opportunity to hang out with staff members I enjoyed, but the booze pushed me away from that very camaraderie I had missed when I wasn't in hockey. Looking back, booze had asked me to choose between those people and it, and booze won. It asked me to choose between it and doing my best in pro hockey, and I chose the bottle. It asked me to choose between it and training, and it won. The only person who held up in the head-to-head fight against the bottle was my wife (and then my son), but the fight was getting fiercer.

In every AHL city, I learned where to go that was close enough to the hotel to be convenient, but far enough that I wouldn't run into players or other staff. I figured out where the liquor stores were, so that I could have something in my room, and it got bad again. There are no cures.

In two years with the team, I only had one alcohol-related incident, a night out with another staff member where I still smelled like booze the following morning, but it was laughed off for an obvious reason: we were in St. John's, Newfoundland, and if you don't go out and drink too much in that town, it might hurt your credibility. Still, I was removed from running the video in the room that day so the team wouldn't sniff me out and deem the staff unprofessional, and I worried I'd racked up my first demerits, knowing that more could certainly come.

I fretted constantly about being found out, and it became clear to me that it was not sustainable to remain in such a demanding position while going through what I was going through. The deception was seedy and embarrassing, and I don't know who saw through me, but I felt the shame. I was exhausted all the time, unhealthy, and my son was growing up at home without me.

In my second year, we found ourselves up against the Syracuse Crunch in playoffs, a team laden with players who would go on to win the Stanley Cup with Tampa Bay. It was a brutally hard-fought series that went the distance. In Game Seven, in Syracuse, we were up 3–1 heading into the third period, and I didn't know how to feel about it. I was torn between the allegiance I'd built to the team and just wanting to escape the year without getting exposed. A win meant at least two more weeks of the season, and not normal weeks. I'd have to throw myself into scouting our next opponent and putting together packages of all their lines, with a PowerPoint presentation for the players that Sheldon would walk them through. A win would've been good for my career, and my pocket too (there were playoff bonuses). I was so invested in that team, I didn't want us to lose—I just dreaded the additional work and time away and additional risk of doing something dumb. I felt I was hanging on by a thread.

When the dust settled a half-hour later, our season was over, and again, I didn't know how to feel. All that effort over the course of the year would've been justified by a championship, and I wanted the best for everyone I had been working with, but getting out of that season without creating a problem brought a great sense of relief.

My contract was up that summer, and a few weeks later, I spoke with Kyle. They offered me another one-year contract, which wasn't overly surprising, but I had already been looking for the exit. I took the Marlies proposed number to an up-and-coming sports media platform, *The Athletic*, and basically asked if they could match it, and the answer was yes.

I saw so many benefits. I saw the chance to leave the Marlies on good terms, without ruining my reputation, and with all relationships intact. I was so fearful I'd blow it before I could get out. In a way, I was trying to protect my own name the way I'd been worried about protecting the family name when I declined a second invitation to New York Islanders training camp. I knew I'd done enough to form good relationships there and hadn't embarrassed myself. By getting out then, I felt I could be like George in *Seinfeld*, leaving the room immediately after telling a good joke. I could leave a good taste in everyone's mouth about my time there.

More importantly by a good distance, I'd get to be around to help raise my son on a day-to-day basis, and I don't think I've yet done justice to just how important that was to me. As Charlie got closer to the years he'd remember as he grew up, I wanted to be present, and ideally the best version of myself. Bri was underwater as a full-time worker raising our young son with no family in town, while I was only around about half the time during the season. With *The Athletic*, I'd also continue to earn well.

And, wait for it, I'd be free to reconnect with my best friends in town, all of whom liked the sauce. Oh, how that was a tantalizing "bonus." I use "scare quotes" on *bonus* because I think it was closer to the core of why I wanted to leave that great opportunity than I admitted to myself then. I'd be free to have midday pints again—the best type of pints, in my mind—and could write whenever my brain felt like it. With only a couple of articles due per week, I felt like I had fallen into the dream scenario for myself.

Somehow I was oblivious to what should have been obvious: every time I had been left alone to work I had started a terrible cycle of alcohol consumption that almost ruined me. And that was literally how this job was designed: fully alone, with a good income, and just writing. That job wasn't the dream scenario for me; it was the dream scenario for my disease, which had been waiting for me, doing push-ups in the parking lot of the Marlies arena, as I walked towards the exit.

9

SPACE TO TURN AROUND

It was as if the words *Do you need to go to rehab?* had torn a hole in the space-time continuum and offered a quick-closing portal to a better life, and I knew I simply couldn't let yet another opportunity pass. I might die if I did.

I managed a quick but meek "I think I do."

I *knew* I did.

I was ready. Fully beaten.

If that unfolded in seconds, the thickness those words lent the air stopped time. The silence that followed was agony.

What the hell would that even mean?

The silence hung.

What would rehab even mean . . . for our marriage, for my son's life, for my work, for my family, for the remainder of my existence on this planet, to say nothing of the perception of the years that had come before. They had been good years, mostly, and Bri and I had loved each other wholly—would we look back at some of our best times with regret?

What was even the most important thing to consider now? Where do you start? How does one even "go to rehab"? Do you just look up *Rehab* in Google search? Does it cost money? How much? Does insurance cover that? How soon should I go? How soon *could* I go? Who would take Charlie to daycare in the mornings? Would Bri have to stop going to work while I was gone? Could we afford one or both of us to stop working? Would my job keep paying me? Would they want me back at all? Could I go to parties? Would my friends drift away?

I was forced to acknowledge that alcohol had worked its way to the centre of everything I did.

Like multiple people trying to walk through the same door frame at once, the questions got stuck and nothing got through. That's a lot to process even when your brain is working properly, and mine was a crusted husk, an abandoned snail shell that had once contained life.

Everyone talks about the first step—"admitting you have a problem"—but what the hell's the second?

More questions hid like land mines that had to be identified before they could be disarmed.

Moments earlier, I had been sitting away from the family at my desk, pretending I had Sunday morning work to do in hopes my wife wouldn't smell the morning booze on my breath. She didn't. But what she had seen was a crumpled bag of Miss Vickie's chips that Drunk Me had curiously stuffed behind the books in the bookshelf, which led her to check behind the other books—hey, she knew I had stashes *somewhere*—which led her to a 1.5-litre bottle of red wine I had mentally reserved for that evening after everyone went to bed. The "jug of wine before bed" routine had become familiar, as it assured me I'd stay "asleep" through most of the night and not sweat through my sheets the way I did when I went to bed less than fully drunk.

With every word after "I think I do," though, that sweating came while conscious. I didn't know what to feel other than this absolutely needed to happen, and I wanted it to start immediately so the hard part could be over.

I also needed her not to find the hidden vodka in the water bottle three books to the left so I could survive *that* day while we figured it all out. I was then, as I would be in the near future, living "one day at a time," but the goal of each 24 hours up to that point had been to not end up where I had suddenly arrived. The jig was up.

In the weeks and months immediately following my time with the Marlies, I had begun living my perception of the absolute dream. Maybe not everyone's dream, mind you, but given my set of priorities at the time, it's an understatement to say I had found my sweet spot. I was happy.

I could find lunch just about anywhere in the city, do work I enjoyed—I have always enjoyed writing—until one or two each day, and still have a couple of pub hours to sip IPAs and read Twitter and hang with whichever of my local buddies had the afternoon free. We had a good-sized group of daily pub-goers, so there was always someone around (and if not, the staff became friends, too). It was our own version of *Cheers*. Plans to get together were rarely made formally; instead, a blanket "heading to the Dew" might be sent to the group chat for whoever's day matched up.

So, that was both the dream and how I practically saw life going forward. I tried to find a sustainable level of consumption that wasn't crushing vodka midday, and I aimed to do that by keeping to my old Marlies schedule, which didn't allow me to drink until about two, when our practices would end. I never wanted to be the husband who came home drunk, and now that I was finally in a position to be around more regularly, I did my level best to avoid that.

"Sustainable" at first was four or five IPAs at the bar, a couple more at home and a bottle of wine at night. With that "meagre" level of intake, I was able to access my brain and write in the morning, and not shake in the a.m. hours.

I managed—for a while, anyway—to maintain that pace without issue (pathetically, that tolerance was a point of pride with me). My wife might have noticed beer on my breath each day, but I wasn't hiding that. She knew I went to the pub by our house after work for a "social outlet" now that I was working alone (though I may not have been upfront about the duration of my visits), and I'd rarely drink so much in the early days that I wasn't mentally present. Hell, I was usually in a pretty good mood.

You're never gonna believe this, but the plan to stay an alcoholic, but a functioning one, didn't pan out. I had learned precisely nothing from my previous swells of alcoholism.

What's funny is that I had come from hockey's highest development league, where I had become fascinated by this vaguely unscientific chart (made by habits guru James Clear) that hung in the team gym and had made perfect sense to me:

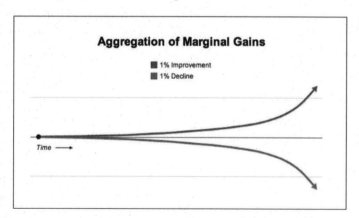

The difference between getting incrementally better and incrementally worse.
© James Clear / jamesclear.com/wp-content/uploads/2016/08
/ABriefGuidetoProcessImprovement-2.pdf

I believed it to be true of our AHL players and their workout habits, and I charitably saw the efforts of my playing days reflected in that upward line when I thought back to the times I had truly committed myself. I had seen the good efforts add up slowly, then more quickly, and it felt relatable.

For some reason, my brain wouldn't let me see my present self sliding along the downward path.

In the beginning of those happy days, I would have spent my paycheque all the way down to zero by the time the next one came. A pint in downtown Toronto checked in at about $10 at my local, and "three to six and often food" every day added up. Somewhere along the way, those cheques were necessary to pull me out of overdraft.

As the numbers in my bank account fought the heavy gravity of zero and below, the numbers on the scale crept up the other way. This was the whole "1 per cent" thing in a nutshell. There wasn't any specific day when things suddenly went egregiously bad for me; there was just a slow erosion of my well-being, with small oversteps just slightly worse than the ones I had made in each preceding month leading me to a new, slightly worse normal. When nothing of note happened in a day, it was on balance a bad day, as I spent more than I made and became less healthy.

My tolerance went up further, which is another way to say my tolerance for *not* having alcohol in my system went down. There would be days, really just after the worst nights of heavy consumption, where I'd sense withdrawal rumbling deep within me before it ever showed itself physically; I'd feel it coming the way some animals know an earthquake is coming. Something about vibrations and an awful combination of senses. I would just know, and I'd be scared. This vibration hung over me, like the moment just before a shudder or a chill materializes, where I just knew I needed alcohol immediately, or else shakes and sweating and nausea were coming rather than release. The fear of those symptoms—or more specifically, how my body could react in the worst-case scenario—was how I let my brain win some days when my disease asked me to make bad decisions: I got back to that place where often I didn't *want* to drink, but unfortunately I *had* to. I was maybe a year or less into living what I thought was my dream when the nightmare began.

The idea of withdrawal became my prison, in that my fear of being without alcohol made me shut down any potential life plan that involved lack of access to a drink. No, I did not want to go apple-picking; no, I could not do a radio hit in the p.m. hours; no, I did not want to "take a trip," which might involve non-drinking events like travel. My life became so limited by what I viewed as a literal need for alcohol in my system, like insulin for a diabetic.

I had liked drinking when it felt like my choice. I came to recognize it wasn't anymore, and I grew to resent it.

I wonder now if those real withdrawal symptoms ever would've come, and if maybe that "feeling"—that sense that withdrawal was coming—was even accurate, or if that was just my alcoholism using its leverage over me to get me back to the bottle.

My chances for a life as a "functioning alcoholic"—which had been a messed-up life goal—all but ended there, though I didn't realize it. I had reached this point where I stopped fighting, like a kid sparring with their dad or big brother, only to realize they were straight-up overmatched. There was no more will to find some geographic or occupational cure. If my condition decided it was going to pin me with my arm behind my body, I came to believe I had zero ability to fight back. On several occasions, I'd curse out loud when I'd just *think* something like *Maybe I could fit in a drink before this meeting,* because I'd know it wasn't the right thing to do in that moment, yet if my brain wanted to pin that arm behind me, I felt entirely submissive. I'd trudge to a pub with all the joy of a kid who's been told it's time for bath and bed.

That's some change, isn't it, from loving my afternoon pints with friends to reaching the point of cursing when even thinking about alcohol? Drinking had been at the centre of our friends' social time, whose greatest hangouts consisted of meeting up at the pub and getting a little too loose, then falling into one of our nearby townhouses to listen to music and crush boxes of wine or whatever else someone had in stock. Those days were great, and I've never regretted them for a second.

The problem was that when those nights ended and we all parted ways, most of those people woke up with some regret and a strong desire for the couch. They wanted to get right.

I woke up thirsty.

It was around 9 a.m. and I had almost finished an article I'd started during the surprisingly clear-headed morning the day prior, meaning I was going to have a day free from much work. Unfortunately, the evening after that productive morning had not been so clear-headed. That meant I was left with one of those dreaded withdrawal/hangover rumblings rising within me, and so, with the bulk of my work done, I decided a pull of vodka might steady me enough just to get me through the work. That would get me to an 11 a.m. bar opening time somewhere, where I could get back to "normal" and just try to maintain during the afternoon.

I felt incredible, almost immediately.

I could feel the alcohol slide down my throat and warm the inside of my stomach, and the corners of my mouth ticked up like the Grinch the day his heart grew two sizes. It turned my near-sick feeling into a lightly shampooed buzz, with all the alcohol from the day before clearly not yet out of my system. Suddenly, the final sentences came easily, full of a natural-sounding kind of good humour. The article ran that afternoon as I sat at Bar Hop on King Street, and it was a hit, with the RTs and likes on Twitter placing me in a positive-reinforcement loop for all the wrong reasons.

While the feeling never became a clearly expressed thought, I learned I could have a little booze in the morning to steady myself and be just fine. Hell, I was a writer, and writers drink, right? Isn't there a popular whiskey called Writers' Tears? I was hardly the first to dabble in the bottle at the wrong hours. *I bet more writers do this than we even know.*

My new comfort with morning drinking was an event befitting the Chinese farmer parable, in that it was unequivocally the worst thing that could've happened to me … in the short term. It all but ended me, *but* it may have eventually ended the worst version of me once and for all, which eventually pulled me free from that hell.

I started to drink so much some mornings (usually the day after publishing something that went over well) that I would pass out on the couch before noon, and by the time my wife got home, I would be waking from an alcohol-induced coma, feeling like my brain was encased in ice, with basic words beyond my immediate retrieval. Those were the days when she truly thought I was wasted; in fact, I hadn't drunk in five or six hours, yet I had no capacity to contribute a worthwhile thought.

An alcoholic's most important commitment is to protect his ability to drink more alcohol, and by the fourth or fifth time this happened—to go with the accompanying marital tiffs—I found a solution: simply not being around on the days I drank so much before noon that I fell asleep. She couldn't tell what a mess I was if I wasn't present, I had decided.

When that happened and I woke up dumb in the early afternoon, I'd immediately text and create excuses to be out of the house for the night. I'd send a note that would clear the path for me to go and sit in bars alone, trying to avoid seeing Bri for more than a few minutes on my way out the door, usually to do something I claimed was work-adjacent (like going to a Leafs game).

That left me free to drink alone until the house went to bed and I could creep back in. And I'd choose *alone* because I didn't want to be around friends with my brain so fried. I couldn't even emote capably, which wouldn't have been fun for them anyway, I told myself. This all led to feeling awful again the next day, more morning drinks, and an unsustainable cycle. Sometimes I'd string together whole work weeks living like that.

What scenarios does "drinking" call up in your mind? Sitting with friends at a bar? Golfing or beaching or hanging with others? Maybe a solitary drink or two to unwind after a stressful day? I ask because what it became for me then was unrecognizable to those who consume in a "normal" way.

I would know that a few of my friends were at a different establishment just a block away, yet I'd hide in a bar I knew they avoided, because it wasn't about being social or having fun. It became just about the alcohol, and consuming as much as I could while hanging on to my wife, kid and income by any means necessary. I was obsessed. I was losing it.

I lived in this lethargic sadness and self-loathing. I looked around some of the dark bars those lonely nights, full of solitary drinkers who had long since lost ties to obligations like a home life, and I wouldn't see myself, but I could squint and recognize a possible future. I couldn't fathom how I'd become one of *them*—which carries an awful connotation, that *them*. Many of the people in those bars had never been given a tenth of the opportunity I'd had in my life, and had been driven to isolation and alcohol by their circumstances. But a couple times a week, I'd find myself shoulder to shoulder with *them*, staring at another amber IPA, that false idol I had come to worship. With a few in me, I'd see that they were beautiful, those bright beers in dark bars, with the lights of beer signs refracting through each honey-coloured glass.

I was hypnotized and couldn't stop, despite knowing an end of some kind was coming.

You can't drink like I was drinking and carry on. At some point someone tells you that you have to stop, whether it's your partner or employer or family. (Or you have a stroke, or you drive your car into a streetlight or—God forbid—a pedestrian. Whatever the case, it just can't continue.) And when it comes for the umpteenth time, you have to either heed that request or lose the person asking. Thus far, the booze had succeeded in separating me from everything, and it would come for the things that mattered most, too.

I felt some fear and uncertainty, but any time I'd feel an emotion, I'd order a shot and drink it away—usually Jägermeister, because who cares, I was an alcohol nihilist. I stopped letting myself process what was happening. I stopped feeling.

It could've been the fourth time that month that I'd been out doing this, or the fourth that week, or the 40th in a row—I don't know—when the call came.

"Just come home. Just come home and walk right past me and up into bed and I won't say a thing. Just come home so we know where you are."

I still don't remember how many times I'd done it. I don't remember all the dive bars I'd hidden in. I don't remember when that particular call from Bri came in all this cycle of shit, but I remember that part of the conversation vividly, her words a life preserver tossed from above, were I only smart enough to grab hold. Bri knew—she always knew on those worst days—and that particular night, it was so bad that she just didn't want to lose me to a reason that wasn't of her own choosing.

I also remember waking up the next morning and lying in bed, knowing I'd have to go downstairs and face her, but not knowing what we'd be talking about, aside from my drinking. Had I seen her, or talked to her, on my way upstairs the day before? At least I woke up at home this time, rather than in a hotel, like the last time she'd caught me in a cycle of lies and alcohol and kicked me out. But digging out from these stretches was getting harder. Work was getting harder. Life had become "unmanageable," to use the language of a program I badly needed.

I needed help, that much was clear, but quitting drinking forever—given how we'd always socialized, and our great circle of friends—seemed like the last resort. And so at that time I verbally agreed to make changes—I told Bri I would dry out and learn to *manage* my drinking—which I all but knew was impossible, as someone who'd stopped fighting back against my alcoholism. I wanted to be able to stop when I wanted, but my obsession was so strong, I couldn't bring myself to put anything ahead of the bottle. Not yet.

It's a funny thing, being at those places in your life where you know you want to be different, just . . . later. There were stretches of time in college when I knew I would eventually settle into a serious relationship—I wanted that at some point—but it just wasn't the time. In my early days as a hockey player, I knew I'd have to take the gym more seriously, but it's like I waited for life to force me to do it. It was the same here—I knew the way I was living had to change at some point, but I wasn't able to make that choice on my own timeline. Every drastic change I've made, it seems I made it defiantly kicking and screaming.

I approached what came next with curiosity, because it would show Bri I was trying and also buy myself—and my drinking— some time. It was at least an alternative on my clear path to forced abstinence. "Managing" my drinking meant going to CAMH—the Centre for Addiction and Mental Health— which offers "harm reduction" programs, where they agreed to help me dry out. I figured I had nothing to lose. At worst, I'd score some free points with Bri, whom I cared about above all when it came to keeping my life together. At best, it would miraculously work, and I'd be able to drink in moderation again without having to quit outright. I figured I was flailing in my personal life, but if I could improve my ability to manage alcohol even a little bit, maybe I could continue life as a perceived "heavy drinker" and not an "utter train wreck." Perhaps being a "functioning alcoholic" was in the cards yet, I mused with metaphorical fingers crossed.

I went to my first "meeting" at CAMH, where people shared details about their fight to manage their drinking. The people I saw in those rooms gave me a first impression that was hard to shake: the path I was on would only take me somewhere worse if I didn't make changes. I had maintained relationships and employment and stayed away from the long arm of the law, which wasn't the case for many people there.

And so, while I saw this experience as a warning, I also got the wrong impression that I might not be so badly off after all. Maybe I had hit what felt like bottom, but hey, it could be worse?

In a dumb way, it was like someone in credit card debt having their limit increased. "Harm reduction" helps many, many people. But for me, at that point, it became just another chore I'd end up sneaking my drinking around.

To further stave off anything more drastic happening in my relationship, I also agreed to go to marital counselling. It was a reasonable request, given how often Bri and I were fighting. The problem was that I suspected it was a waste of time, because I knew what the problem was; I just couldn't *say* I knew what the problem was. I knew I loved and respected Bri and wanted to be with her, full stop. (I think the mutual love/respect Bri and I showed the counsellor had her wondering why we were there at all.) But I was in so deep with the bottle that I couldn't act in a manner that represented those feelings in our daily life, so I had to create other problems to blame, in hopes that neither Bri nor the counsellor would blame the alcohol. I did have some anxiety, which is largely how I excused away the excessive drinking at the time, but most of that (all of it?) stemmed from having an alcohol-fried brain, and that made me self-conscious.

Everything I was going through had been a product of fighting—or worse, not fighting—my addiction. My anxiety was just a symptom of my real condition.

Back at CAMH, part of the program began with a day of supervised sobriety to ensure that someone like myself—who was dependent on alcohol—didn't have a seizure, or worse, as they went through withdrawal. At the time, I probably hadn't had a 0.0 blood alcohol level at any point in any day in five months—no exaggeration there. I had no clue what to expect when I committed to that day, though I did love that I was encouraged not to stop drinking until the date arrived. I felt that meant I had a free pass in the weeks that led up to the beginning of my program, which was to kick off three weeks entirely dry before the Christmas holidays.

When the day came, I'm not sure I ever made it back down to a flat 0.0 after all. Contrary to recommendations, I drank a ton the night before, and by "night before," I mean I took a couple tugs of some vodka I had hidden in my bedside table at about 4 a.m. I was still drunk (by medical standards) when they gave me a breathalyzer before my dry-out day. The guy taking my blood alcohol level rolled his eyes at me as if he was thinking, *Great, another one of these guys*, before he left me to lie in a hospital bed and stare at the ceiling for the day. They checked in on me and gave me a pill or two that I took without question (I believe they were lorazepam). I spent the day scrolling through Twitter. Later that night, I'd drink a little straight vodka when the house went to sleep, on what was the first night of the three weeks I'd agreed to go sober. I told myself I just had to hold off the shakes and bad symptoms, and that I'd wean myself from there. We were going to New York for Christmas at the end of those three weeks, and sobriety during the holidays, at that point in my life, was just not possible.

It breaks my heart to say this, because it meant the world to my wife that I was trying, but I didn't go a day without a drink those three weeks. It's sickening to reflect on that. Every sneaky sip felt adulterous, as if getting caught would instantly end my relationship, but I felt helpless against the booze, my brain a Nerf sword in the midst of a medieval battle. It wasn't just that I was lying to Bri, though; I was lying to myself. I talked myself into the "self-weaning" theory and persuaded myself I was actually doing better than I had been (low bar), and that I was on the right path. I told myself that if I could just get through those three weeks without getting caught, using the "discipline" I was practising during those days, I'd be able to carry myself as a more normal drinker on the other side. All of that, in hindsight, is irrefutable proof that my ability to process logic was simply not functioning properly.

I was so wrapped up in my own fight I had no chance against the rest of the world.

I tried to consume as little as possible throughout the days so as not to get caught when Bri was between work and her bedtime (weekends involved hiding ample booze on Fridays and desperately trying to disguise my breath with Halls and Fisherman's Friend lozenges). But I stopped my drinking by noon those days and resumed at 9:30 p.m. (that was a legitimately good stretch for me, by my low standards), when she would head to bed for the night.

We checked off my daily successes on the calendar, which crushed me emotionally, because I was failing her. But I was drinking less and feeling physically better than I had as a result, so I picked myself up by telling myself things were going in the right direction. *Maybe I'll get dry one day soon?* I wondered. By the time we got to New York for that Christmas, and I had the green light to openly have a few drinks, my descent was back in full effect.

In the public view, I drank an appropriate amount, but truly, someone like myself in the Gillies house at Christmas was just a rough pairing at the wrong time. They have a busy house—guests aplenty and a full bar in one room—with a sort of steady party feel from the afternoon on. People come and go, drinks are constant, and it's impossible to keep tabs on anyone's intake. And so, I in-took.

I managed to use the old alcoholic shuffle (excessive lying) to convince the family I needed to sleep on the couch there (we had our young son in our room, and the bed was smaller than our own), meaning that when everyone went to bed, I'd be alone with the bar. Clark noticed his bottles being drained at an alarming rate (as I learned retroactively), and I put myself right back where I'd started before my few weeks of "sobriety"—or, more accurately, my "slightly restrained drinking." I rediscovered the constant need for alcohol I'd never really dropped the weeks before.

Something was different, though. That "need" used to be a conscious process. I would want alcohol, then need it, then seek it and enjoy it. My brain had become so addled by now, though, that I sucked up alcohol like a Roomba cleans a room, just moving about and doing its assigned job without a thought or care, bumping into whatever is in its path and changing direction without complaint.

When we arrived home, it was just before New Year's Eve, the welcoming-in of 2019, which would prove to be the most emotional, monumental, important year of my life.

In the weeks that followed, Bri watched me fall apart. She saw the return of my alcoholic coma naps, my excuses to be out in the evening, and the utter disappearance of the man she thought I was. I was poisoning myself, constantly sick.

All through this, my boy Charlie remained the most important thing in my world. (Our daughter, Molly, born in 2020, would eventually join him in that standing.) I knew I would do anything not to have him taken from me, always. But instead of working to get better, I worked to be allowed to continue to drink while keeping him and Bri in my life and staying employed. This is the equivalent of driving a Lamborghini at 150 miles per hour towards a brick wall while saying, "The most important thing to me is just driving this Lambo and keeping it intact," as the wall looms a few hundred feet away.

In truth, employment must've been hanging on by a thread, as my work output and quality had gotten so poor, I'd been forced to explain away missed deadlines by offering vague statements about my health. Not having written anything one week, when a couple of articles should've been completed, I'm embarrassed to recall saying something like "They don't know what it is," which implies some truly awful things. I was aiming for pity, letting them think I was very sick. I justified it to myself because I *was* sick. I just wasn't ready to take on the cure.

My fight against this thing had brought ups and downs for years, but those months I'd describe as pure suffering, free from even the false happiness that alcohol used to bring. There were no moments of being drunk that felt good. I was hiding from everyone who cared for me, alone.

In the mornings after I'd drop Charlie off at daycare, I'd take a pull of whatever booze I had hidden in the house, and often my body would reject it, leading to me throwing up in the sink by 8 a.m. But the solution wasn't to *not* drink, because my body rejected sobriety, too. I'd have to slowly introduce small sips in the morning to sort of prime the engine. By the time I picked up Charlie at daycare for the walk home, I'd have to hide myself from other parents for fear of being found out. I was a weird kind of drunk—not goofy or happy, just blurred and faded. If another parent was arriving at the daycare at the same time, I'd pretend to be on a phone call to avoid a conversation with them. It was strange, because I still believed I was a good dad; I was, as much as I could be, but I was busy killing myself. I tried to lean into that "good dad" side of me, as it was the only thing that made me feel useful then. Charlie loved to play with me—loved me, period—but only I knew I couldn't go on being this guy, or else I'd lose that.

I could barely stomach the underlying thought I truly never let myself think: that I could lose him. I knew I would just never let that happen, no matter what I had to do.

I was losing it slowly on the physical front, but emotionally I was already mostly gone.

At home in the late morning, I'd stare at myself in the mirror, bleary-eyed and swollen, and try to get myself to care more about my dwindling life than alcohol. I barely ate, because I couldn't. I don't know the medical reasons—a swollen liver, or swollen organs in general?—but I constantly felt "full." Food repulsed me, and often the first time I'd try to eat was dinner, when the family was around.

I just wanted the whole shitty ride to stop so I could get off. I was exhausted.

Some version of *Do you need to go to rehab?* was inevitably going to tear a hole in my world at some point, and I just knew that whenever that portal to a better life presented itself, I had to be ready to jump through it.

When it came, I said, "I think I do," but yeah . . . I knew I did.

I was drunk when I called Rich Clune, or "Dicky" as I'd come to know him. We might have had a Twitter spat once upon a time, but when I was with the Marlies, we laughed that away, and in time we grew close. He had been a leader on that team, and spent time in the coaches' offices as a result, particularly if he was a scratch and I was the only one in the room, logging video during a game.

I knew when I was with the Marlies that Rich had gotten sober. I knew then that I was an alcoholic. And I suspected even then that one day we'd be closer than Rich expected.

And so I called and told him I had said "I think I do," because I thought I did. He assured me I definitely did. He also assured me he'd be there for me, and he became my first ally outside of my wife and family, the first person I had exposed my problem to beyond that inner circle.

I had been lonely, as by that point, almost nobody knew me, including myself. Brianna was right there beside me as I committed to starting anew. My family was, too. And Rich was the first person from the 12-step program that I invited in to get to know the real me.

EIGHT DAYS LATER

REHAB JOURNAL, FEBRUARY 19, DAY ONE

Sitting here on my first day awaiting room assignment. Eating one of the gingersnaps Mom sent me with, about to read a note from Bri with a heart on it. Just completed my assessment where I was basically told I'm one of the lucky ones who hasn't lost anything . . . yet.

There's a lot ahead that's not appealing—a whole lotta God talk, some sketchy characters, sharing a room . . . but I can't help but feel lucky. I've got a real chance here to be a better me and I aim to be open-minded enough to find that guy again.

Guess I better go start being nice to people. Month is a long time without friends.

It had been a little more than a week since "I think I do." Five days were spent figuring out what would come next, which featured that fully wasted and weepy phone call to Rich Clune, just about the only person my age I knew who'd been through this and could understand my predicament. His support was imme-diate, immense and meaningful—in a weird way, I needed him. I needed someone like me, who had been in the midst of obvious opportunity but almost lost everything.

My wife and mom spent time then calling the provincial gov-ernment to figure out how one goes about "going to rehab," who had an extra bed and what wait times were like. (I sure couldn't have processed making those arrangements.) Did you know you can't just "go to rehab" in Toronto on your own timeline unless you've got about $10,000 handy? We did not know that, nor did we have all of a spare 10k, but I did have *some* money, and a mother who was so desperate to help that she was able to squeeze her retirement savings some, a piece of shame I'll get further into in a minute. You *can* enter treatment without spending that money, but then you're not going until a space opens up, which can take months. For the people who need it most, those months can kill. At best, I knew that another month or two might be the death knell for the positive things I was desperately trying to keep a part of my life. The logistical hurdles were not easy for someone in the midst of mental anguish. I'll never know how—or if—anybody can piece it all together without support. My wife and mom guided my sinking ship towards the nearest port.

Making plans and committing the extra money for an imme-diate bed was followed by an excruciating 72 hours in which I had to be clean and sober before the treatment house (Renascent) would allow me to show up. I wasn't sure I could manage a single one. We had decided I would attempt this task under the care of those two special women. I had wanted to do it in a hospital set-ting (I was at least partially worried I'd sneak drinks; I didn't even trust myself anymore), but there wasn't room available for me anywhere. My mom had flown out from Kelowna to spend the month with Bri and Charlie so that things at home could remain quasi-functional. Their concern, and that of my extended family (thanks yet again to my uncle Ken), led to me getting in touch with a potential "sponsor," which was another phone call I had to make during those tough hours to appease everyone who wanted to help me get my life straight. I was not in a place yet where I *wanted* to make a call like that, and even when I did, I bluffed and "yeah'd" and "OK'd" everything to get it over with as quickly as possible. I knew nothing about anything recovery-related at that point, and didn't have the brainpower to process complex thoughts. But I at least had the sense that I owed it to Bri and Mom to get started down this forever life-altering path.

The blips would come: *What am I* doing *right now? Are there solutions less drastic than this?*

That call was the first time I would speak with Glenn Vogelsang, a man I've not gone a week without speaking to since. He had worked for my uncle many years earlier and gone AWOL, before calling years later to make amends for his behaviour during those toughest of life stretches. He had gotten clean and was in a position to give back to those who needed the same. With that relationship patched up and our connection made, Glenn was more than willing to offer me the same metaphorical toolkit he had found in sobriety.

I was different than others in rehab—which, let's be clear, is not the same as *special*. I say *different* because rehab doesn't always kick off with heart notes and cookies from family. I say *different* because I came to know numerous alcoholics who left that building not to support, but to pressure to get back drinking. Maybe *uncommon* is the better word. One guy had his mom ask him to hit up his "plug" (dealer) and get her drugs on his first night back home. Meanwhile, again, I had a Tupperware container full of cookies from Mommy and a heart-bearing note of *You can do it!*–style encouragement from my wife, disappointed or disgusted as she might have been with the person I'd become. I recognized that I had no excuses for not succeeding, which is still a common position from which alcoholics fail. The heart on the note signified that if I did have success, there was hope of salvaging a happy life on the other side. That alone was *different*, or *uncommon*, in that building. Or at least that's how I saw the opportunity there for myself.

Thinking back now, the things that qualified me as "different" were circumstantial and luck-based. I was born into a loving family with financial stability, whose members cared and gave me a chance. The positive relationships I had seen throughout my extended family led me to seek out a positive one for myself as well. But really, it was the similarities I should've been focusing on. All of us in treatment had fallen off a brighter path of some sort; most just hadn't had the safety net I had. We had all had moments where we just said, "Fuck it," knowing there were other expectations on us but we preferred the drink or drug to the right thing. Most of us were not just accepting but at times *wanted* people to give up on us so we'd have more space for our vice.

These realizations came later, though. Initially, I worried about any attempt at a positive attitude branding me as an outsider, mostly because the first group of guys I saw in the main sitting area looked like they'd been through the wringer. They mirrored the outside world of February in Canada: cold and spiritless and grey-brown. Rock bottom doesn't look good on anyone, and the current of frustration and confusion running through the men there meant that not everyone looked at someone new walking through the door and saw an opportunity for a hug and friendship. My initial perception was *This is rough*.

But any concern about my new roommates was overridden by a self-defence mechanism my brain employs that I'm pretty proud of (apparently, it still worked even then). When I sit in front of a challenge without any way around it, for some reason I'm able to not spend any mental energy on it, because "you gotta do what you gotta do." That's all there is to some things. Whatever anyone thought of me, I'd survive, whether there were tough moments or not. Fear or strategy wouldn't help; I just had to get in there. As a hockey player, I hated fighting, but there were times I felt I had to do it in order to prove my commitment, and so I did it. When my jaw was broken, I had simply said the accepting "OK" and got started recovering. And again, I just had to buck up, as it had become black-and-white. I could carry on with the positive things I had in my life or be involuntarily divorced and unemployed in my late 30s and have to start over, to say nothing of the pain that would come with letting my family down. As much as I wanted the fix to be a sprint, I was lined up at the start of a marathon, and the starter's pistol had been fired.

Even with my optimistic-leaning opening mindset, I made three journal entries that first day and the tone of the next two deteriorated quickly from that hopeful first offering. I was placed in a room I'd charitably classify as "austere," with three single beds, one of which I could've touched from my own, the other a few feet from those two. The picture below isn't that exact room but the one I was upgraded to later in my stay, a room with just one roommate (though his bed was still an arm's length away):

Accommodations at Renascent near Spadina and Bloor.

This is not a comment on the quality of the housing—Renascent did a tremendous job with the resources they had—but the white linens I was initially given had darkened like pages in an old book, and the pillowcase had a faded orange blood spot on it, while its contents were yellowed from sweat. We had all put our clothes—everything we brought—through the dryer on hot as soon as we checked in, to ensure that nobody brought bedbugs into the building—the second floor was being fumigated for some at the time. A lot of people churn through that building, and they aren't exactly laden with excess funding.

This was not "rehab" the way we think about celebrities getting help. I've seen pictures of places like that, where gleaming white marble slabs surround a pool, an oasis amidst a vast expanse of Arizonan desert. Renascent was clean, though (despite 20 to 40 guys living there at any one time), and it was organized, and it was professional. The unavoidable impression of the place as somewhat worn and threadbare was merely a by-product of the heavy use everything saw.

My brain had lost vibrancy, and the colours of those days were reflected back to it. It was that palette of greys and browns and grey-browns, and the wet saltiness of the outside touched everything within 15 feet of the doors.

My second journal entry on the 19th noted that at that exact time of day, my son would be running around after his bath with nothing but his hooded towel on his head, his junk flapping about, yelling, "I'm Batman" up and down the halls. Instead of being there, I was bracing for my first church basement and an introduction to the 12 steps. My stomach churned. It was the depths of winter, and after they checked our names off to leave the building for our nightly meeting, we stepped outside and the wind blew. There was no buddy system, just grown men trying to find their way. I felt invisible and lost amidst dozens of people, my mind reeling.

But I went to that first meeting, and I listened.

FEBRUARY 20—THE NEXT MORNING

The thing that sticks with me most from last night's meet-ing is the girl who spoke about the 12 steps—the program in general, I think—is that it creates "space" to turn around.

I imagine it like Austin Powers trying to turn that vehicle around in the narrow hallway. That's how getting it turned around alone has felt. This could move the walls to get going the other way.

I had considered sobriety at various points before this, but getting clean without help had felt impossible, partially because the phys-ical addiction meant it wasn't as simple as just overcoming some powerful thoughts. In my mind, that meant I couldn't simply turn around and stop drinking. There was more to it, and it was beyond repair. But with proper help now, I was clinging to the bursts of positivity I could find at the beginning of treatment, as the fear of uncertainty nearly crushed me in those first few days. I was told that the days ahead included some time with counsellors, and I greatly dreaded what I assumed would be an honest accounting of who I had become, and the following in my dad's footsteps, and how I ended up where I was. I never wanted to confront that stuff, but I knew it was coming. I was also definitely not a "God guy," and since I badly wanted to have success in the program, I was worried I was going to have to spend time lying about believing in whatever it was they were trying to "sell" me so I could get good reviews and let other people *think* I was buying in. "God—yeah, yeah sure, big fan over here." It's not that I didn't intend to buy in—I truly wanted to get sober—it was that I believed myself "too smart" to suddenly become a God guy, and so I expected to have to bluff on that part. (Incidentally, that arrogance—the whole "I can handle this my own way" thing—revealed itself as a constant threat to my sobriety.)

Trying to get a grasp on my feelings at first was an exhausting exercise of constant self-evaluation. I lived in worry and low-level fear. Every physical twinge triggered a *Here comes the stroke* thought, and every bad mood raised the question *Am I an angry person now?* I didn't know myself or know what it would feel like to get sober. That was a trip, thinking, *I hope sober me isn't an asshole.* But I was also awaiting a mental clarity I hadn't allowed myself to have in years, and I had a hidden fear—that alcoholism had taken from me one of the ways I self-identified: as a pretty smart guy. For years I had had trouble processing complex thoughts (which was why I began to lean on that listicle-style writing to avoid having to produce a coherent 1,500 words), but I had comforted myself all the way along by blaming the day's fog of alcohol, rather than considering that I had legitimately lost processing power. I still don't have a conclusion about what I mentally lost by living the way I did (I certainly wasn't doing any fancy book learning, so I'm pretty confident I didn't get *smarter*), but at this point I was relieved that the weeks and months would at least shuck a few layers of ice off my brain like a scraper on a frozen windshield.

New feelings and thoughts and plans appeared in my mind in the quiet moments, and I batted down fears like I was playing whack-a-mole. In the very immediate short term, I was still worried I wouldn't be accepted by the others at rehab, which you wouldn't think would be a big deal, but I admit I was wary of some angry young guys to whom life had yet to offer a chance. Small disagreements flared quickly, and they cropped up over everything from skipped chores to snoring to stolen vape supplies. Taking any 30 guys and making them involuntary roommates at the lowest point in their lives is bound to cause some tension. I'd spent time with big groups of dudes with different motivations in dressing rooms, but at least those guys were trying to pull in the same direction. Some fellas in treatment had seen some things on some tougher paths than the ones I'd traversed, and I wasn't sure ol' Captain Gingersnaps would've been the most popular guy if someone had decided I was a problem.

I had no idea what would happen with my wife and son while I was away—would they find it just so much easier without me causing problems that they'd just get over me? Maybe my wife would find some sympathetic stand-up guy to help her through the tough times. I didn't know. What I did know was that if I tried this and failed, she'd almost certainly be moving back to Long Island, where her immediate family still lived. In treatment, you learn that for many, relapse is a part of recovery. I couldn't see a world in which I'd relapse and she'd want to spend another day with someone so utterly unreliable, whatever the cause might be. It's scary sitting on your last chance.

Maybe my employer would find a better use for my salary. I was paid well enough but couldn't be counted on to produce over the past few months. I have no doubt things were hanging on by a thread there. What was left of me if I lost my hockey media role, another label I had come to put on myself? I was worried I wouldn't have a clue who I was.

What about my soft, heavy body? How was it going to take going cold turkey after years of abuse? I was scratching the skin off my upper thighs and calves every night and sweating through my sheets.

Maybe I couldn't do this whole getting-sober thing at all—I'd never had success yet—and I'd venture off in a couple of days and get blind drunk in disgrace. Hell, the Madison Pub and the Puck (a hockey bar I somehow hadn't seen before, of all the cruel temptations) were both within a five-minute walk from our residence just off Bloor Street. (On day two, my journal shows I first wondered if I was really, *truly* an alcoholic—which is baffling—before confessing I had considered just having a beer or two a day while I was in treatment, followed by a stick of gum to hide that. *Then* it acknowledges, "OK, that wasn't good, turns out I am really, *truly* an alcoholic." That was how quickly the thoughts could come and go, and I wasn't confident I'd be able to fight off every thought in every mental state, happy, sad, tired or mad.)

All these worries vied for my attention at a time when I didn't know where it should be focused. All I wanted to do was use the house pay phone and call Bri and be reassured that she and my mom and son all loved me and for them to heap praise on me for actually going . . . but it wasn't their job to pull me through the position I'd put myself in. Agreeing to treatment was great, but at some point, that praise had to end and the work had to begin.

The cold seeped through the windows, human interactions were chilled, my facial expression stayed frozen no matter the situation. I was ice.

I knew that in the days ahead, I had to be selfish, to focus on myself, to get right and work on my own brain, or I'd never be able to be there for anyone else again. I had to organize my head in a way that allowed me to stay sober. They asked us to rank our priorities early in my stay, and hey, I'd written plenty of power ranking articles. I could do that. Like everyone else there, I knew to include "staying sober" as a priority in my life.

I'd say "Obviously I put family number one," but that ended up being the point of the exercise. Anything you prioritize above your own sobriety is something you'd better be willing to lose, because without the sobriety, you won't be able to keep . . . anything.

What was so hard was confronting the one practical thing I was there to do—to learn how to stop drinking—while reconciling all the embarrassing things I'd done and how I'd hurt my family and what I'd become. There was no guarantee that clearing out the cobwebs was going to reveal a person I liked. Hell, some people put the cobwebs there for that very reason: to obfuscate their view of themselves, who may have become something a great distance from who they set out to be. Had I?

How had it gone so far? I was in my first week sober at a time when I hadn't gone one *day* in years, and both my mind and body were in grave condition. I was trembling and unsteady. During my time drinking, I always described the feeling of those cobwebs clearing as my brain "coming back online" to myself, because that's what it felt like. As much as I craved access to my brain, the second it would come was when I'd feel the guilt about how I was living, and I'd need to drink that away again. Here I was left to face it. In the years before, anytime I'd start to get too sober, I'd feel a static-electric-like crackling in the front of my head, a physical sensation that felt as if my brain had been a deflated beach ball and someone had started to blow air back into it. I mean it when I say I felt that physical sensation. It only happened when it had been a short time (12 to 16 hours, maybe?) since I'd had a drink. I'd get red, hive-like marks on my forearms, which had led to many a Google search that convinced me I had cirrhosis (a diagnosis I was certainly looking to find amongst the possibilities). I had also tied those physical symptoms into my work—as they showed up, I knew they meant I had better get working fast before the worse symptoms began and I'd be "forced" to start drinking again. My grey matter "inflating" meant it was officially time to get writing, whether I had an idea or not.

That brain and I had become enemies. For me, that didn't mean facing tragic things like abuse and loss like so many in treatment—I was lucky there. But it meant confronting what a desolate *loser* I had become, how I had squandered all of my abilities and the love of many and a life that offered me every opportunity. It's one thing to struggle when life has chucked you lemons, but there's a weird shame in being thrown perfect, catch-able spirals only to drop the ball over and again.

A big part of my early struggle in the program centred around the fact that I *wasn't* suffering from abuse or tragedy, and that my biggest issue was just a true physical and mental addiction to alcohol. So many men and women were dealing with things so much more severe than I was, to the point where I even had imposter syndrome about being an alcoholic, a thing I defini-tively was. It took some time to accept my own condition as *worthy* of the help I was being offered. I've heard it said that people can drown in 7 feet of water as easily as 70, and I had to appreciate that although my pool wasn't as deep, it was still worth pulling myself out of.

I also learned this truth about alcoholism, which I've referenced earlier in the book: people think you hit "rock bottom" and that's when you know it's time to stop digging . . . but that's not what happens. You hit *a* bottom, but you get to *pick* your "rock bottom," because the truth is that there's always another, *lower* bottom if you go back out drinking. Drunks think they've bottomed out, then pull themselves together just long enough to fire up the metaphorical excavator and dig lower. Almost every alcoholic in every recovery meeting has a story about hitting what they thought was the bottom . . . before doing worse.

My problems were mounting and about to collapse upon me. If I kept drinking, those lower bottoms I saw in the room—DUIs and accidents, incidental deaths, jail time, wet brain, cirrhosis and cancer, estrangement, legal woes and dying—were all there for me, too. And so, knowing that a lower version of rock bottom was always there, I tried to make the decision—as best an alcoholic can commit to anything—that this bottom I'd found was going to be *my* "rock bottom," and that I was worth this intensely focused month despite the additional burden on those closest to me.

FEBRUARY 21, DAY THREE

I woke up a few mins ago with the thought "as soon as possible I want this to not define me." I remember in psych classes discussing how we self-identify. Hockey guy, Canadian, husband, Dad, etc. So many alcoholics in recovery wear their recovery like a Cup ring. For them it may be as or more important. I want my healing to be just another scar I have, another hurdle I cleared, not who I am.

Last night at AA I heard a metaphor for when I leave here that was relevant. Just because I stopped drinking doesn't undo damage. Farmer and wife hide in storm cellar, hurricane wipes out house and barn. Husband after: "This is great! Aren't you glad the wind stopped blowing?" But damage already done.

I wrote that from my single bed, on sweat-soaked sheets from which you could've wrung a 750-millilitre bottle Absolut-ly full. It tells you a lot about where my mind was at then—not just in treatment, but in general. I always wanted to do things the easy way, and wanted the challenging things to pass quickly. The last thing I wanted was to look the pain in the face.

But in rehab, they make you face it.

I was still physically struggling. My bedroom was on the second floor, and the small cafeteria-style dining room was in the basement, meaning I had to go down two flights of stairs to get there and then walk back up them—which was hardly the number of stairs I used to run up while training in the summers, but there were days when I took the elevator. My body's search for homeostasis left me unsettled and exhausted. It felt like I was missing something at all times, and I guess, from my body's perspective, I was.

Being able to relate to the other men there was a comfort, in that I knew the guys there would at least understand what I was going through. But the way everyone is forced to rely on one another through chores and group work took some getting used to. Y'know what nobody wants to do when they're trying to rise up from the depths of their personal rock bottom? Scrub baked cheese off a half-eaten lasagna dish shoulder to shoulder with someone else whose life also presently sucks. The others were just trying to fix their own lives, and none of us had practised much care for our immediate families for a while, let alone for relative randos. As a result, there were few moments of the days to look forward to, just more exposure to the pain I'd caused and the reality I'd built, and I constantly wanted to escape. And, like many people in that house, I knew of a liquid that would offer that.

Was I really never going to escape again? I had always loved a Frank Sinatra quote: "I feel sorry for people who don't drink. When they wake up, that's the best they're going to feel all day." I had always laughed, knowingly, at the line. Me and Sinatra, two peas in a pod, y'know? Now *I* was the shlub who didn't get to be in the inner circle of the quip?

Somehow being "a drinker" had been part of how I had come to see myself, and I was so worried about what becomes of a person who loses foundational pieces of their self-identity. I had forgotten what the rest of me was even about. I think I used to be nice to people and liked reading—those were self-identity things, I guess? When "hockey player" was knocked off that list of self-identities, maybe that made room for "drinker." Maybe it had for my dad, and others like us, too.

In wishing for my alcoholism not to define me in that journal entry, you can also see that I had some fear of becoming a person I'd thought uncharitably about in the past: those non-drinkers. That was because my drinking buddies and I had consistently made fun of non-drinkers, who in our eyes didn't know how to let loose, how to have fun, how to laugh. That was no life at all to us. Everyone around the bar talks about how they'd rather live a shorter life of fun than whatever the opposite was (and I have unfortunately since seen several people get that wish). Non-drinkers were boring and dull; they were nerds. I didn't want to say the words *I don't drink* for fear of the assumptions people would make about me.

Desperation had pushed me so far past all that. I say "that was no life at all to us," but what was the life I had been living? I was willing to suffer through the physical and emotional pain of rehab just to live any other way. For what seemed like forever, I hadn't wanted to become a sober person—ugh—but here I was, suffering and staring my failings in the face, just so I didn't have to be a drunk for another day.

DAY FOUR, FEBRUARY 22

Had my first "I don't know if I can do this" moment after dinner. I've just been here three days some-fucking-how, 25 days to go? Bored, lonely (not a person here worth considering a long-term friend), hate not being able to contact wife and Charlie. He's gonna get used to have me not around.

I mentioned I needed to be selfish, but I meant in terms of caring for myself, not whatever selfishness is bleeding out of the words above (there were numerous people there worth long-term friendships, I learned—what an awful line). The boredom I felt left room to think, and as the fog cleared from my brain, the pain came more clearly into focus.

There was my mom, and the guilt I felt for what I was putting her through, that I had pushed her to spend her money to look after me at my grown-ass age. She had always been so proud of me, and here I was, a source of shame for the family. I was embarrassed by it all, and not just about the money. A part of the embarrassment was . . . I was supposed to be the easy one, right?

I had seen what she went through with my brother—all his hospital time and needs—while working a full-time job. Jeff worked his ass off to be as independent as possible as he got older, but in his younger years, amidst what seemed like endless surgeries, he deserved help, and Mom was constantly at his bedside eager to give it. She took every scrap of vacation time she had (and more) driving from Kelowna to Vancouver to see specialists and ensure Jeff got the best care possible.

My dad did his best to be there for Jeff, but in the years immediately following a divorce, the situation was very stressful for Mom. I saw her face as we were picked up to spend the weekend at Dad's new place. I saw the pains she took to keep their discussions away from us, knowing the tone with which they were carried out. I'm a pretty emotionally attentive guy—not always seeing those conversations play out doesn't mean I missed the mental weight she carried in their wake.

And so, the last thing I had wanted was to be a burden, ever. I wanted to be something good she could count on. With the work she put in for everyone else, she deserved that. In a way, I guess that's what I always wanted—and want—to be for those I care most about: a *reliable positive* in their lives. And there I was being the opposite in such a drastic way. I had felt like such a capable guy, able to do just about anything I set my mind to, and I'd let myself become just another line item of dread on everyone's docket.

Speaking of my brother, he had always been so proud of my path. He was always the first guy wearing the gear of whatever obscure team I played for or whatever outlet I worked for. Sometimes, because of his physical limitations, I felt like I had accomplished everything I'd achieved for both of us, and so to have failed him—and what I aspired to do for us—hurt, too. We had always been best friends, but I hadn't let him close enough to see what I'd really been going through during those years.

The clearing mist from my brain was laying it all clear, and I was realizing I'd need to find beginnings and ends to all these feelings.

There was my dad, whom I had inadvertently become. It's easier to reflect now on how highly I must have regarded my dad growing up without ever really acknowledging it in those years. I don't know how much my pursuit of the sport was tied to trying to follow in his footsteps. But when you look at it, boy, howdy, it's tough to miss that maybe I had some issues there, no? It could be that in the years when I really start to remember everything about him, I wasn't seeing him at home during the monotonous day-to-day routine, but at events (or as a coach in a locker room), where just about everyone was applauding him and praising him and showing him respect.

Without ever consciously aiming to follow in his footsteps, I had become a pro hockey player who had gone through the New York Islanders system and played in Utah—and who had ended up with a drinking problem.

Is it possible that a lot of that was subconsciously motivated by a desire to be like my dad? Or is that just some hippy-dippy psycho-babble that's easy to put together in hindsight? It's just impossible to miss how similar we were, and are, and rehab screamed at me to LOOK AT IT. We've always gotten along famously; we're like two peas in a pod when there aren't bigger issues in the way. But I had seemingly taken on *all* of his traits, not just the ones I liked. I still don't entirely know how it all came to be. I loved him then as always, but I came to recognize how we had always just hummed along as if everything was peachy keen, even when problems surfaced. A more honest assessment of how I ended up where I was had to start with a sober look (quite literally) at my past. I'd need it to stay clean going forward.

All these thoughts were just vague feelings that needed to be dug up and cleaned off and identified—emotional archaeology, really—before they could be dealt with. And the digging hurt.

For my home life, I knew that if I got myself right, Charlie was so young that I could salvage things with him. My worst fear in any of this was the idea of not being around for him, and I felt that fear so strongly it actually gave me a belief in my ability to stop drinking. I felt guilty, but confident that a better me had plenty of time with Char.

I was less sure about his mom. I had taken advantage of my best friend in Bri. First as kids and then as grown-ups, we had always been "us," Justin and Bri, a team with a foundation so impossible to shake that I took it for granted. Maybe I'd just assumed I would always have her, but now the threads on that safety net were nearly worn through. It's one thing to let the great stuff about a relationship slide—the dates, the laughs, the connection—but it's another entirely for one person to be a flat-out burden on the other. Women have left men for less than what I'd put her through, I knew that for sure.

I had been blessed with something in a partner not everyone gets: someone who believed in me every step of the way and trusted me to handle my own business, whether that be in my career or now, in my commitment to getting sober. I was sure it would be the last time she'd extend the faith that I would be able to figure out the next, correct steps. And I wanted that faith—it was only then that I realized how much I cherished it and craved getting it back—but I hadn't proven myself worthy of it. I was so worried it was lost forever.

Something that gets lost in a relationship when one person is such a shell of themselves is how little the *other* person gets to be themselves. Bri was forced into being my babysitter, as well as a watchdog protecting herself and Charlie from the worst of me, and because of that, I had stripped her of the best parts of herself. I hadn't allowed her the sense of humour and lightness I loved about her. I had taken a relationship with so much joy and connectedness and turned it adversarial. I had put a stranger in her home—myself—and she was forced to react accordingly.

For years I had noted the differences between the Gillies family and my own—two families that had very similar beginnings during the Islanders years and beyond—and I had seen how drastically divorce changed things. My brother and I had such a happy childhood, but I came to envy the simplicity and structure of the Gillies unit, and I wanted it for our family in the years ahead. I worried about having brought Bri to Toronto, away from that unit, and then messing up so badly that she'd be raising our boy alone. *God, maybe she'll take him to New York without me.* I simply could not believe I'd ended up where I was, and would do anything to undo the damage I'd caused.

As the fog slowly began to lift from my brain, the clarity brought the realization of just how close I'd pushed "bend" towards "break" with Bri, and how much I missed *us*. That's the inscription on the inside of our wedding rings—"You're my *us*." I didn't know if we'd ever get that back.

THE ROUTINE

It turned out that the worst of those personal pains would become nocturnal, as the day hours were full. They existed like vampires, staved off by the sun, but unfortunately it was still the dark season, so they had plenty of hours to haunt me.

During the days, I got to the work at hand. What else could I do?

Wakeup time was 7 a.m., and everyone was to be showered and ready for breakfast at eight, with their rooms clean and beds made. Bed inspections were carried out, and it is remarkable how much pushback the staff got from a house of alcoholics about bed making. Someone bitched about it every day. I learned that the policy wasn't so much about the bed being made as it was about establishing a good, consistent routine, like in the army. It's been said about making your bed that it may be a theoretical "waste of time"—you're just going to get back in it later—but it's nice to feel like you've accomplished something before breakfast, and it's nice to get into a neatly made bed each night.

This call for consistency is everything an alcoholic hasn't had the faintest interest in during the years before trying to get sober. We had become unreliable by choice, keeping our schedules clear so that we could follow any whims we desired. I was someone you simply could not make plans with, because I'd inevitably end up breaking them to do . . . whatever I wanted (usually drink in a dark pub for eight straight hours). Being reliable means being accountable to something or someone—and here we were, being asked to be reliable in our routine. Baby steps, right? It was the beginning of tidying up my mental mess.

After breakfast there was a guided meditation, usually something involved with our "chakras"—just 10 to 15 minutes of trying to get our disordered brains at peace before the day. And then we started learning, sitting in a classroom setting (read: the lunchroom, but with notebooks), listening to a mix of counsellors at the whiteboard who were trying to help us understand our conditions. What an "alcoholic" does and looks like varies wildly, but there are trends that tie us together. Identifying those, coming to grips with the costs and learning how to break the cycles—this was all so essential to making permanent change. (Understanding some of the physiology of alcohol abuse interested me, too.)

It was there I was exposed to the "Two Wolves" parable. The idea is that a kid is angry at another who has wronged him, and he's taken that frustration to his grandfather. The grandfather explains that hate wears you down, that it's like taking poison and hoping your enemy will die. He explains that he can relate to the feeling, and that it's as though there are two wolves inside of him.

One wolf is good, and lives in harmony with the surrounding world, without taking offence where none is intended. He will only fight when it is right, and in the proper way. The other wolf fights everyone and everything without cause. The constant anger blinds him. The grandfather says it's hard to live with both those feelings inside, as each tries to control his spirit.

When the grandson asks which wolf wins, his grandfather smiles and explains, "The one I feed."

"Feed the good wolf" became an early pillar of my new belief structure, as I tried to pile up little morsels of good to strengthen my famished good wolf.

The one colossal change I felt in those classes was that, for the first time in forever, the loneliness abated. I could raise my hand and comfortably share something about my past behaviour—something that would've seemed absolutely absurd in any other setting—without feeling like a complete pariah. There's nothing quite like revealing that you used to put vodka in travel-size shampoo bottles to have a secret stash, only to have someone respond that they used to inject vodka between their toes so that their wife wouldn't smell it on their breath. Or that they drank the hand sanitzer while they were in the ER recovering from alcohol poisoning. Or that, in a pinch, vanilla extract used to get the job done. The non-drinker response to these things might be "No, not really, nobody actually did that—did they?" In this room, nobody batted a goddamn eyelash, because of course they did.

That part about not feeling lonely anymore shouldn't read as a comment on my wife or friends or family. I had just been lying to everyone for so long, I felt like nobody knew me, and I bet they were feeling the same way. When I was drinking alone in the a.m. hours, I would wonder if anyone out there had been living like me and would be willing to talk about it (I knew that the ones who want to continue that lifestyle sure don't wanna talk about it, because they know others will try to take it away). Despite the divergent walks of life in that room, I came to feel I was among my people. Those people could understand why I'd done some of the more embarrassing, stupid things in my life.

Still, let's be clear: it was not fun. On top of those classes and lectures, our daily routine included doing dishes, mopping and cleaning bathrooms (including the toilets in an all-men's facility), among other things. The work needed to be done, and we needed structure and small victories. Each night, we trudged into a dark and cold Toronto to a rehab meeting, then back home to kill a little time before bed, just to do it all again the next day. It was then that I'd have to ask a counsellor for permission to take my pre-approved vitamins, which included melatonin to help my body find more natural sleep, something I hadn't had in years.

Comforts were few. One-on-one sessions with counsellors challenged me to look at my relationship with my dad, my relationship with my life compared to my expectations for myself, and how I'd treated those closest to me. Uneasy conversations with Bri on the lobby pay phone were what I looked forward to most, but I was so emotionally exhausted, I could barely express any happiness I felt. I didn't cry much, yet I felt being on the verge of tears as a steady weight, particularly on those calls.

Learning as a kid is hard, but I'd always found that if I paid attention, whatever I took in generally stuck. It felt like stocking empty closet shelves with information. What's much harder as an adult was that this learning felt like I had to make room on the packed shelves, so I had to pick through what was already there and move things around for new ideas.

In some of those recovery meetings, I learned that a big hurdle for the program is the misunderstanding of what is perceived as a religious aspect, which was the concern I mentioned I had heading into the whole thing. I wasn't religious, and no desperation for sobriety was going to rework my brain to become a literal believer in all the stories within the Bible. I wasn't seeking heaven so much as I just wanted to stop seeking the Skyy— vodka. But it was in those meetings with counsellors that I opened my mind to the phrase and loose concept of a *higher power*, which within the program means anything that holds a greater meaning for you than yourself. After all, "yourself" is the thing most alcoholics had been prioritizing in staying alcoholics.

The word *God* is included heavily in the 12-step texts, but the program opens itself up to that "higher power" ideal, which for some alcoholics may just be the collective strength of those who are sober in the meeting rooms. That's a pretty powerful collective. For others, it might be nature, or a long-lost family figurehead. Since I was a kid I've been floored by the vastness of the universe and not so naive as to think I'm capable of processing what's going on in the big picture around me. There's some sort of spirituality in that, and that awe I held helped me keep an open mind and search for something. The "higher power" I came to accept, then, became my familial ecosystem—and I mean my extended family here too—and it hinges on how dependent everyone is on one another for us all to thrive. I don't think I can process how connected that group is, and how we all hold one another up, but I know my contribution to the unit is greater when I'm a better version of myself. I came to see how integral I was to our collective happiness, and how integral each of them was to me, and how I feel like, combined, we make up something bigger. When I say "God" in any recovery context, I feel it's a proxy for me as I draw on the strength of that family group, of that something that's bigger and means more than just . . . me.

That relationship ecosystem branches from my wife to my son (and now daughter), to my mom, dad and brother, aunts and uncles and cousins, and reaching far beyond that. It now includes a group of men, all sponsored by Glenn, whom I talk with each week. It includes our closest friends. I've leaned on each of them for something in my life, and I want to be someone they can reach back to. As George Bailey learns in *It's a Wonderful Life*, one person touches a lot of lives. And here's a shocker: that whole community doesn't exist solely for my benefit. That humility was wrought from reflecting on how I had been living before, examined through the microscope of the program's spirituality. A healthy version of me can be a far-reaching force for good for those people and more, and that's what I want for my life and for those connected to it.

I wouldn't have to find a religious God for the program to work for me, or to pretend to for counsellors and sponsors in the program to accept my commitment to staying sober. I just had to find a higher power: something that meant more to me than me.

MARCH 7, DAY 16

I'm at the point where I feel good, and I'm worried about work plans when I'm out. I'm ready to make plans, reconnect with Bri and home and our routine. But I'll try not to waste my remaining days here. Will try to build a stronger foundation and better connection to the real sober me whom I had forgotten I really love. I still have work on myself to go.

I wrote a mission statement yesterday that opened with a line I really like, as written below:

I will live with the care of those closest to me in my heart.

While I was working towards my sobriety and dealing with the pain that I had both dealt and received, I was finding pillars to build on within the program.

I will live with the care of those closest to me in my heart.

There's a phenomenon in addiction recovery that's referred to as the "pink cloud" phase, which in most cases comes when you finally get to the other side of physical withdrawal. That was me in that last journal entry. You can feel euphoric and joyous, which are things you hadn't been able to feel for years without being drunk or high. You can have a hopeful outlook, you can be positive and optimistic about your recovery, and you can have confidence in your ability to remain sober. There's real shock in the epiphany *Holy hell it is possible for me to feel good for moments at a time just taking life* au naturel. You can fixate on all the good things, the ability to be emotionally in touch, and . . . and you can overlook the hard work ahead of you, including the reality that *life is often a tremendous pain in the ass, even for the sober.*

It's really funny to head out into the world feeling like *Now that I'm sober, I can handle anything!* Then you walk through your front door, lock it . . . and the key breaks off in the lock, and your coffee spills while you're trying to pull the key out, and then your sleeve rips on the shard of key sticking out of the lock. Life still being life is what turns the short-lived pink cloud into rain once again. *Wasn't getting sober supposed to fix everything?*

When the pink-cloud phase ends, being clean and sober doesn't cut it. You have to manage your emotions and repair your relationships and keep up on all the menial, mundane details of a balanced lifestyle. You have to deal with other people, and let's face it, dealing with certain people can be about as fun as accidentally drinking someone's chew spit on a bus in the minors. And sometimes you just wake up in a shit mood. *I got sober for this?* is an early threat to those who've just committed to processing the still-challenging world with a clean brain.

But that's part of what you're fighting for: the ability to feel all that, and process that, and experience the highs and lows as they come, which is the essence of living.

Here's one of my final journal entries before being thrust back onto the hamster wheel of everyday life:

MARCH 16, DAY 25

I'm having a tough night.

The time here has started to feel like a waste of time. Not all of it—but this past week. And today, a ton.

I am irritable.

I saw Charlie and Bri and Mom today which was good, but seemed weird. Almost home, so no "fit in the time" desperation. No time to talk cause Charlie is mayhem. Love seeing them all, was just weird today. Limbo. Purgatory.

I'm reminded that real life means not being lauded with praise all day every day after rehab.

———

Real life lay ahead. And though it never seemed like the end would come that first time I sat down in that well-worn common space, time had kept on ticking.

On March 19, 2019, I rolled my Marlies-branded suitcase out through the wide wooden door of Renascent and onto the front porch, and the world was hardly waiting. Life had sped on. I had my personal goals tucked in my back pocket. Healing my relationships with my family. Getting physically healthy. In my career, a lofty one: getting on *Hockey Night in Canada*. I was left to figure out how to get the world to include me once again, but this time in a positive way.

At my exit meeting from Renascent, I sat with "New York Tom," easily the gruffest and most direct of the counsellors encountered during my stay. Everyone who'd been there a while had warned me of his infamous manner when I arrived, and I did the same for those who came after me. I'd tell those who were just arriving not to fear him, that he was your prototypical "hard-ass with a heart of gold" whose approach can feel rough but genuinely has your best interest in mind. Some people in those rooms need to hear hard truths that make them bristle, and he excelled at providing them. So, Tom was going over my plans for the weeks and months immediately out of treatment, trying to put together a daily calendar with me, when he told me I should do "90 in 90," which means attending 90 meetings in my first 90 days out of treatment. I couldn't fathom the idea—I had just done a damn month of daily meetings, so I figured I got the picture, you know?

I told him I didn't think that would be possible, but that I'd be sure to get to as many as I could, hoping to sweep that discussion under the rug and move on. But that wasn't good enough. I explained that I had completely abandoned my job to be in rehab, and I needed to get back to not just working but doing exceptional work, to keep my employment. At *The Athletic*, you're on a fixed-term contract (or at least I was), so proving myself before it ran out was important, I said.

I had also abandoned my family and had a wife who needed her husband back and a son who needed his daddy back. We had no family in town, so my taking off over dinnertime to go to a meeting would just pile more on my wife's plate. I also wanted to exercise and get in shape. I had so many things I wanted to do, and none of them included constantly finding meetings around Toronto, commuting to and from, sitting for an hour at a time, hearing the same message over and over.

I was, in retrospect, an oblivious dumbass. Have some self-awareness, Bourne.

In a nutshell, Tom was having none of it. He said that earlier that morning, he had made a return-to-life daily plan for a single mother of three who was willing to do it, so basically, what the hell was my excuse? Was I less committed? I was still struggling to find the humility to recognize the work it was going to take for any of my oh-so-important "plans" to be possible. If I didn't get sober, my family wasn't going to be there at all, nor would any jobs. I had to make sobriety my everyday focus in the early days, and so I did— with the help of the intense focus and resolve of my wonderful wife.

This was where I had to constantly remind myself of the life priority list they had me create in treatment, and to understand that putting even a single thing ahead of "sobriety" on that list would make me more likely to lose it.

My schedule took some juggling—well, *our* schedule as a whole did—but I found meetings at which I'd become a regular.

There was one at 6:30 a.m. at the OISE building on Bloor Street; a 7 p.m. "Love and Tolerance" meeting that had a couple of locations and became my home group; and a 5:30 p.m. session at the little church beside the Eaton Centre on Fridays, for starters. (I loved the 5:30 p.m. Friday meeting because that had been my prime drinking time, and focusing on my sobriety at that time firmed up my resolve for the night and into the weekend.) Sometimes there'd be 100 people in a meeting, sometimes there'd be 4, but I stayed through them all, and learned to share with the groups as I got more familiar. Really, it was the first public speaking reps I'd ever had.

Days passed slowly at first, but they did pile up. One month after my month-long stint at rehab, I picked up my two-months-sober medallion at a meeting and started to find myself a little. The motto on those little medallions is 24 HOURS AT A TIME, and how that plays out is effective. You aren't trying to stay sober for the rest of your life. You're just trying to stay sober *today*, and you can worry about tomorrow tomorrow. It makes the commitment that much less daunting. Every time you enter a challenging situation and make it out sober, the confidence of knowing you can do it builds for the next time you encounter that scenario. You're just accruing these little bits of belief in yourself as you go, and doing so is monumental for those who have come to see themselves as flaky and unreliable. I was feeding my good wolf.

Part of what had given me such severe anxiety during my alcoholic days was the constant feeling that I wasn't at my best, and I was now determined to know just what my best looked like. At the root of that anxiety was a confidence, really, because I believed my best had always been pretty good before I destroyed myself. I started pounding the treadmill during the days, too, and walking to all my meetings, and I started shedding pounds now that I wasn't taking in the IPA-related calories and carbs—equivalent to about two loaves of bread—each day. I played at around 190 pounds. At my most unhealthy, I had been around 230, but with a totally different body makeup. I entered treatment at about 220, and within six months I had it down to a less muscular version of the 190 I had once been, which was a handful of pounds below where I'd eventually settle in when I stopped running excessively.

Food started to have real taste again, and my memory started to come back to me, and I believed I was on top of the world. This was a grander version of that "pink cloud" I mentioned earlier, a false sense of security that you've made it, you've figured it all out, you're cured. For some, it can be the precursor to relapse if you let that confidence get away from you. But I stayed tethered by developing that great rotation of AA meetings, having unquestioning support at home, and resuming writing and getting paid. With those achievements, I felt like I had some purpose in my life, which kept me moving forward. Purpose and support—what a concept for a healthy life.

The transition to my life now wasn't sudden, but I had finally found the upward line on the "aggregation of marginal gains" graph. When it seemed like nothing happened for a day, my life quietly got one per cent better, rather than worse. I made more than I spent. I got healthier. I earned more trust.

We moved in early 2021 and spent months getting settled. That summer, travel was allowed again, so after our yearly pilgrimages to Kelowna and New York, we set our sights on October 2021, which was to be the official relaunch of our new life. I would be sober, my job would be stable, our two-kid family would be complete and we'd be in our "forever" home.

My wife was to return to work after an 18-month maternity leave (thank you, Canada), my son started senior kindergarten at his new school (as well as before-and-after care with a neigh-bour), and my daughter started daycare. Lineup changes at Sportsnet 590 led to the launch of a new show: *Real Kyper &* *Bourne*, a Leafs-focused show I co-host with former NHLer Nick Kypreos. It felt like, for the first time since rehab, I would find a steady routine again, with a normal season, in our home and school and all the rest. It seemed like I was building towards a new life.

The pandemic complicated that plan in reality, adding virtual schooling and other challenging times, but we moved closer to consistency.

Hopefully, as you're reading this—knowing how that year went—you'll see it as having been a success. Regardless of the outcome, having reached this point feels like a win. When this book comes out, it will be February of 2023, and I will be four years removed from my dry date and the start of treatment. It's been a lifetime and it's been the blink of an eye, and it all happened 24 hours at a time.

10

REFLECTIONS

I didn't live with my dad much, and when I did I was very young. I didn't reach my teen years with some fully formed opinion of the man he was. I know both my brother and I loved him and enjoyed all the time we had with him. I remember how he'd make the three of us scrambled eggs: a full dozen at a time, usually in one solid piece by the time it was done, just an absolute brick of eggs with a brown bottom. They were great. I remember the camping trips, and the golf, and the good times. When we were together, he always *tried*, which is a lot more than can be said for a lot of divorced parents without much visitation time. So, for me, hearing stories about him as I've gotten older has been a strange education, and the lessons have usually gone one of two ways: I've heard from people who knew him during his playing days, who would tell me what a wonderful man he was, how kind he was, and how he was smart and well-liked and caring. I saw plenty of that in him, and often benefited personally from that side of him. I also hear stories from people who knew him later in life, and sometimes those played out in a manner that left me less full of pride. I saw that side personally, too, when things were tough. I don't believe all that good stuff ever went away— I still see it now and felt it over the years—but as his life became increasingly unstable, I think it became harder for him to display his more positive traits. Wouldn't that be true of any of us? When you're fighting for your own life, isn't it hard to prioritize others?

There are two hockey stories about my dad that have been volunteered to me primarily because their severity stuck with people so many years later. In the first, Dad is playing junior hockey for the Saskatoon Blades. He's leaving the defensive zone, and he's doing the very thing that would make him a Stanley Cup champion and Islanders Hall of Famer: *he is flying*.

He's moving too fast, though, a step ahead of the play, and the pass comes too late. He has to look back for it, and . . . you've seen this hockey movie before. With his head turned down towards the arriving puck, he eats the shoulder of an onrushing player in a catastrophic way. The shoulder hits low on his face, snapping his head back, and the material of those old cheese-grater knit jerseys did him no favours—the fabric basically peels the skin off his face all the way up. He's out, and it's bloody, and the team doctor says, "I'm not going there, he's dead."

Years later, in practice, the Islanders are in one of the end zones, working on a full-team drill, and a defenceman steps into a slapshot. Dad isn't wearing a helmet, something he chose not to do for a year of his career and which was common in practices in those days. The shot hits him square in the forehead, with the *crack* sound described to me as "like a gun going off."

People close to my dad claim he wasn't quite the same in the aftermath. It seems like something changed for him *somewhere* along the way. He doesn't know how many concussions he had, because in his day, they were waved off with euphemisms like "seeing stars" and "getting your bell rung." Personal concerns like "bright colours give me headaches" were greeted with "Keep your head up next time" and some Advil.

I can't forget the best side of Dad. I've seen so much effort on his part with my brother over the years, which is not a given from parents of kids with disabilities. (Around my brother's wheelchair sports teams, I've occasionally seen what the opposite looks like.) What comes next for our relationship leaves me guarded, though, because because of the way some of my family may feel about me: "Fool me once, shame on you, fool me twice, shame on me." To let down your guard is to be vulnerable.

And so the fundamental question, when the bad stuff undermines the good, is how much I fairly get to be upset about, and how much I should acknowledge the reality that he's been suffering, too. And while that sounds like a question specific to my relationship with my father, that's not my aim here. My aim here is to grapple with the baffling conundrum so many involved with alcoholics are left asking: *Where does the alcohol end and the person begin?* You can substitute "those who've suffered brain trauma" for "alcoholics," because trying to figure out what's authentically them, and what's the product of whatever happened to them, leaves so many twisting in the wind without answers.

That I'm on both sides of this situation, as an alcoholic myself, as well as someone who's been doinked on the head a few times, pushes me towards being charitable.

With life questions so murky, there simply can't be a grand blanket conclusion. All I can do is try to sort out my own situation, but I know many in the world have these internal debates about their own family members, or even themselves. (Assessing how much to blame one's alcoholic self for the visible damage after being the very hurricane that blew through can be challenging work.)

Is my dad a victim of the NHL and the way it was in the '70s and '80s, when players suffered countless head traumas but weren't paid enough to survive without a career after hockey? Is he someone who needed more help than he's got because of what the game took from him?

It's tough for me to come to that conclusion, because the NHL Alumni Association has gone to great lengths to help Dad overcome some post-career struggles. They've paid for his time in treatment. They've paid copious amounts for dental work. They have not abandoned him; they've been there when he's sought help. At varying points, I believe they helped him collect a little extra money, which I was so grateful for when I worried about how he was going to make ends meet. There's not a chance he wouldn't have been willing to assume the risks he did when he started playing, even knowing what could happen. Just ask him. So, I have trouble pointing a finger at what his NHL days left him with, despite the league's role in his post-career hardships.

So where does the responsibility for his actions lie? Surely you can't just give a pass to a person forever, no matter what they do?

And what about the alcoholism? If we're being compassionate, and we should, we have to understand that alcoholism isn't just some recurring set of bad choices. It's more formally known as "alcohol use disorder" and it's a legitimate medical condition. How much of a pass should a person get for the things they do because of alcohol when they're fighting that condition? How can I push him away for booze-related actions, knowing what *I've* been through, knowing how it feels to be so warped and single-focused? But then, how can I let him in, knowing what a wild card every day has been, unable to reliably trust the events that may come next? How can I forget the past? Watching someone drown while a life preserver floats beside them is maddening, but you can't grab it for them.

Al-Anon is a support group for the families of alcoholics and all they go through—my wife went through a similar program meant for the spouses of alcoholics—and it's not just an education in how to take consistent pain. At some point you learn you've got to cut off ties to protect yourself. But where is that line?

Months after agreeing to put these questions into a book in 2021, my dad and I had a falling out, the only lasting one we've ever had. (It was unrelated to the writing of this book, which I'm forever grateful was written with his blessing.) Something small had led to a text, then a small confrontation, and moments later I would learn that Dad had unfortunately relapsed. The messages leading up to my stepping away from communication for a number of months cut deep. Even through our more stressful incidents in the past, including his taking back of the Cup ring, we had stayed connected. At worst, we'd talk less frequently (going from once every couple weeks to a month or more between). We would always find a way to try again—two alcoholics, two hockey players, two fathers whose lives would intersect at various stages of rising and falling.

After the blow-up via text messages, he made the decision to seek help for a third time. That was admirable, but forgiveness is getting harder. I know it's getting harder for my wife, too. She has only been around to see the last 15 years, which have been the hardest. It's possible that my own ability to stay sober so far—in the face of potential life losses, like those he faces—has made understanding his battle *more* challenging. I get the struggle, and the challenges don't go the same for everyone, but the changes that come with sobriety are monumental . . . aren't they worth it? But I also recognize how much harder it is with less support.

Following his latest bout of treatment, he's done great during an extended run of sobriety. We've reconnected, and we're once again in a good place with legitimate hope. Back and forth I go, like so many children of parents fighting this awful disease.

I've reflected on hockey's role in all of this—by which I mean both my dad's issues and my own—and I see the game as a contributor, in part, but not the villain. Over the past century, hockey has failed in many ways, and the NHL would say the same about its own past. There have been terrible, life-altering incidents and bad people. There is still so much room for the sport to grow. The reason I don't sit here and point my finger at hockey is because, at every turn of my story, there have been exponentially more good people than bad, by an unquantifiable margin, all trying to right wrongs from the inside out. There's a thousand good people for every villain, and just based on the sheer numbers of humans involved, there will be villains. There's a reason we're seeing a long-needed push for more inclusion, because for the included, hockey is generally a positive world to exist within. I believe in the sunnier direction of the game, even if it's coming from a place that had shadows. In sum, I believe in the good of hockey.

The NHL Alumni Association has supported my dad. The shady doctor I dealt with was discovered, removed and jailed, an anomaly in a sport with so many good ones. Crazy coaching methods have softened, hazing has gone the way of the dodo, and the NHL's substance abuse program is helping more people than you can possibly imagine, becoming its own thriving community behind closed doors. Signs of growth include the attempts at welcoming those from marginalized communities; the fact that more women are playing, managing, coaching, and covering the game than ever before; and the way that skilled players have pushed the face punchers down from the edge of the bench to the floor. Hockey culture has led to some egregious failings, yet I see a concerted effort from so many to strive for better. Whatever the varied beliefs about whether the sport's culture is worth fighting for, I don't blame it for the negative parts of my family's story.

When considering hockey's role, I just can't look at the condition I share with my dad and imagine a walk of life free of people like us. There are alcoholic lawyers and doctors and philosophers and mechanics. We both liked to party, but that's not unique to the sport. When I look around, no occupation is spared.

As for the physical damage incurred, I see that as a part of having selected a physical line of work. If I'm a writer and my nose got broken by my editor, I gotta tell ya, I'd be pretty upset about that. But if I choose hockey and get a slapshot to the face, or an opponent turns my nose into an expired pomegranate, I see myself as on the hook for that.

Is there pressure to behave in certain ways within the game that maybe aren't your preference? For sure. At times I had to put on the "alpha" bravado when it's not in my nature. It's pro sports. But such are the complexities of numerous professional lives. There's pressure in most lines of work to behave in ways that aren't exactly your own choosing. From there you can choose to do those things either their way or your way. I never felt a pressure that wouldn't have allowed me to make my own decisions.

Is my forgiveness weakness?

Maybe there's some irony in my conclusions, that I have to live with my choices as *my choices* while debating how much to hold an alcoholic accountable and wondering how much I was accountable for the very things I did during my worst days. It sounds like some version of personal responsibility, yet I know my tendency is to look at my own worst drinking months and years and say, "Well, I was an active alcoholic then," as though that somehow means the things I did never happened. So, do I just get a pass for it all, even though it was me making the bad choices?

Maybe this devolves into a philosophical conversation, one about free will, and a scientific discussion about the brain, or maybe a consideration of family and how, at some point, you can choose to live with the imperfections of an imperfect life or reject them entirely, and reject part of what makes us human. The ways people handle complicated questions about the decisions of family and their causes and blames are part of what defines us as people.

All I see are grey areas, with no hope of their becoming black-and-white, which for me is a fundamental truth about most existence. Hot-take sports analysts get clout by picking black or white every day and excelling at arguing, but they're almost always missing something—usually the more accurate truth—because most fans prefer it that way. Most listeners don't have the time or mental effort for nuance, anyway; they're on their way to sort through their own personal bullshit.

It isn't concussions alone that have caused my dad's struggles, or alcohol alone, or hockey's culture, or the frustrations that came with a challenging second act of life. But they all played a part. And there's no fix for any one thing, or the whole of all these things. But there's a way, with time and work, that my relationship with my dad can be salvaged. And there's a way I can salvage my own life from alcoholism, and try to give back to help others salvage theirs.

There's nothing left here but time and work and effort. That's all there is. On playing hockey, on managing our relationships, and on managing our personal conditions. It's that part that matters most, and to exist within it comfortably involves managing the grey between our ears.

I'm a lucky man in so many ways. I have a loving family and my health and I've had opportunity. My personal story is not one of hardship. Yet still I deeply believe in the expression "Be kind, because everyone you meet is fighting a battle you can't see." (It's a real shame that Instagram and home decor have wrenched the meaning from some of these more useful axioms.) There's not a person you could pick out at your workplace or school or anywhere whose full story consists of "Everything is fine and has been fine."

So I'll end on gratitude, which will make my sponsor, Glenn, proud. I'm grateful for him and the program for preserving the good in me and, in turn, my life. I'm grateful for what hockey has given my family, imperfections included. I'm grateful for the challenges that have forced me to appreciate the daily process, rather than some outcome. I'm grateful for the loving support of that family—my wife, mom and brother, and my dad, too. I'm beyond grateful for Charlie and Molly, who fill my heart with a love I didn't know could exist.

The most famous expression tied to the program achieved its stature because it captures a healthy way to live, and it has nothing to do with alcohol. It's a daily message I wake up and aspire to, as challenging as it can be. It's called the Serenity Prayer, and it's as simple as it is poignant. You don't have to be religious to appreciate the message at its core:

God, grant me the serenity to accept the things
I cannot change, the courage to change the things I can,
and the wisdom to know the difference.

Life has no instruction book, and no promise of contentment, but there is good within it. I'm grateful for the few core beliefs that give me guardrails to stay on the right path and keep feeding my good wolf.

That path: Accept the things I can't change. Change what I can. Know which is which and move on. And do it all with the care of those closest to me in my heart.

EPILOGUE

It's important to me to note that I never set out to write this book. I had been approached some years back about writing a hockey book, and had kicked around a dozen ideas without ever nailing down a firm direction. (Part of the reason for that process dragging on can be better understood in the context of everything I've just shared. For a long while I made plans better than I delivered on them.) After going to rehab and reflecting on hockey and my career, we came to believe there was enough of a story there—my story—that was worth sharing. It felt like real good could come of it, and so it felt natural.

After the writing began and I shared some of the early work with my excellent editor, Nick Garrison, it became clear that my story couldn't be told without parts of Dad's, and that there were more interesting insights (beyond just hockey) to be mined by going deeper into that emotional territory. While digging in there was personally difficult, I realize that this would have been hard for Dad, too, and I'm grateful that he was supportive of my telling those less glamorous parts of our story.

In the years ahead I hope to become something that I was looking for when I was struggling: a person who wasn't forced to stop drinking by some awful loss, but rather chose to stop before that inevitable loss occurred. I picked my "rock bottom," and so far that decision has given me the best years of my life. That option is there for others, too.

I don't claim to be "fixed," and I don't know if I'm ready for the sobriety of someone else to be dependent on mine. But I do know I can at least provide a willing ear and heart for others who feel alone in their struggle. I hope I can raise some money for those who weren't as fortunate as I was in cleaning up my life. I know that part of the deal of having a program and a sponsor is giving back, and just as my sponsor laid the "toolkit" at my feet to help myself, I hope I can offer it to others.

ACKNOWLEDGMENTS

I hope that somewhere in the book I have properly conveyed the following:

I am extremely grateful for the love of my life, Brianna. She saved me. I don't know if it was in the life/death sense or not, but she certainly took that extreme outcome off the table with her support and patience. She gave me back my *life*, with her and our kids and our house and all those good things. I'll forever be indebted to her for that show of love, and for allowing us to reclaim what we'd both cherished so much—"us." (Her ability to bear down when things get tough? Extremely "playoff performer" mentality—must be those good Gillies genes.) I love you, Breezy.

There's not enough I can say about my mom and the support and love she's given me in my life. I don't know if you've seen *Moana* or not, but she is our family's beating heart of Te Fiti. Her myriad sacrifices to put my brother and me in a position to succeed (whether we've succeeded or not) have always demonstrated how she's put herself second for our benefit. It's never gone unnoticed or underappreciated. I won the lottery with her as a mom, and I hope to pass on to my own kids what she's been to me. If I even get halfway there, I'll be a great dad.

My brother, Jeff, isn't in the book nearly enough for someone who's such a huge part of my life. We've unfortunately lived apart for a long time, but he and my sister-in-law Sarah are two of the most important people in my life. Their love and support (there are those words again) of not just me, but also Bri and their nieces and nephews, are a foundational part of that "familial ecosystem" that I consider my Higher Power. I'm so proud of them both.

And to those special kids Charlie and Molly, who will likely read this when they get older: I could not love you more. Truly, like, I can't even believe how much I love you. When my mom used to be over-the-top lovey and tell me how great I was as a kid, I used to say, "Stop, stop," and she'd say, "Wait until you have your own kids, you'll get it then." I GET IT now, because you are both so great, smart, kind, cute and wonderful. I'll always do my best to offer you the support all the people mentioned above gave to me. I love you.

And to my dad, I'm grateful that, from the good times to the bad times, which are outlined in this book, you always cared so much about Jeff and me. We've been through it all, but you've believed in me and rooted for me along the way, and having your permission to write this book is an example of that. I still believe there's a happy chapter ahead and will do my part to make it so.

I also want to thank someone who's existed at the intersection of my career and family, and who's mentioned several times in the book without enough follow-up: Ken Juba. It's not just that this book wouldn't exist without him, but my career wouldn't, either. He's guided me along throughout the years as an intelligent, thoughtful mentor who's helped me make sense of my place in the world and the best avenues to pursue with my skill set. There's a reason my "higher power" didn't end up just being my immediate family. Uncle Ken has gone so far above and beyond for me over the years (it's no small side note that he was the first person to talk to me about my drinking) that I've grown to appreciate how connected my greater family really is. There's a lot of love that goes into that connectedness, and Ken's a crucial part of that circuit. I'm just so thankful for him.

In my sobriety today, I lean heavily on the group of guys who are all sponsees of our sponsor, Glenn Vogelsang. The five of us (including Glenn) meet via Zoom once a week and talk through how we're handling the various pressures that life throws at us. It's like group therapy, and I'm blessed to have those moments each week. It's a core part of what's kept me sober, and what helps me stay balanced today. Love you guys.

I want to thank my editor, Nick Garrison, who's believed in me and my writing going back many years (I believe we first talked in 2016), who was probably like, "Boy, some writers are flaky but this guy is on another level." I know his encouragement to push myself on certain topics is what gives this book whatever legs it may have, and I'm thankful to have someone who didn't just think I could write a book but who also pushed me to write a better one. I had no idea how to write a book, none, and still don't after writing this one. So big thanks to Nick for steering the ship to make it all come together.

And finally, my thanks to hockey, including the NHL, AHL, ECHL, NCAA and minor hockey, down to the very last parent, volunteer, and coach. I love the game, and I don't take for granted all that it's given my family over the years. A fresh sheet, a bucket of pucks, and that cool breeze in your face—man. Every day is a chance to write your story anew.